BUSINESS ETHICS

EDWARD STEVENS

PAULIST PRESS
New York/Ramsey

Library of Congress
Catalog Card Number: 79-91409

ISBN: 0-8091-2244-8

Published by Paulist Press
Editorial Office: 1865 Broadway, New York, N.Y. 10023
Business Office: 545 Island Road, Ramsey, N.J. 07446

Printed and bound in the
United States of America

CONTENTS

CHAPTER 1
ETHICS AND BUSINESS:
AN INTRODUCTION

Show me a 35-year-old executive with an MBA from a very good school who wants to stay in direct sales because he likes making customers happy, who likes his colleagues and wishes them every success, and who would never do anything unethical, and I will show you a man known as a "religious type," as a "loser."[1]

While it remains true that "business is business," it also is true that I would rather do my business with a gentleman who realizes that there are certain types of profit for which he has no need.[2]

OBJECTIVES FOR CHAPTER 1

1. To understand the relation of ethics to business, and the advantage of clarifying the philosophical premises that underlie one's own business ethics;

2. To arrive at a preliminary definition of "morality" and at a strategy for judging the adequacy of a given business philosophy as a basis for ethics;

[1]Albert Shapero, "What Management Says and What Managers Do," *Fortune* (May 1976), 276. The sentiments expressed in the quotation are not those of Shapero. Rather they represent an attitude that he is attacking.

[2]John Andrew King, "Business Ethics," a reader's letter to the editor in *Business Week* (July 12, 1976).

1

3. To see the justification for the order of treatment in the rest of the book. If you are impatient to see what this book is about, go directly to Section 3.

Introduction. This chapter sets out to answer three questions: (1) Why study business ethics? (2) What strategy can we adopt for judging the adequacy of a business ethic? (3) What business ethical philosophies will be treated in this book and why?

1. WHY STUDY BUSINESS ETHICS?

Two stumbling blocks stand in the way of anyone who would undertake to study business ethics. The first is the apparent opposition between good business and good morals. A "religious type" in the business world, it seems, can only be "a loser." Second, even granting the practicability of ethics in business, is business ethics teachable? An adult functioning in the business world is already either an ethical person or not. No philosophy course in business ethics, it seems, is going to change that person. Let's examine more closely these two difficulties.

"Good medicine is good morals." This ethical maxim has traditionally been cited to guide the physician in making responsible medical decisions. And the maxim has a plausible ring to it. Until recently, at any rate, the image of the medical profession has been enveloped in an aura of dedication, responsibility, and service. Morals and medicine appeared to be comfortable bedfellows.

"Good business is good morals." Now this maxim enjoys no such ready plausibility. Rather it tends to evoke the same kind of cynical reaction as greeted Charles Wilson's assertion that "What's good for General Motors is good for the country." I might get away with making such a statement about General Hospital. But General Motors? Never!

Of course, businessmen, no less than politicians (and indeed no less than any one of us), want to put the best moral face on their activities. Corporations would have you understand that they have the common man's best interests at heart, and that they are selflessly and ceaselessly investing vast resources into research that will make his life easier and happier. Their image-makers tirelessly work at projecting the same aura of integrity, selflessness, and dedication around the corporate world that the medical world enjoys. Indeed, "good will" has a dollar value and finds its way onto the accountant's sheet as a quantifiable, albeit intangible, asset.

But can business's dalliance with morals blossom into a marriage firm and secure?

The critics of business are willing to grant that a certain "honesty among thieves" prevails. Businessmen know the game and within the fraternity observe the rules of the game. But outside the fold lies the Adversary in the form of government regulatory agencies, consumers' rights advocates, ecology groups, and underdeveloped nations. Is business to hold itself morally responsible to these groups? Or to use terminology more comfortable to the business person: What is the social responsibility of business to these groups?

Answers to these questions are not obvious. Common sense is not enough. What seems obvious at a National Association of Manufacturers convention is heresy to a Ralph Nader. Common sense of one group is arrogance to the other. And the polarization between business and society at large is becoming ever more acute. During the 1960's, universities were challenged to expand their traditional preoccupation with academic matters to include an activist concern with problems of the cities, the nation, and even of the world. More and more is business being confronted with a similar challenge. Traditional business ethos has been narrowly focused on economic and technical values, much as traditional academics focused on detached objective research. Each did what it does best. It is no small moral demand to claim that business should now be concerned with social values as well. The business person rightly asks, Why? And s/he deserves an answer. Moral conversion is mindless if one has not seen the light. Does skill in handling society's economic functions render business competent to cure social ills as well?

A business person cannot help but have economic values in the center of his decision-making and behavior. This assertion is redundant. The very meaning of the term *business* is "the development and processing of economic values in society."[3] The laws governing economic values are not violated with impunity. Business people know this and therefore bristle at any outside pressure that would force them to violate these laws. A governmentally enforced price freeze would be an example of such a pressure. Such an arrogant attempt to suspend the law of supply and demand is just begging for an economic backlash. Interferences like this with the "natural" economic process are therefore anathema to business. What about *moral* values? Should the enhancement of economic values (profit-maximization) yield to *moral* values? Is not the effort to introduce moral values into the business decision-making process an irrelevant external interference with the "natural" process of developing economic values? Would not

---

[3]Keith Davis and Robert L. Blomstrom, *Business and Society: Environment and Responsibility* (New York: McGraw-Hill Book Co., 1975), p. 19.

this likewise be an arrogance that cannot fail to go unpunished? Would not the business person be forced ultimately to pay the economic piper if he allows his business sense to be seduced by the blandishments of morality? He would seem justified, then, in keeping his economic decision-making uncontaminated by moral values and distinct from his moral life. A businessman's function is skillfully to maximize economic values. This being the case, can ethics (a concern for moral values) in business ever be more than a matter of lip service and image-making? It is easy to mouth expressions like "good business is good morals," "honesty is the best policy," and "follow the Golden Rule." But do these principles really obtain in the nonutopian world in which business functions? Such is the *prima facie* opposition that appears between good business and good morals.

In response, we point out that the conflict is only apparent. Every freely chosen human decision necessarily has an ethical dimension. And business decisions are no exception. So business and ethics, far from being opposed to each other, are inextricably entwined. Every business decision is an expression of a philosophical and ethical outlook on life. In this sense, every business decision is also a moral decision. It says something about the kind of person you are morally. Morality is not moral*ism*. Narrow moralism concentrates on abstract unempirical rules and codes. These latter can easily seem to conflict at times with the realities of business life. But a broader view would look less to the particular do's and don'ts, and more to the ideology, or philosophy of life, or social philosophy that underpins the do's and don'ts. It is here that we see the shape of the ethics that business decisions reveal.

This brings us to the second difficulty. If ethics is first and foremost a matter of one's philosophy of life, how can it be taught? How can a book teach philosophy to anyone? That would be as fatuous as handing a book to a grown man or woman on how to walk, talk, or tell right from wrong. These are things that are learned in the doing. You've been walking and talking for years and decades. By now you have your style. That's you. No book is going to change it. It's unconscious to be sure. We don't see and hear ourselves as others do. But it's there and it's real, nonetheless. The same seems to go for right and wrong—moral values. Your moral values have been built up over a lifetime of hard decision-making tested by that good and strict teacher, experience. Isn't it silly to hand a grownup businessman or woman a book or a course on "business ethics" and say, "This will teach you how you should behave." You've been developing your brand of business ethics for years. It's already there. By now you have your moral life style. That's you. It will doubtless continue to evolve. But no book is going to change it.

There are three major theories of moral education: (1) *indoctrination,* (2) *values-clarification,* and (3) the *cognitive-developmental* approach.[4] The debate about whether virtue can be taught goes back as far as Socrates. Morality, it seems, is something that we teach to children. Moral values are not simple facts. They involve feelings; they involve calls to action. Whence morality is commonly taught by methods of *indoctrination.* Appropriate perhaps for children, does indoctrination make sense for adults? We indoctrinate by *persuasion* (e.g., a pep talk by the company president on "responsibility"). We appeal to *good example* (e.g., to the hard work and honesty of the company's founder). Indoctrination uses *reward* and *punishment* to cajole or threaten (e.g., paying bonuses or docking pay to manipulate desired behavior). Indoctrination *rationalizes* the "correct" course of conduct (e.g., by giving 10 reasons why employees should observe safety regulations). Such methods of indoctrination when used on adults suffer from one common flaw: they often work poorly or not at all. Whence the skepticism about whether moral values can be taught to adults who have already attained a kind of ethical maturity.

This book is not an effort to indoctrinate business ethics in the reader. The first alternative to *indoctrination* in teaching morality is *values-clarification.* This method assumes that you, the reader, are already an ethical person. Can you clarify for yourself what this ethics is, what its premises and consequences are? Then, more importantly, can you evaluate it for yourself, and even change it, if you see fit? Moral values, in this view, are defined by the individual for him or herself. This is the way it has to be in a pluralistic society where commonly held conventional norms have broken down. The operative assumption is that reflection upon one's own values in a nonthreatening, conflict-free environment is the most successful way to get a firm and intelligent grasp on them. Moral education is essentially a matter of self-awareness. In this sense, ethics can be "taught" to adults. Values-clarification is a matter of reflecting on and evaluating for oneself one's own philosophy of life and ethics.

Your decisions about right and wrong in the business world express your business philosophy, indeed your philosophy of life. Impatient as you

---

[4]Psychologist Louis E. Raths, following in the tradition of philosopher-educator John Dewey, of whom we'll see more below, introduced the *values-clarification* approach to moral education. See, for example, Louis Raths *et al., Values and Teaching* (Columbus, Ohio: Merrill, 1966). Lawrence Kohlberg, dissatisfied with both the dogmatism of *indoctrination* and the moral relativism implicit in *values-clarification,* evolved the *cognitive-developmental* approach to moral education, following the work of Jean Piaget. See, for example, Lawrence Kohlberg, "The Cognitive-Developmental Approach to Moral Education." *Phi Delta Kappan* (June 1975), 670–77, and Jean Piaget, *The Moral Judgment of the Child,* translated by M. Gabain (Glencoe, Illinois: Free Press, 1948).

may feel about "philosophy" as an academic exercise, you do as a matter of fact already possess a philosophy that is uniquely your own, hammered out in your living experience, and which is the guide of your decisions, actions, and values. For most of us, that philosophy remains unconscious and unarticulated. But it's there and it's real, nonetheless. Values-clarification seeks to make the unconscious philosophy conscious and articulate. To this end, values-clarification exercises are included throughout this book.

A second alternative to *indoctrination* is the *cognitive-developmental approach* to moral education espoused by Lawrence Kohlberg. To Kohlberg, *values-clarification* can be a first step, but moral education doesn't stop there. Kohlberg agrees that *indoctrination* into socially approved conduct leaves much to be desired, especially in the moral education of adults. But neither does he want to subscribe to the moral relativism implicit in *values-clarification*. The freely chosen and affirmed values of the individual are not self-validating. Moral education should invite a growth in *principled reasoning* about one's ethics. I don't get off the hook by claiming that a dubious value is "right for me." There can be conflict in reasoning about values. One philosophy challenges another. There is no assumption that one philosophy is as good as another. Moral growth is possible as the reasoning becomes more mature, more principled, more universal. Whence Kohlberg's approach is *cognitive-developmental*. The dialectic of conflicting business philosophies in this book as applied to moral dilemmas in business is intended to assist such growth in moral awareness.

Do I blow the whistle on what I know to be a defective and dangerous product under production in my factory at risk of my job security? Do I seriously recruit and train disadvantaged and minorities at a higher cost than that of current recruitment practice? Do I use dubious hardsell tactics to entrap inexperienced buyers into purchases they neither need nor can afford? Do I go to the expense of enforcing the use of safety equipment and attending to health standards of my employees on the job? These are not mere "image" problems. My decisions will inevitably involve philosophical value judgments. Implicit in these business decisions are philosophical judgments about human life and health, about the economic price of both, about human rights in society, and about the relations of subgroups in a community. It is inevitable that business decisions carry a moral and philosophical dimension. Every business decision is also a moral decision. And every moral decision implies a philosophy of life that consciously or unconsciously is backing it up.

As long as my ethics remains inarticulate and unconscious, I remain an uncritical slave to it. When I become reflective and conscious of what exactly my philosophy of life and ethics is, only then am I in a position to evaluate it and ratify or modify it in dialogue with others. Such is the value of *values-clarification* and *cognitive moral development*. A small parable may help to illustrate this point.

An introductory parable. Suppose one day you walk into a bank and see an armed robbery actually in progress. Customers are cowering on the floor. A tall, stocking-faced bandit has a gun trained on them. Two other younger-looking thugs are behind the cage prodding terrified tellers to empty the cash drawers into their sacks. Two bank managers exchange a nervous and calculating glance as if devising a way to sound the alarm. Your heart sinks. Why did you ever pick this time to come to the bank? How could you stumble into a mess like this? The stocking-faced bandit catches sight of you. A shiver runs through your body and your breath grows short.

Suddenly there's a shout from the corner of the lobby, "Cut!" With that barked command, the tension evaporates. The bandits pull off their masks, the tellers smile as the customers get up off the floor. And the light dawns. This is not a robbery, but a movie-take of a "robbery." The "customer," "bandits," and "tellers" are, in truth, actors. The robber-world has been transformed into an actor world. The crime has become a "crime."

For you blundering innocently into this situation, the whole reality has shifted. Though the reality, as you saw it, was instantly turned upside down, note that the personages, their actions, and their words during the scene were exactly the same for you as they were for the movie director. Yet he saw a movie-take of a "robbery" while you were witnessing a robbery. If the events were the same for each of you, what was different? Simply this. The director had one set of assumptions about what he saw, while you had a completely different set of assumptions. Your basic taken-for-granted assumptions about the world not only color the way you see the world, they actually determine the reality of what you see. On the basis of this reality, you declare certain things to be true and others to be false.

One value of philosophical reflection is to make you aware of worlds that are alternatives to the one you've been taking for granted. Unaware of alternatives, you'll remain trapped in your taken-for-granted world. To return to the parable, had you suffered a fatal heart attack on entering the bank, you'd have died convinced of the *truth* that a *real* robbery was going on. When the director shouted, "Cut!" alternative assumptions came into play for you. The reality changed, and truth changed. You were able then to escape from your previously taken-for-granted world and criticize it. Your philosophical assumptions yield a very definite view of business "reality" from which certain truths in business ethics logically follow. But you need not be trapped in this world. You, as philosophical critic, can evaluate the truth of its assumptions.

The question is not what *should* be your business philosophy with its consequent morality. The question posed to you is rather what *is* your business philosophy and its consequent morality. This is an essay in clarification, in making the implicit explicit, the unconscious conscious. Are you a Machiavellian in your business decisions? Or are you a pragmatist? There is a difference. Legalism, objectivism, relativism—these are some of the business philosophies that we will examine. All these *isms* sound very abstract. But when acted upon in daily life, their consequences could hardly be more concrete and practical. The choice is not between operating or not operating according to a given business philosophy and morality. The question is rather whether you go about your moral life with eyes open and well aware of your operative philosophy or with eyes shut, unconscious of the assumptions and moral consequences of your decisions. The fact that you never give morality a second thought doesn't mean, as we have seen, that your decisions have no moral import; it simply means that you are unaware of the moral dimension. The fact that a person cannot spell or even pronounce the word "philosophy" doesn't mean that he has no operative philosophy in his life; it simply remains unconscious. Once you have made conscious and explicit the philosophy and morality that you actually do have, then *you* decide whether this morality is for you or not. Look at its assumptions; look at its consequences; look at the picture of the world and of society that forms the working framework of your business decisions. Is that picture true to the way things are? Can you live with the consequences it has for your decisions? When your hidden assumptions are brought to light, do you like what you see? Are these the principles that you want to guide your life? In making your implicit philosophy explicit and conscious, you are no longer an unwitting slave to it. You are free to examine it, criticize it, ratify it, modify it. This is what Socrates meant by saying that the unexamined life is not worth living. The examined life becomes a free life. When critics attack your values as a business person, you can then respond in terms of philosophical reasons rather than merely of public relations and "image." What some people consider a present crisis in business ethics may well signal the need not so much for a change in the climate of business morality as for a coherent, rational philosophical defense of why business operates the way it does, and indeed of why morally it *should* operate the way it does.

The best teachers of business ethics are not philosophers and religionists, but the business people who, consciously or unconsciously, are living out and practicing a morality. In choosing which business philosophies to examine in this book, we have listened to businessmen. We have heard them speak in Machiavellian accents (though they would not so label it themselves), and so we examine Machiavellianism. We have heard pragmatism and legalism defended (again, not always under those labels), so these philosophies have been selected for examination. Business people have been our teachers. After all, it is they who have hammered out such philosophies for survival and growth in the business world. When business people make their philosophies explicit, they will be more able to be defenders of rather than defensive about the moralities that make business possible and good. Such will be our method.

A Committee for Education in Business Ethics funded by the National Endowment for the Humanities has adopted the following goals for a course in business ethics:

    a. improvement of moral reasoning about issues in business ethics.

    b. sensitization to basic spiritual and other values of this society.

    c. recognition of the many variables in most ethical issues in business.

    d. understanding the more subtle criteria for deciding ethical issues in business.

    e. recognition of the diverse ethical theories one can use in analyzing business-ethics problems.[5]

It is hoped that the method of clarification and cognitive development

---

[5]The present work is not connected with this two-year NEH curriculum development project, but this author shares these goals. The institutions cooperating in the project were:

    a. Center for the Study of Values, University of Delaware

    b. American Philosophical Association

    c. School of Business Administration, California State University at Long Beach

    d. School of Management, Northwestern University

    e. University of Minnesota at Morris

    f. University of Pittsburgh

    g. The Wharton School, University of Pennsylvania.

I might single out four centers for values studies, among many, that have been particularly helpful in making available information and materials concerning business ethics and economic value-issues:

    (1). Center for Business Ethics
        W. Michael Hoffman, Director
        Bentley College
        Waltham, Ma. 02154

    (2). Center for the Study of Values
        Norman E. Bowie, Director
        University of Delaware
        Newark, De. 19711

    (3). Center for the Study of Human Dimensions of Science and Technology
        Rensselaer Polytechnic Institute
        Troy, N.Y. 12181

    (4). Institute of Society, Ethics, and the Life Sciences
        360 Broadway
        Hastings-on-Hudson, N.Y. 10706

(as opposed to indoctrination) used in this book will assist the reader in attaining some of these goals.

Preliminary values-clarification exercise. As a way of pulling together some of the points made so far, reflect on the following statements. Indicate your position regarding each by writing a number in the blank before each statement:

1 = strongly disagree, 2 = disagree, 3 = not sure
4 = agree, 5 = strongly agree.

___*5*___ (a) Good business is good morals.

___*1*___ (b) No business person who is "going places" can afford the luxury of worrying about morals.

___*4*___ (c) Every business person operates on the basis of some moral philosophy, whether he is aware of it or not.

___*2*___ (d) In the business world, moral values have more to do with ideals than with practice.

___*4*___ (e) Stay within the law, and you can't go wrong morally with business decisions.

___*4*___ (f) Business ethics is mainly a matter of conforming to the expectations and practices of the people you are dealing with.

___*2*___ (g) Business decisions involve economic realism, not moral philosophy.

___*2*___ (h) Moral values and religious values come down to the same thing.

___*4*___ (i) There is a justifiable crisis of public confidence in the ethical climate of business today.

___*2*___ (j) Business ethics is a nice public-relations phrase, but there is really no such thing.

Discuss and compare your answers with the answers given by others. When you disagree, try to figure out why. How do you answer the question, Why study business ethics?

We now move on to the second task of this chapter.

2. A STRATEGY FOR JUDGING THE ADEQUACY OF A BUSINESS ETHICS

The focus of this book is not on values in general but specifically on *moral* values in the business world. This can be confusing. Many values get mixed up with morality that don't necessarily have anything to do with it. Consider our most frequently used value words, "bad" and "good," and all the nonmoral uses to which we put them. Here are some of the meanings that could be implied by the bad-good distinction.

First, "deviant-conforming": This is the sociological sense of bad-good. For example, New York City lawyer Carl E. Person recently proposed to sell shares in his litigation in order to finance it. As of this writing, such a plan would be deviant behavior for the legal profession. Proposals for doctors to advertise their fees would fall into the same category of sociological deviancy, at least in many states. Such a plan is "bad" in the sense that it doesn't conform to accepted practice in the profession. But whether it is "bad" in the sense of "immoral" or "unethical" is another issue altogether.

A second usage is "sin-virtue." This is the religious sense of bad-good. A Baptist minister may well be branded a sinner if he were to open a liquor store. Does that make him an immoral person? Religion and morality need not go hand in hand. Religious prescriptions can be criticized on moral grounds.

Another common use of good-bad is in the sense of effective-ineffective. A "good" salesman, in this sense, knows the use of power. He understands that Marine Corps formula for partisan warfare: "You Can't Win Over Their Hearts and Minds Until You Have Them By the Balls." He can sell color TV sets to welfare recipients, no money down, knowing well that the sets will give out long before the payments that the buyers unwittingly contracted for. He is a good, i.e., effective, salesman. But his morality is another matter.

Bad-good in a fourth usage is synonymous with odd-proper. Value is assigned to the conventional, disvalue to the unconventional. A recent psychological experiment has concluded that businesswomen who wear pants are simply not taken as seriously as those who wear dresses. Males and females alike perceive the dress-wearers as the ones who are going places. But from conventionality of dress one does not rightly draw conclusions about morals.

Finally, bad-good is often used to express the distinction between criminal and law-abiding. Does violation of law imply violation of morals? In a case documented by Travelers Insurance Company of Hartford, a worker who sped up the operation of his machine by removing a safety device, consequently causing the machine to malfunction and cause an accident, sued the manufacturer for $2 million and won. The court decided that the manufacturer was at fault for not providing a second safety device to prevent removal of the first. So there was held to be legal liability. But would you assign moral culpability to the designer of the machine?

So values come in many varieties. You have to ask—value for what? Valuable for getting the job done? This is a practical value (effectiveness). Valuable for being a good citizen? This is a legal value (observance of law). Valuable for getting along with others? This is a social value (conventionality). Valuable for being a God-fearing person? This is a religious value (virtue). Well, what about *moral* value? For what is moral value valuable? We have seen that it does not necessarily mean law-abiding, effective, virtuous, or conforming. What *does* it mean?

An action is *morally* valuable when it is responsive to the total realities of the situation. The morally good business person is true to himself/herself in the fullest sense of that phrase. A morally good action is one that is true to the totality of what it means to be a human being. It is this sensitivity to the total meaning of human that characterizes the moral dimension of life. Note that in being true to myself as an individual, I must be faithful to all the social systems that enrich and confer upon me my identity as an individual. If my personal identity is bound up with being a spouse, a parent, a salesmanager, a citizen, a religious believer, and a human being, then being true to myself involves fidelity to all these facets of my identity. And conversely, moral evil is infidelity to oneself as a human being in all that this implies.

And we can deal with the morality of a business corporation in the same kind of systems framework as used for the morality of the individual business person. Corporate morality means responsiveness to the total reality of the corporation's identity. When corporate policies, decisions, and actions are faithful to all the social systems internal and external that make the corporation into the reality that it is, then we can talk about corporate policies, decisions, and actions that are ethical and morally good. Failure to be responsive to these systems is precisely what is meant by corporate immorality in its many guises.

So a legally correct action is *also* moral if it meets this test: Is it true to the total reality of the situation? Is the individual business person true to himself and all the relationships that are part of himself? Are corporate policies and behaviors true to the business entity with all its interacting parts? The practice of "red-lining" by banks may be legal. Does it pass the *moral* test? Refusal by a Catholic hospital to perform abortions may by religiously virtuous. But does it meet this moral test? Payments by multinationals to foreign government officials may be expedient. Are they also moral? Do such payments reflect a sensitivity to the total realities of the situation? "I don't know the answer to these questions," you rightly reply. "It depends. What exactly do you intend by saying 'the total reality of the situation, be it that of the individual business person or of the business entity'? How do you spell it out? In conflicting systems and transactions, where do the priorities lie?"

The objection is well taken. We have a broad definition of what a moral value is. We're in the right ball park. But in the moral ball park there are many seats. There are many business philosophies. Tell me your philosophy, and I'll tell you the ethics that follows from it, that is in harmony with it. But the root question is: What philosophy of life, implicitly or explicitly, guides your decisions? It is your business philosophy, whether or not you are aware of that philosophy, that determines priorities and defines that "total moral situation" to which the ethical business and business person is responsive.

The following chapters will examine several currently popular business philosophies together with their implied ethics. They are not meant to be reviewed as so many packages in a philosophical supermarket—"take your pick," "one is as good as another." No. The purpose is to evaluate these philosophies with a view eventually to evaluating your own philosophy as a basis for ethics, and for business ethics. The measure of a philosophy is its ability to comprehend consistently what it means to be a human being. Economist Paul Heyne puts it well:

> If an ethical businessman has to be defined, we would define him simply as a man who is the full measure of what a man should be.
> No serious ethical inquiry can escape the question of what it means to be human. What is "the nature and destiny of man" to use Reinhold Niebuhr's phrase? . . .
> The situation of the businessman is just a special instance of the human situation, and no temptation befalls him that is not common to man.[6]

The question you will put to each of the upcoming philosophies is, Does it take the full measure of what a human being should be? This is the strategy for evaluating and comparing theories of business ethics one with another and with your own theory. Of course, "what it means to be human" needs to be specified. And this is precisely what the upcoming business philosophies will attempt to do. How well and completely each does so will be yours to judge. In this way, you can determine which philosophies (and what ethics) best interpret the meaning and guide the direction of human life in society, and particularly in business society. We turn now to an overview of these particular business philosophies to be examined.

3. BUSINESS PHILOSOPHIES AND THEIR ORDER OF TREATMENT

Business ethics: individual or institution? There is a tension in business ethics that we will not resolve at this point, viz., the tension between the individual and the institution. When I move from my personal life and ethics at home to the life and ethics of the business institution where I work,

[6]Paul T. Heyne, *Private Keepers of the Public Interest* (New York: McGraw-Hill Book Co., 1968), pp. 113–15.

do the rules of the game change? Business philosophies divide on this issue, as we will see. For some, the conscience of the corporate institution is as good as the consciences of the individuals who work there. This view will stress the responsibility and integrity of individual business people to maintain an ethically healthy business climate. Others, however, see a difference *in kind* between the ethics of people in an institutional setting and their behavior in their personal lives. This view insists that a sound ethical climate cannot safely be entrusted to the vagaries of individual consciences, and seeks enforceable institutional codes and procedures. This tension between individual business person and business institution will find differing resolutions in the different philosophies we are about to treat.

Philosophical approach vs. economic approach. In taking a philosophical approach to the moral situations confronting the business person, we go beyond the behavioral sciences and economics. Obviously, business decisions heavily involve psychological, sociological, and above all, economic considerations. But the empirical sciences cannot, either singly or together, define the total *moral* situation. Science is not enough. Science taken on its own terms cannot examine either the breadth or the depth comprised by the moral dimension of experience. A decision made on scientific grounds alone is necessarily incomplete. It is not and cannot be responsive to the total reality involved. And such unresponsiveness is what we call moral evil (see the previous section). Let's look for a moment at the limits inherent in scientific methodology that make necessary a philosophical grounding for morality.

It is perfectly reasonable, for example, to adopt an economic approach to business decisions. But in opting for an economic framework, the business person must *presuppose* certain things about the world and the human beings affected by his decision. The economic viewpoint involves certain very definite assumptions. And if the economic question ("Does it make money?") becomes the sole measure of a business decision, then economics begins to operate as a philosophy of life underpinning a morality with certain specifiable values. To philosophize is precisely to make explicit such assumptions, consequences and values. Philosophy examines the truth or falsity of what science presupposes. Operating in his own framework, the economist might quite rightly assume that economic decisions are better than uneconomic ones, that it is impossible for any activity to be too profitable, and that a profitable economy is a healthy economy and best for the human beings involved. What the economist assumes, the philosopher examines. The business person, after addressing himself to the economics of the situation, in his philosophical moments might ask himself: Is it true that economic results are better than uneconomic? Is there any limit beyond which profits, while remaining an economic plus, become a human minus? Does the situation in question reveal noneconomic values that clamor to be taken into account, in addition to the economic concern of returning an adequate profit in terms of money? Such questions are philosophical, not scientific. Economics cannot deal with them on their own terms, and in answering such questions, the business person reveals the moral climate and direction of his use of economics.

Assumptions of this inquiry. This book, then, is an invitation to reflect on the philosophical framework that you bring to questions like these. We assume as a starting point the experience of moral obligation, of moral good and moral evil, viz., that in the decisions you make at work, your own integrity as a human being is on the line. There do exist human beings who are completely devoid of all moral sense. We call them sociopaths. This book is not for them. Adopting the moral experience as a starting point, we saw three of its characteristics. The experience of moral obligation is (1) unconditional, (2) involves the whole human being, and (3) is based on one's philosophy of life. In other words, morality is more than mere expediency, more than mere success, and requires something more than the social sciences for its full explanation. To examine the moral dimension of the business world means to examine your philosophy of life. At stake are your most fundamental values as a human being.

Moral values are in a class apart. They provide the test to which the responsible business person submits his other values. Law, convention, conformity, religious virtue, effectiveness—none of these is a guarantee of morality. A moral value is one that is in harmony with what it means to be a human being in all that that implies. Each business person will spell this out differently. In other words, each operates on his own business philosophy. This philosophy is the foundation for ethical decisions. So much for the general groundwork. Let's get down now to specific business philosophies.

Business philosophies to be examined. We will examine the following theories of ethics:

Group A: Social Darwinism (Chapter 2)
         Machiavellianism (Chapter 3)
         Objectivism (Chapter 4)
Group B: Conventional Morality (Chapter 5)
         Legalistic Ethics (Chapter 6)
         Accountability Model of Ethics (Chapter 7)
Group C: Pragmatism (Chapter 8)
         Marxism (Chapter 9)
         "Economic Humanism" (Chapter 10)
Appendix on the John Rawls Debate about Distributive Justice

Reason for the order of treatment. As a rough principle for ordering these philosophies, I have used psychologist Lawrence Kohlberg's[7] three stages or levels of moral maturity. Kohlberg discovered that moral life and decision-making functions first of all at a level of what he calls *pre-conventional morality*; then it moves to a second level—*conventional morality*, and finally to a third or *post-conventional* level. Without pressing the classifications too rigidly on these philosophies, the theories in Group A (social Darwinism, Machiavellianism, and objectivism) share many of the qualities that Kohlberg assigns to the pre-conventional level of morality, as do those in Group B (conventional morality, legalism, and the accountability model) share characteristics of Kohlberg's conventional level, and Group C (pragmatism, Marxism, and "economic humanism") Kohlberg's post-conventional level. This is one way of relating the philosophies in question to put them in some perspective. These classifications certainly could be quarreled with.

Pre-conventional morality is morality at the level of the child. It is calculating and self-centered, even selfish. Altruism is an alien concept at this level. The first cluster of business philosophies in a greater or lesser degree could be said to manifest such tendencies. "You scratch my back and I'll scratch yours." "What's in it for me?" "What have you done for me lately?" Such is the level of moral motivation that characterizes pre-conventional thinking. The story is one of power games and of marketplace reciprocity.

Social Darwinism will put *survival by natural selection* at the heart of ethics. Let those who are not strong enough to survive perish (see Chapter 2). Machiavellianism as a business philosophy makes *expedience* the rule in business decisions. Ethically speaking, business decisions involve little more than a calculus of private benefits (see Chapter 3). Ayn Rand's objectivism is perhaps not so crudely egotistical. She makes *rational self-interest* the rule of moral right and wrong, self-interest understood in a very individualistic way (see Chapter 4). All three theories tend to take a manipulative view of other human beings. But generalizations are dangerous. The positions are not quite as blunt and simple as they may appear here, as you will see.

Conventional morality represents a quantum leap upwards in ethical maturity and social sensitivity. The moral focus shifts away from egocentric selfishness outward toward the expectations of society. Loyalty, duty, obedience become the central virtues. Conventional morality is governed by the laws, taboos, and expectations of the groups in which one moves

---

[7]Lawrence Kohlberg, "Stages of Moral Development as a Basis for Moral Education," in *Moral Education: Interdisciplinary Approaches*, C. M. Beck, ed., (Toronto: University of Toronto Press, 1971).

and works and lives. Loyalty and law are more important than selfish pre-occupations. How business policies and business decisions would look in the headlines would be a ruling concern. Heteronomy—focus on others—is the ethical rule. The story is one of social rules and respect for formal authority.

Conventional morality makes the *approval and disapproval of the group* the norm of moral good and evil (see Chapter 5). When we look to this approval and disapproval insofar as it is formally encoded in laws, we have legalism as a business ethics. *Law* defines good and evil. Legal means ethical; illegal means unethical (see Chapter 6). Law can be used as an ex-trinsic ethical norm as legalism proposes. Law can also mandate proce-dures to ensure that internal business decisions be made in a responsible fashion: this use of law will be discussed as the "social-accountability model" of business ethics (see Chapter 7). Each of these three theories is concerned about others and the expectations of others. There is an altru-ism and social concern here that is missing at the pre-conventional level.

Finally, Kohlberg's post-conventional morality represents a quantum leap in ethical maturity over the conventional level. It represents morality at the level of the mature adult. The moral focus shifts again, this time away from group expectations and back to the self. But this is not a return to the selfishness of level one. Not egotism but autonomy is the rule—the self as autonomous. I'm less concerned about how others see me, and more concerned about how I see and judge myself. Ethical decision-making at this level submits even laws and moral conventions to the test of universal moral principle to which the autonomous self is committed. Ethical princi-ples appeal to comprehensiveness and logical consistency.

Pragmatism as a business philosophy and ethics puts human *reason* operating on the *scientific model* in the ethical driver's seat. Rational method becomes the central ethical principle to which laws, conventions, and decisions must submit (see Chapter 8). Marxism as an approach to just economic distribution is even more confident in human reason than is pragmatism. Whence Marxism is less experimental and more sure of *rea-son's* ability to plan *a priori* a humane ideal economic society (see Chapter 9). Finally we look at representative critics who pronounce a plague on both the house of pragmatism and of Marxism. E. F. Schumacher, Tibor Scitovsky, and Ivan Illich, each from his own ethical perspective, criticize on *humane* grounds the industrial West and the ideals of the industrial West as these are propagated to the Third World (see Chapter 10). Post-conventional morality relies on universal ethical principles like the pri-macy of reason and of humanism to overcome both the selfishness of pre-conventional morality and the heteronomy that characterizes conventional morality. Ethical autonomy is the key value.

Finally, one can't deal with ethics and economic values today without adverting to John Rawls on justice. The theory of Rawls represents the highest stage of post-conventional morality. Debate on his theory still rages hot and heavy and perspective is not yet easily attained. But an Appendix is included in which the student is briefly introduced to John Rawls, to Robert Nozick his libertarian critic, and to the utilitarians, themselves objects of Rawls's philosophical criticism and, more than incidentally, themselves representative of yet one more approach to business ethics today.

How to use this book. So much for the organization of the book as a whole. The chapters, with some modifications, are organized as follows. The *objectives* at the head of each chapter will give you an idea of what the chapter contains, and of the main points to be understood and mastered. Then there will be a *values-clarification exercise.* The purpose of this exercise is to help the student become aware of his/her present attitudes toward the issues to be raised in the chapter before reading the chapter. The exercise could be done individually, with the answers compared and discussed in groups afterward. This can prepare the student to assimilate the *premises* of the business philosophy in question and the associated *business ethics.* Does the philosophical reasoning presented change any of his/her preliminary attitudes? When the philosophical ethics is understood, there comes time to *evaluate* the philosophy and its ethics using the strategy proposed in Section 2 of this chapter above. Objections and answers, pro and con, will be presented for the student's reflection.

At the end there will be a couple of short *cases for discussion* intended to point up concretely the key issues raised by the business philosophy examined in the chapter. This is not a case-study book, nor does it intend to discuss the wide range of concrete issues afflicting business today. It intends to elucidate alternative business philosophies that might be brought to bear on such issues so that students can evaluate these with a view to articulating their own approach. Cases are included at the end of each chapter to highlight important philosophical points and to illustrate the kinds of concrete ethical issues a business person must confront. Teacher and student will want to supplement these by developing their own cases, and exploring in depth one or more concrete problem areas on which a business philosophy is brought to bear. The brief cases included in the book lend themselves to discussion in small groups. The students can thereby consolidate their understanding of the chapter and their evaluation of the business ethics in question. In the process of evaluating other philosophies students will be assisted in articulating their own business ethics. At the end of the case discussions, the student might profitably use 5 or 10 minutes of class time to write up his/her conclusions and reasoning about some aspect of the case. In this way, the discussion can come to a point and not wind down to an aimless end.

Finally, each chapter includes a short list of suggested readings wherein the reader can explore in more depth the business ethical topics that the chapter treats in a necessarily oversimplified and outline way.

DISCUSSION QUESTIONS

1. Economics professor Paul T. Heyne of Southern Methodist University defines the ethical businessman as follows:

> If an ethical businessman has to be defined, we would define him simply as a man who is the full measure of what a man should be.
> No serious ethical inquiry can escape the question of what it means to be human. What is "the nature and destiny of man," to use Reinhold Niebuhr's phrase? . . .
> The situation of the businessman is just a special instance of the human situation, and no temptation befalls him that is not common to man.

(a) Do you agree that your business ethics basically rests upon your philosophy of what it means to be a human being, as Heyne asserts?

(b) In taking an ethical stand in business, when it comes to the crunch does your personal philosophy override considerations of social convention, law, and religion, or is it the other way around?

Consider the following case:

> David Decker worked as chief bookkeeper in a small lumber-furniture company for nine years. He is a 45-year-old bachelor, somewhat introverted, the kind of a person who keeps pretty much to himself. He supervises a small clerical staff competently enough, a modest job suited to his moderate talent. He had to fire one of his typists, Anne, who, though popular with her co-workers, was extremely lazy and careless. Anne subsequently accused David of making obscene phone calls to her. He was arraigned and charged, and waived a jury trial. The judge found him not guilty on grounds of insufficient evidence. When he returned to work, many of the workers, male and female, refused to associate with David. Office procedures were disrupted. Some of the female workers ask you, the manager, to get rid of David, since they do not like working under "a creep and pervert."

(c) What conflicting values are you faced with resolving?

(d) What would be your managerial decision? Why?

(e) Is there a moral dimension to your decision, i.e., a challenge to your conscience as a morally responsible human being? Explain.

(f) Do you sense any conflict between a good managerial decision and a good moral decision?

2. Albert Shapero, Professor of Management at the University of Texas at Austin, describes as follows an attitude common in many segments of the business community:

> Why not bribe officials if it will get you the sales and make the annual report look good? Why not lower product quality to just about the lawsuit level? Why provide more than the minimum of service to maintain profits? You will swiftly be promoted to another department if you can keep the numbers right. Show me a 35-year-old executive with an MBA from a very good school who wants to stay in direct sales because he likes making customers happy, who likes his colleagues and wishes them every success, and who would never do anything unethical, and I will show you a man known as a "religious type," as a "loser."[8]

(a) What business philosophy would you say is operative here?

(b) Would you prefer your salespeople to be imbued with this philosophy, or would you prefer "religious types"? Why exactly?

Consider the following case:

> Louie Rodriguez is a cabbie at a large metropolitan airport. He has begun bribing dispatchers to give him long-distance runs, a practice well accepted at the airport. Those who don't offer bribes may make "a halfway decent living," he says, "but only if they're lucky. Most of the time, unless you pay them, you're just not going to get anything." Since "joining them," Louie has made what he calls a decent living: $45-$55 a day for 12–15 hours work. Occasionally he goes downtown where he's not licensed in order to "steal fares. I could get a $60 ticket for that. But you get to the point where you have to make some money, and how else are you going to do it? Desperate situations call for desperate means."

(c) Does Louie give some indication of his philosophy of "the nature and destiny of man," to use Niebuhr's phrase again?

(d) Would you characterize a cabbie who never paid a bribe and never broke the law as "a loser"?

(e) Is Louie's behavior unethical?

[8]Shapero, op. cit.

SUGGESTED READINGS

1. Business Ethics

Beauchamp, Tom L., and Norman E. Bowie. *Ethical Theory and Business,* Englewood Cliffs, N.J., Prentice-Hall, Inc., 1979.

Cavanagh, Gerald F. *American Business Values in Transition.* Englewood Cliffs, N.J.: Prentice-Hall, Inc., 1976.

Davis, Keith, and Robert L. Blomstrom. *Business and Society: Environment and Responsibility.* New York: McGraw-Hill Book Co., 1975.

De George, Richard T., and Joseph A. Pichler (eds.). *Ethics, Free Enterprise, and Public Policy: Original Essays on Moral Issues in Business.* New York: Oxford University Press, 1978.

Donaldson, Thomas, and Patricia H. Werhane (eds.), *Ethical Issues in Business,* Englewood Cliffs, N.J., Prentice-Hall, Inc., 1979.

Garrett, Thomas M. *Business Ethics.* New York: Appleton-Century-Crofts, 1966.

Garrett, Thomas M. *Business Ethics.* New York: Appleton-Century-Crofts, 1966.

Heilbroner, Robert L., and Paul London (eds.). *Corporate Social Policy: Selections from Business and Society Review.* Reading, Ma.: Addison-Wesley Publishing Co., 1975.

Heyne, Paul T. *Private Keepers of the Public Interest.* New York: McGraw-Hill Book Co., 1968.

Johnson, M. Bruce (ed.). *The Attack on Corporate America: The Corporate Issues Sourcebook.* New York: McGraw-Hill Book Co., 1978.

Kohlberg, Lawrence. "Moral Stages and Moralization: The Cognitive-Developmental Approach," in *Moral Development and Behavior: Theory, Research, and Social Issues,* ed. by T. Likona. New York: Holt, Rinehart and Winston, 1976.

La Croix, W. L. *Principles for Ethics in Business.* Washington, D.C.: University Press of America, 1976.

Sutton, Francis X., *et al. The American Business Creed.* New York: Schocken Books, 1962.

Weber, Max. *The Protestant Ethic and the Spirit of Capitalism.* New York: Charles Scribner's Sons, 1958.

Wish, John R., and Stephen H. Gamble (eds.). *Marketing and Social Issues: An Action Reader.* New York: John Wiley and Sons, 1971.

2. Some Sample Case-Sources in Business Ethics

Bauer, Raymond, and Robert Ackerman. *Corporate Social Responsiveness.* Reston, Va.: Reston Publishing Co., 1976.

Eckel, Malcolm W. *Case Studies* [in Business] *From the Ethics of Decision-making.* New York: Morehouse-Barlow Co., recent undated partial reprint from the original 1968 edition.

Garrett, Thomas M., Raymond C. Baumhart, Theodore V. Purcell, and Perry Roets. *Cases in Business Ethics.* Englewood Cliffs, N.J.: Prentice-Hall, Inc., 1968.

Litschert, Robert J., and Edward A. Nicholson. *The Corporate Role and Ethical Behavior: Concepts and Cases.* New York: D. Van Nostrand, 1977.

Luthans, Fred, and Richard M. Hodgetts. *Social Issues in Business: A Text with Current Readings and Cases.* New York: Macmillan Publishing Co., Inc., 1976.

McCloy, John J., Chairman. *Report of the Special Review Committee of the Board of Directors of the Gulf Oil Corporation.* In the United States District Court for the District of Columbia, Civil Action No. 75-0324.

Seidler, Lee J. *Social Accounting: Theory, Issues and Cases.* New York: John Wiley and Sons, 1975.

CHAPTER 2

SOCIAL DARWINISM: THE IRON LAW OF SURVIVAL

As every individual, therefore, endeavors as much as he can both to employ his capital in the support of domestic industry, and so to direct that industry that its produce may be of the greatest value; every individual necessarily labours to render the annual revenue of the society as great as he can. He generally indeed neither intends to promote the public interest, nor knows how much he is promoting it. . . . [B]y directing that industry in such a manner that its produce may be of the greatest value, he intends only his own gain, and he is in this as in many other cases led by an invisible hand to promote an end which was no part of his intention. Nor is it always the worse for the society that it was no part of it. By pursuing his own interest he frequently promotes that of the society more effectually than when he really intends to promote it.

Adam Smith, *The Wealth of Nations*[1]

The growth of a large business is merely a survival of the fittest. . . . The American Beauty rose can be produced in the splendour and fragrance which bring cheer to its beholder only by sacrificing the early buds which grow up around it. This is not an evil tendency in business. It is merely the working-out of a law of nature and a law of God.

John D. Rockefeller, Sr.[2]

---

[1]Adam Smith, *The Wealth of Nations* (New York: The Modern Library, 1937), p. 423.
[2]John D. Rockefeller, Sr., as quoted by William J. Ghent in *Our Benevolent Feudalism* (New York: Macmillan, 1902), p. 29.

OBJECTIVES FOR CHAPTER 2:

1. To clarify one's own present attitude toward "The Iron Law of Survival" as a basis for business ethics;

2. To understand the philosophical assumptions that underpin the philosophy of Social Darwinism;

3. To be able to explain Spencer's view of

(a) how natural selection operates in human society

(b) why Social Darwinism requires a policy of laissez-faire;

(c) why Social Darwinism is an optimistic philosophy;

(d) why survival requires cooperation as well as competition;

(e) why survival and morality are not opposed to one another;

4. To understand the main objections brought against Social Darwinism, and replies that can be given to such objections;

5. To evaluate for oneself how true and complete a picture this philosophy gives of what it means to be a human being, and therefore how adequate the business ethics is that flows from this philosophy of Social Darwinism.

1. THE IMMORALITY OF MORALITY

A moral decision is just that—a decision. There are alternatives. You have a choice. Without freedom, there is no morality. We examine in this chapter the claim that freedom is exactly what is lacking in the business world. It follows from this that morality in the business world is irrelevant because impossible. There really are no alternatives. Business decisions are determined by forces greater than you or me or any individual person. It is not free responsible decision that directs the course of industry, but rather impersonal inevitable law. Thus classical economist Adam Smith sees business guided by the "invisible hand" of economic laws, while biological law—"survival of the fittest"—determines the growth of business, says John D. Rockefeller, Sr. So the burden of moral responsibility is shifted off the shoulders of the individual and onto "nature." Leave natural laws alone and all will prosper. Paradoxically, to introduce moral considerations into the inevitable working out of natural laws may be the one real immorality.

> By pursuing his own interest he frequently promotes that of the society more effectively than when he really intends to promote it.[3]

[3]The following is an attempt to expound Spencer's philosophy in as favorable a light as possible. This book does not intend to advocate any one particular philosophy. Rather it will present alternative philosophies for the reader's own evaluation. This writer's own predilection lies with pragmatism, to be presented below. This philosophy, too, has its difficulties that will likewise be submitted to the reader's own evaluation.

So Adam Smith. Follow nature's laws if you would best serve business and society. The "robber barons" were not such in their own eyes. They were nature's servants. Let's now examine and evaluate the business philosophy that supports such an approach to life.

2. SOCIAL DARWINISM

Social Darwinism was one of the most eloquent examples of this business philosophy with its associated ethics. "Struggle for existence" and "survival of the fittest" became the slogans that men lived by. I'm talking about the third quarter of the nineteenth century and of the shattering impact on human thinking of Darwin's arrival on the scene. But it wasn't Charles Darwin who spoke to the business persons of those times. It was Herbert Spencer (1820–1903). The name, Herbert Spencer, is hardly a household word today, but the fervor that he inspired in his contemporaries was literally religious. He filled a gaping need. Darwin's evolutionary hypothesis had seemed to deal a death blow not only to traditional biology but more importantly to religion and morality as well. Spencer picked up the pieces and showed how the world could make sense again, even when seen through Darwinian eyeglasses. In fact, Spencer showed how a vigorous and optimistic morality could be founded on evolutionary principles drawn from biology.

It is hard for us to imagine today what a comfortable little universe Western man lived in before Darwin's time. Why, one even knew the date of creation. It was 4004 B.C. Just count the years of the biblical genealogies leading back to that day "in the beginning" when "God created heaven and earth"—in six days, resting on the seventh. The species were fixed and unchanging, and Adam named them one and all: "This is a giraffe, that's an elephant, and there goes a rabbit." And to the divinely created world corresponded a divinely established moral law. Man's place in the sun was clear, his duties clearly defined. All was stamped with the authority of Holy Writ.

When that authority collapsed, this secure little universe caved in with it. Darwin did the damage. There was no fixed and tidy date of creation. Plant and animal species had developed over thousands and millions of years. In fact, there was no creation. Evolution sufficiently accounts for the various forms of life. Not only does life appear in diverse forms, but these forms themselves are not fixed and unchanging but rather are constantly evolving. And more importantly, man was not created specially by God. Man, too, evolved from lower forms and is evolving still. And since there is no divinely established and fixed human species, there is no correspondingly fixed moral law established by God for humankind. Moral duties were no longer clearly defined. Mankind had lost his place in the sun. The authority of Scripture was overturned and with it went traditional morality.

Spencer stepped into the breach. He repaired the damage, not by getting around Darwin, but by taking the evolutionary hypothesis itself as the cornerstone of a whole new world of science, philosophy, and ethics. Beginning in 1860 he started turning out a series of volumes of his "synthetic philosophy." His aim was to synthesize physics, biology, philosophy, sociology, and ethics into one coherent structure. He took Darwin's evolution by natural selection and applied it across the board. Darwin's hypothesis was no longer to be confined to biology. It would serve to interpret the foundations of philosophy, the workings and progress of society, and the basis of ethics. This "biologizing" of philosophy resulted in Spencer's grand, all-encompassing system. A framework for hope and morality had been restored, but on new terms. Let's see how. But first:

3. IS THERE A SOCIAL DARWINIST HIDDEN INSIDE OF YOU?

Before getting on to Spencer, let's look to ourselves. Spencerian values are still alive and very much in the air. Perhaps you espouse them yourself. The following statements may provide a clue. How strongly do you agree or disagree with them? Give yourself an honest test. Before each statement fill in a number.

VALUES-CLARIFICATION TEST

1 = strongly disagree, 2 = disagree, 3 = not sure,
4 = agree; 5 = strongly agree

_____ 1. Human nature doesn't change. There's no moral breakdown in business. The economics of competition has always followed its own ironclad laws. The so-called "robber barons" understood and obeyed these laws. They were not robbers in any moral sense at all. Nor are business persons today.

_____ 2. Competition and profits are ideals in their own right; it is empty idealism to speak of higher purposes for business.

_____ 3. Society is served best when competition is allowed free rein; restraint on competition can only hurt society; it violates a fundamental natural law.

_____ 4. In an auto-insurance claim or product-liability suit, I as a consumer will sue for all I can get, however small the injury I actually sustained; my survival comes first: let others look to themselves.

_____ 5. As a supermarket shopper, if I can switch price labels or shift butter into margarine packages, so much the better for me: let the seller beware.

_____ 6. As an employee, I help myself to supplies from work. While this practice is not officially approved of, it's done widely enough, I'm the better off for it, and no one is hurt.

_____ 7. Sick leave in my nonunionized company is only for the sick; to me, however, it's time due off, pure and simple; I'll call in sick whenever I want a holiday.

_____ 8. Self-restraint in the pursuit of higher wages by the worker is just as self-contradictory as self-restraint in the pursuit of higher prices by the producer; the iron law of supply and demand inevitably should prevail.

_____ 9. The suspicion of excessive dividends or of unethical practices in a company are of no concern to me the shareholder; my only interest is maximum return of my investment.

_____ 10. As a business manager, I am the key player in a game; he who understands the inevitable operation of economic laws will win the day; winning is what matters.

Note three things. First, business ethics is a net that catches many fish. There are many roles in business. Business involves shareholders or owners, customers or consumers, directors, managers, producers, sales persons, laborers, etc. Decisions made in each role have a moral and ethical dimension. As we will note in a later chapter, there are both differences and similarities between individual flesh-and-blood business persons and the fictitious, legal corporate *persona* of a business institution. Business ethics as applied to each will reflect these similarities and differences. While we will not neglect business ethics at the institutional level, the stress will be on alternative business philosophies as they are embodied in and are acted upon by individuals. At times the corporate *persona* will closely reflect the ethical standards of the executive officers and other personnel, to the point even of encoding and institutionalizing these standards. More often, no such merging of individual and institutional ethics can be assumed. But always the two levels are closely connected. On the other hand, the moral decisions of individual business people must take into account institutional constraints. On the other, the ethical climate of the institution will often be very much a function of the kinds of decision-makers who happen to be in the business at a given time and place. In this latter sense, assurance of ethically responsible corporate conduct is pretty much left to chance—a problem that will be dealt with later on in the book.

Secondly, note that the interests of the various business roles are often in conflict. Were your answers to the above questions consistent? Do you as a customer or employee feel justified in grabbing everything you can, while condemning a business manager for doing the same? Or would you, the boss, applaud managerial survival tactics while frowning upon customers who connive for their own survival?

Thirdly, the more strongly you agreed with the statements in the above values-clarification exercise, the more sympathy you'll doubtless feel for Social Darwinism as a business philosophy. It's a question of what value priorities you feel are operative—must be operative—in the business world. Competition, survival, profit-maximizing, self-interest, and facing up to economic inevitabilities all are values that no business or business person can afford to ignore. But not everyone would assign them first place. Everyone would admit that these are constraints on business decisions. But do these constraints carry a moral weight as well? In the Social Darwinist view, these values function as crucial moral determinants of business decisions. They are inevitably woven into the very fabric of economic life as it is carried on. Compare with others your agreement or disagreement with the value-statements above. Compare the reasons for your answers with the reasons others had. It is entirely possible, however, that the reasons for your answers don't coincide with Spencer's. We need now to look at the operative philosophy.

4. THE ASSUMPTIONS

Social Darwinism need not be understood as a prescription for cut-throat capitalism. One of its inspirations lies in the work of the eighteenth-century economist Adam Smith, who sought to reconcile private interest and public virtue. His answer was a marvel of simplicity. There is no conflict: the pursuit of private greed will result in public good. Leave the market mechanism alone, and the self-interest of one business person will be balanced out by the self-interest of the others. The "invisible hand" of economic law will keep prices down and employment up. The competitive struggle for goods begets a well-ordered society. This was Smith's ideal. He held no brief for grinding down the worker or trampling upon the poor.

Herbert Spencer wedded Darwin's evolutionary theory to Smith's "invisible hand," and Social Darwinism was born. What assumptions about life, the world, and the business process underlie this philosophy? Not very inspiringly, the law of conservation of energy was Spencer's starting point. As he put it, everywhere in the universe, matter and motion are incessantly redistributed. Two processes are involved: evolution and devolution. These are contrary, and they complement one another. *Evolution* is the progressive integration of matter with the dissipation of motion. The jogger's cardiovascular system evolves and grows strong as he spends his energy around the track. Effective decision-making, a productive work force, skillfully invested capital: such expenditures of energy make a business evolve and grow strong. *Devolution* is the reserve side of the process. It is the breakup, the disorganization of matter, with the absorption of motion. As matter is spent, energy is gained. Think of the fiery heat given off by the oxidation and breakdown of wood. It is the expenditure of matter that fuels the wheels of industry. Energy doesn't come from nowhere. As Spencer put it, matter and motion are incessantly redistributed. Progress requires energy at every level. There will be a material cost and a human cost. To lament this fact is sentimentally to close your eyes to a universal law: evolution and devolution are contrary and complementary.

The life-force is essentially *evolutionary* (rather than devolutionary). And that's good news. This life-force has a direction. It moves from the less complex to the more complex, i.e., from incoherent homogeneity to coherent heterogeneity, as Spencer says. This is inevitable. Homogeneity is essentially unstable. Give every person in the world $1,000, no more, no less (homogeneity). In 24 hours, you'll have millionaires, paupers, and every economic level in between (heterogeneity). There is an inevitable thrust toward diversification, complexification, growth.

We see this law of progressive complexity operative everywhere. For example, from the nebular mass the solar system was formed. In the course of evolution on earth, the relatively simple amoeba evolved into the complex organism called man. And biogenesis recapitulates phylogenesis. In the evolution of a single human organism, the relatively simple zygote evolves into the mature, diversified, many-faceted adult human being. Intellectual evolution follows the same pattern and direction. The mind of the infant is what Aristotle called a *tabula rasa*, a blank tablet, and that mind grows into the experienced, many-dimensioned intellect of the wise man. And it is intellectual evolution that Spencer is especially concerned with. This sets him apart from Darwin. It's not just biology, but the les-

sons learned from biology as they apply to humankind. That's the focus of
Spencer. And in the realm of society itself, we find evolution from small
tribal units to larger units, provinces, confederations of provinces, the nation state, and eventually perhaps a world-wide global society. You may
well challenge each and all of these assumptions, but for now let's accept
them and see where they lead. Why does the life-force, why do human beings, why do societies evolve in the direction of increasing complexity? The
answer to that question is quite simple. Complexity has a survival value.

The winners in evolution's relentless forward push are those who best
exemplify this survival law. The baseball player who can hit, run, play in-
field and outfield is likely to have a longer career than the slow-footed
power-hitter. The college student with the hyphenated major, biology-phi-
losophy, psychology-management, physical education-art, will go further
than the one who puts all his chips in one basket, say, nineteenth-century
English literature. The manager who knows his way around sales, finance,
and personnel is more valuable than the expert cost-cutter who knows little else. An oil company that has integrated control of oil from well to
pump and is reaching out horizontally to control plutonium, coal, and natural gas as well is another illustration of the survival value of diversification. In these ways do we live out the Spencerian evolutionary law for survival and growth.[4]

Businesses survive because they're fit. They're fit because they're in
tune with the natural laws of evolution. It was Spencer, not Darwin, who
coined the slogan "survival of the fittest." That expression, which has become a cliché, is the key to how evolution works. Implicit here is Spencer's
optimism. This is the secret of the hold he had on his contemporaries and
of the enthusiasm he inspired. Spencer's was a gospel of progress. And
businesses carried on in Spencer's terms were at the very forefront of the
progressive wave of evolution.

Darwin saw the biological species survive and grow by nature's selecting the best and the most fit for survival. Spencer extended this biological
optimism to human society. He made it a general law of evolution that embraced and explained not merely biological improvement but human moral
progress as well. And indeed the American scene after the Civil War gave
a ready plausibility to this picture of evolution as a struggle for existence
where nature selected out only the fittest to survive. Human failures were

---

[4]If diversification and complexification have a survival value, what about the divestiture
battle to break the tight hold that oil has on the energy industry? The test of natural selection
holds true here as well, we might say, using Spencerian principles. Environment is the selec-
tor, and the social environment in which the oil industry operates cannot be ignored with impunity. An industry's anticompetitive stance can be a detriment to survival when society per-
ceives this as threatening to itself. As we'll see below, Spencer points out that cooperation as
well as competition is required for survival as civilization advances.

shunted aside; competition was desperate; exploitation was the rule of the day. Not only did the winners in this struggle survive, but their very survival marked them out and set them apart as good and as morally superior. In the Darwinian framework, their survival alone was without further qualification a boon to the human race. For, who survived? Those who had skill and self-control. Those who had the intelligence and power to use technology to adapt to the environment. This natural environment stood as the norm, implacably weeding out the weak and rewarding the strong. And the strong by their very survival were revealed to be good—good in themselves and good for the race.

5. CONSEQUENCES FOR ETHICS

It is not surprising that businessmen of the time instinctively embraced this philosophy, which so perfectly reflected the climate of their day-to-day operations. There was a sense of having finally discovered a scientific basis for ethics. Darwinian biological evolution, extended by Spencer to human social evolution, reveals the fundamental principles of moral right and moral wrong.

Ethical progress, then, involves improvement of human character. Natural selection, left unimpeded, guarantees this improvement. "The best and the brightest" will survive to carry the race onward and upward. Adaptation of human character to the stern selective conditions of life is good. The root of evil, on the other hand, is the attempt to interfere with this process of selective adaptation for survival. Why evil? Because this is the same as interfering with the progress and improvement of the human race. Whether you are talking of a human being or of a business, if it is not viable it should go under. Artificially to preserve an unsound business weakens and slows all business, much like the artificial preservation of human defectives pollutes the gene pool, as some modern biologists like to say.

This immediately leads to a second consequence of Social Darwinism for business ethics, viz., the doctrine of laissez-faire. The biological law of natural selection provides a scientific basis for the political philosophy of governmental nonintervention in the business process. The struggle for survival benefits society as a whole. It weeds out the weak in favor of the strong. Government intervention would only hamper this progress, whence the doctrine of laissez-faire. This doctrine guarantees the natural right of every person and of every business to do as it pleases so long as it does not infringe on this same equal right in others. The sole function of government is a negative one: to insure that this freedom is not curbed.

Such unimpeded growth by natural selection has its price, to be sure. Nature puts everyone to the test. There's to be no cheating. Nature insists that mental and moral defectives no less than physical defectives be swept aside to make room for their betters. The poor, the crippled, the idle and the stupid are all in the same boat as far as natural selection is concerned.

These are harsh words to contemporary ears. But a harsh philosophy is not necessarily a false philosophy. If it gives a true picture of reality, one does not violate it with impunity. Reality will strike back. And indeed, even today we hear Spencer's accents, for example, in debates about business's dealings with the Third World. Consider the question of global famine. Here, many argue that we should apply the *triage* concept of medical treatment in time of disaster. The "sick" nations should be divided into three groups, the argument goes. The first group would comprise those we can cure; the second, those we can help cure themselves; and the third, those that are beyond cure. The last group should be allowed to go under. To prolong the survival of the terminally ill only weakens the health of all. This aspect of Social Darwinism might be viewed as an extreme application of the "lifeboat ethic." If the raft can't support all, some must die so that some may survive, else all alike will perish. Spencer is concerned not merely with survival but with a survival that is progress.

Artificial attempts to forestall natural selection, then, only end up staying the advent of the ideal society (to be described below). Government intervention in business penalizes the superior and perpetuates the inferior. Political science (or sociology, as Spencer called it) is not the study of how to direct society, but the study of why society cannot be directed. No one, not even the state, can suspend the law of natural selection. Nor should anyone desire to. In the eyes of the nineteenth-century industrial magnates, to obey nature's laws as enunciated by Spencer was an act of worship, a bowing down to the divinely established order of things. Listen to John D. Rockefeller, Sr.:

> The growth of a large business is merely a survival of the fittest. . . . The American Beauty Rose can be produced in the splendour and fragrance which bring cheer to its beholder only by sacrificing the early buds which grow up around it. This is not an evil tendency in business. It is merely the working-out of a law of nature and a law of God.[5]

And Andrew Carnegie, one of Spencer's most ardent followers, says:

> I remember that light came as in a flood and all was clear. Not only had I got rid of theology and the supernatural, but I had found the truth of

[5]Ghent, *op. cit.*

evolution. "All is well since all grows better," became my motto, my true source of comfort. Man was not created with an instinct for his own degradation, but from the lower he had risen to the higher forms. Nor is there any conceivable end to his march to perfection. His face is turned to the light; he stands in the sun and looks upward.[6]

What place was there in Spencer's mind for charity and for religion? He himself did not speak with the religious piety of his devoted followers. He granted that religion could come in where science fell short. However much we learn, there is always much we don't know. There'll always be, then, a place for the "worship of the Unknowable." This unknown "X," which is the object of religion, conveniently leaves every person free to fill in the blank as he or she pleases. Nor did Spencer's harsh strictures against interference with natural selection cause him to condemn charity shown to the poor and the weak. Charity ennobles the giver; this spiritual enrichment of the giver presumably outweighs the harm to the human race resulting from the material enrichment of the unfit receivers whose elimination charity impedes. Such concessions to charity and religion do little to mitigate a seemingly harsh and callous picture that Spencer paints of business's relation to society. It would be wrong, however, to rest the case for Social Darwinism on such a dismal note.

6. A UTOPIA, NOT A JUNGLE

Spencer was thoroughly optimistic, a fact which accounts in large part for his popularity. To him, natural selection is a process that guarantees the gradual disappearance of evil. Utopia is not a dream but an inevitability. In his own words:

The ultimate development of the ideal man is logically certain—as certain as any conclusion in which we place the most implicit faith; for in-

[6] Quoted by Richard Hofstadter, *Social Darwinism in American Thought* (New York: George Braziller Inc., 1959), p. 31. It would be instructive to compare and contrast the management styles of Andrew Carnegie, John D. Rockefeller, Sr., and Henry Ford. Clarence Walton in *Corporate Social Responsibilities* (Belmont, Ca.: Wadsworth Publishing Co., 1967), Chapter 2, suggests that each could be viewed as adumbrating a particular model of business's social responsibility. The Carnegie prototype would today be called the "investment model" of social responsibility, with survival as the main goal and the firm as the main beneficiary of a business's activity. John Rockefeller, more than the others, reflects what we would call a "civic model" of responsibility, more aware of the good of society at large and characterized by philanthropy on a grand scale. Ford, with his sensitivity to workers' needs, was the proto-type of the "household" model. See Walton, pp. 122–41, where various models of responsibility are set forth. Carnegie, above all, epitomized Social Darwinism. Rockefeller was not far behind with his "American Beauty Rose" doctrine, by which he amassed his fortune.

stance, that all men will die. . . . Progress, therefore, is not an accident, but a necessity. Instead of civilization being artificial, it is a part of nature; all of a piece with the development of the embryo or the unfolding of a flower.[7]

This vision of the society to be achieved is certainly attractive. But the means by which it is to be achieved—natural selection—strikes many of us today as ruthless, callous, and offensive to our humanistic feelings. To point out that this is the way it is with all of the animal species does little to assuage our moral sensibilities. It is true that the business world even today has place for what Michael Maccoby calls "the jungle fighters."[8] They are found especially in the highly competitive industries. In auto-parts sales, for example, and in the garment industry, the survivors are the jungle practitioners of ruthless cost-cutting, of risk-taking bordering on the reckless, and of sharp sales practices. But however much the harsh law of ruthless competition rules in the jungle, we like to think that human society is, or should be, different. This objection causes many people to dismiss Social Darwinism out of hand as unable to provide a viable framework for business ethics in these more humanistic times. However, the dog-eat-dog struggle for survival is not Spencer's last word about natural selection. With the advance of civilization, he saw a change in the mechanism by which natural selection works. And new forces operative in today's business world tend to bear him out. Jungle-fighting can undermine the cohesiveness necessary to the survival of the modern corporation.

In the past, a competitive struggle for survival among individuals, businesses, and nations *did* have a socializing as well as an eliminative effect. In other words, the struggle served to build up society as well as to eliminate unfit individuals. It was dog eat dog, true; but the very fight

---

[7]Herbert Spencer, *Social Statics* (New York: D. Appleton and Co., 1886), pp. 79–80. In Charles Darwin and Herbert Spencer we have the seeds of the genetic approach to moral evolution by natural selection which today has eventuated in Edward O. Wilson's controversial socio-biological approach to ethical behavior. The reader might pursue the implications for business ethics of Wilson's *Sociobiology: The New Synthesis* (Cambridge, Ma.: The Belknap Press of Harvard University Press, 1975), and especially his latest book, *On Human Nature* (Cambridge, Ma.: Harvard University Press, 1978), in which he spells out the implications of socio-biology for human behavior, including religious and ethical.

[8]Michael Maccoby, *The Gamesman* (New York: Simon and Schuster, 1976), Chapter 3. See also Albert Carr, *Business as a Game* (New York, 1968). Norman C. Gillespie in "The Business of Ethics," *University of Michigan Business Review* (November 1975), 1-4, tackles head-on Carr's reduction of business to the level of decisions made by a player in a poker game. A business person, for example, may be forced to compromise his/her moral principles out of fear for the family's economic security. Gillespie admits that perhaps a business person is not rightly condemned for compromising on such occasions. But that doesn't make the business game itself all right. It points to something rotten in the rules of that game, rules that put a player in such a morally compromising position.

served to bring the dogs together in a way that a world without competition never would have done. The Vietnam war turned Asian names and places into household words in America. They were the enemy, but they were no longer strangers. Terrorists of every variety understand this socializing effect of competitive aggression. Their very acts of kidnapping and extortion make their causes familiar, and thanks to the media these acts serve to introduce their leaders to the public consciousness. A John L. Lewis or a George Meaney is an adversary to management, but the resulting confrontations forge links between labor and management unthinkable in nineteenth-century sweatshops. Right now blacks, other minorities, and women have entered the fray.

In the past, the mode of competition has tended toward outright belligerence, be it the wars of competing nations, the strikes and lockouts of competing economic classes, or the protests, violent and otherwise, of the minorities competing for their place in the sun. The fittest meant the strongest, and these survived. Might made right. But with the development of civilization, Spencer saw natural selection producing a new human nature. This new humankind would be more adaptive to the increasing complexity of industrial society, and hence *it* would survive. There would evolve a world in which strategic arms limitation talks would seem a better bet for survival than war; a world in which negotiated no-strike agreements and compulsory arbitration would seem superior to the kind of mutual defiance that could bring an industry or an economy down; a world in which communication and education seemed to promise more for advance than would violence. As civilization advances, then, survival demands a new set of virtues. The fittest are now those who are responsive to others and honest; they know how to cooperate and communicate; they can be assertive without being belligerent.

When viewed in these revised terms, "survival of the fittest" is no longer the old harsh cliché. When natural selection results in business and business people taking on these new survival qualities, we will then have Spencer's ideal society. Humankind, he says, is ineluctably tending toward a stable, harmonious, completely adapted condition; in this final form it will have reached the greatest perfection and most complete happiness.

7. RUTHLESS CAN MEAN ETHICAL

Is this movement away from *competition* for survival and toward *cooperation* for survival the same as a movement away from an unethical society toward a more ethical state of affairs? Suppose I do what has to be done in a world where the ruthless competitor carries the day. Am I the less moral and ethical than the one who does what has to be done in a world where the skillful cooperator rules and survives? Survival *or* morality? Is this the question?

Not at all. It is not uncommon, however, to hear business people express their moral dilemmas in such terms. And if they see the question boiling down to survival or morality, not surprisingly they'll most often opt for survival; and they will justify themselves on what they consider to be hard-nosed Social Darwinist grounds. Following right along, their moral critics chide them for putting survival first.

Such a debate is all very legitimate, but it's not Social Darwinism. Spencer's claim is that survival *is* morality. The two are not to be opposed. When survival favors the strong, the competitive, the superior, then those who possess these qualities become morally virtuous and those who don't become depraved. When survival favors fairness, cooperativeness, sensitivity, then these become the cardinal virtues and vice is their opposite.

By what right do Spencer and the Social Darwinists legislate such a catalogue of virtue and vice? The answer is that nature legislates, not Spencer. See Chapter One. The morally good person, like the morally sound business institution, is the one who is faithful to what it means to be a human being. To be true to oneself as an individual and to be responsive to the social environment in which one operates as a business is the touchstone of morality. And when Spencer looked at the environment of human evolution both individual and social, he saw that same natural environment ruthlessly selecting who would live and who would die. He saw further that this selection favored the improvement of society. The moral imperative of social Darwinism, then, is not to thwart this natural law that works in favor of social progress. He does not invent such an imperative. He discovers it in nature. That's the way things are. A business philosophy is a clear-eyed view of the way things are. A business ethics follows from this. It is an injunction to operate in accordance with the way things are.

8. IS THIS THE WAY THINGS ARE?

Now to the question of truth. The choice of a philosophy is not rightly a matter of whimsy or of temperament alone. In fact, most typically, a philosophy of life is acquired unconsciously through the years in the process of living, deciding, and acting on decisions. I wake up one day to discover that I have a philosophy of life that colors the way I approach the world both ethically and otherwise. Upon reflection I might conclude, for example, that much of what Spencer says resonates with my own business experience. If this is the case, then the question of truth presents itself.

Social Darwinist ethics is only as good as the world-view that underpins it. Does Social Darwinism present a true picture of the world? Are things really the way that Spencer says they are? The following criticisms are offered for the reader's consideration to help him/her come to a just estimate of how true a picture social Darwinism gives of the business world, and consequently of how valid the Spencerian ethics, proposed for that business world, is.

(1) The stronger and fittest businesses deserve to survive; the unfit should be allowed to go under. Sounds good. But consider. Isn't it possible that the business could be very fit in itself, but that the environment is what kills it? Imagine a small ghetto store with smart management keenly attuned to the needs of the neighborhood and with a firm economic base. It needs a loan really to "take off" and by all ordinary standards is a good credit risk. But the banking community with an arbitrary "red-lining" policy effectively stifles the loan. The store goes under. What would Spencer say? It seems that the environment can kill fit and unfit alike. What about the environment changing so that the fit might live?

(2) Price-fixing is illegal, of course. But practices of "administered pricing," "price-leading," and "orderly marketing arrangements" abound. This is but one example that raises the question of whether the business world really presents a picture of fit and unfit, all competing on equal terms so that the fittest will survive. If pure competition does not flourish, then businesses are evolving not according to the law of natural selection but of unnatural selection! Artificial pricing arrangements may well drive out the fit while keeping the unfit breathing through artificial lungs. How much unnatural selection is there in the business world to distort the Spencerian vision of unfettered natural selection?

(3) What are they fit for, those survivors in Spencer's world? They are fit for survival, that's what. Are there other values equal to or better than survival? If so, might not these be morally valuable as well? Is Spencer too quick to identify morality with the ability to survive? Whooping cranes are an endangered species. Will the world be a fitter place if they are allowed to go under? Are there no whooping cranes in the business world, poorly adapted to survive on their own, but possessing other moral attributes that might justify their existence and even artificial support? Must private schools, mad inventors, the publishers of starving poets' verse, and yes, even the Post Office all alike be allowed to sink or swim on their own according to the Spencerian logic?

(4) In connection with the above Social Darwinism has been called a doctrine of the survival of the survivors. Qualities conducive to survival are selected in. Qualities not conducive to survival are selected out. Might

not the latter variations enhance the quality of social evolution, even though they are quite precarious from the standpoint of survival? Why do Super Bowl champions often appear to be so dull, and maverick last-place teams so appealing and endearing? Is it truly to the best interests of the professional sports industry to let the weaker sisters die? What about other industries and small businesses everywhere?

(5) Does Spencer's stress on the survival of individuals, both persons and firms, do justice to the profound and complex interdependencies today experienced in the economic world, above all? Yes, Spencer might reply. I've pointed out that competition as a survival value will give way eventually to cooperation. (See Section 6, above.) And indeed Spencer does point this out. I wonder if present-day Social Darwinists fully appreciate the meaning of "survival of the fittest" when pronounced in these friendlier accents of cooperation rather than competition.

(6) The next objection is so fundamental that I've saved it for the last. The law of natural selection, according to Spencer, operates inevitably and implacably. His philosophy is a determinism. There is no freedom. You can't fight evolution and its laws. If this be the case, there is no room for either moral good or moral evil. There is no basis morally to condemn any person or any institution; nor basis to praise or recommend any either— including laissez-faire government policies toward business! What will be will be. Spencer's philosophy is the story not merely of the way things *are*, but of the way they *must be*.

This is not to deny that decisions are indeed made. And there is the appearance of responsibility, and of the feeling of moral satisfaction that comes with the success signaling nature's blessing. But can Social Darwinism give a satisfactory account of this apparent freedom, responsibility, and moral praise and blame? If apparently free, responsible decisions turn out on closer inspection to be nothing but the human organism's inevitable strivings for survival in the evolutionary struggle, then human behavior loses its moral bite. The human deserves no more or less credit than the weeds pushing up through a summer garden, a fledgling struggling to fly. Morality without freedom is unintelligible. And freedom by definition is eliminated when all behavior is reduced to a biological struggle governed by the iron law of evolutionary survival through natural selection.

Spencer's "robber-baron" disciples were not philosophical sophisticates. They were more likely than he to speak of moral praiseworthiness in the same breath with evolutionary determinism. But moral praise and moral blame make no sense if there are no free moral alternatives. Doubtless this incoherence is a symptom of a kind of schizophrenia that besets us all. Business people are not immune from this tendency to split their professed creed from their day-to-day operational practice.[9] "Do as I say, not as I do," is the usual injunction intended to remedy such schizophrenia. With business people, the injunction should be reversed: "Forget what I say; look at what I do," for more often their practice comes closer to truth and to expected morality than does their ideology.

The six aforementioned objections are meant to challenge social Darwinism. Is it a liveable, realistic philosophy or is it a doctrinaire ideology that distorts the business world as it really is? The questions below can further this discussion.

We move on now from the "no-ethics" of survival's iron law to the "bad ethics" openly professed by the Machiavellian business person.

DISCUSSION QUESTIONS

1. The following conversation is from Michael Maccoby's *The Gamesman: The New Corporate Leaders* (New York: Simon and Schuster, 1976), pp. 202–03. The "gamesman" is the type of corporate leader who plays the role in an emotionally detached, utterly objective fashion. Here is a portion of Maccoby's interview with one such person:

> "It's a mistake for the Government to give money to people who don't work." I asked him, "What about old people, the handicapped, and mothers with dependent children?" "These must be a small minority," he said. I said his view seemed a kind of social Darwinism which stated that those who cannot adapt to the system should fall by the wayside to be sacrificed to progress.
>
> "Yes," he said, "the system works that way."

(a) "The system works that way," says the corporate gamesman. Keeping in mind Section 8, above ("Is This the Way Things Are?"), do you agree with the gamesman's assessment of how the system works? Why exactly?

(b) Is the gamesman's conclusion defensible on social Darwinistic grounds, as Maccoby implies? Show how.

2. Edward Stevens in "What Good are Old People?" *Marriage* (April 1972), 16-18, says of America's view of the elderly:

[9]Francis X. Sutton *et al.* in *The American Business Creed* (New York: Schocken Books, 1965), thoroughly and persuasively documents the split between ideology and practice affecting business people in every area of business activity.

The young are flexible; the old are "out of it."
The young are the healthy, beautiful people; the old are sick and wasted.
The middle-aged bring home the bacon; the old are an economic burden.
The middle-aged are society's producers; the old produce nothing. The middle-aged occupy respected roles; the old have no roles to play.
In the agrarian society of the past, the old farmer became wise in regard to the ways of the seasons, the land and the crop. His experience had much that was useful to tell the young. But the old farmer today will be driven out of business by the smart young upstart wise in regard to the latest in agricultural science and marketing techniques, including commodity and futures markets, management and forecast advisory services, and incorporation for tax purposes. And the same is likely to hold true for the old church pastor, the old production manager, and the old college president.

(a) In American society, the fittest for survival are the movers, the doers, and the producers. What, if anything, does a business owe to an older employee who is being outproduced by a younger? Consider a salesman, a teacher, a ballplayer, a middle manager. Does the nature of the job make a difference? Why?

(b) Would a Social Darwinist agree with your answer? If not, what in Spencer's premises accounts for the difference?

(c) Would a Social Darwinist argue for a mandatory retirement age of 65? Why or why not? Would you?

3. Who has the better opportunity and likelihood of achieving and maintaining a successful business position in American society: (1) John, an intelligent and healthy 16-year-old boy, born youngest of six children in a fatherless welfare family in a poverty ghetto with a wretched school system, or (2) Dora, a 16-year-old girl, average or less in intelligence, very overweight and a hypochondriac, who inherited several million dollars and a thriving family business? "She's a born business woman—inherited the company from her father," to paraphrase a "*Wall Street Journal* cartoon (June 17, 1977).

(a) Give two or three likely scenarios of John's and then of Dora's economic situation and prospects at age 25.

(b) Give two or three unlikely scenarios for each at age 25.

(c) Do your scenarios tend to confirm or disconfirm the Spencerian picture of the way the business world works? Why?

SUGGESTED READINGS

Collier, Peter, and David Horowitz. *The Rockefellers: An American Dynasty.* New York: New American Library, Inc., 1976.

Fleming, Donald. "Social Darwinism" in *Paths of American Thought*, ed. by Arthur M. Schlessinger and Morton White. Boston: Houghton Mifflin, 1963.

Gillespie, Norman C. "The Business of Ethics," *University of Michigan Business Review* (November 1975), 1-4.

Hofstadter, Richard. *Social Darwinism in American Thought.* New York: George Braziller, Inc., 1959.

Maccoby, Michael. *The Gamesman.* New York: Simon and Schuster, 1976.

Nevins, Allan, and Frank Hill. *Ford: Explosion and Challenge 1915-1933.* New York: Charles Scribner's Sons, 1963.

Smith, Adam. *The Wealth of Nations.* New York: Modern Library, 1937.

Spencer, Herbert. *Social Statics.* New York: Kelley, 1851.

Wall, Joseph Frazier. *Andrew Carnegie.* New York: Oxford University Press, 1970.

Walton, Clarence C. *Corporate Social Responsibilities.* Belmont, Ca.: Wadsworth Publishing Co., Inc., 1967.

Wilson, Edward O.: *On Human Nature.* Cambridge, Ma.: Harvard University Press, 1978.

————. *Sociobiology: The New Synthesis.* Cambridge, Ma.: The Belknap Press of Harvard University Press, 1975.

Wish, Harvey. *Society and Thought in Modern America.* New York: Longmans, Green and Co., 1952.

CHAPTER 3
MACHIAVELLIANISM: THE RULE OF EXPEDIENCY

Any person who decides in every situation to act as a good man is bound to be destroyed in the company of so many men who are not good. Wherefore, if a Prince desires to stay in power, he must learn how to be not good and must avail himself of that ability, or not, as the occasion requires.

Niccolò Machiavelli[1]

Contrary to the general impession, Machiavellian behavior isn't based on craftiness or duplicity. But when necessary, those "skills" may be called into play.

Arthur J. Kover, "Machiavellian Business"[2]

OBJECTIVES FOR CHAPTER 3:

1. To become aware of one's own preliminary attitude toward expediency in ethics;

2. To see how the analogy of business as private government allows Machiavellian political ethics to be applied to business;

3. To understand and apply the principles of Machiavellian business ethics:

[1]All citations of Machiavelli are from his classic work *The Prince*, using my own free translation. This passage is from Chapter 15.

[2]Arthur J. Kover, "Machiavellian Business," in *Business Secrets* (New York: 1977), p. 5; reprinted with permission of *Boardroom Reports*, Management's Source of Useful Information, 500 Fifth Ave., New York, N.Y. 10036.

(a) that "is" takes precedence over "ought";
(b) that private morality gives way to public expedience;
(c) that business decisions are guided by hypothetical imperatives;
(d) that business is a self-contained organism determined by laws that can be bent but not overturned;
(e) that "virtue" means effectiveness in reaching goals, even using craftiness and duplicity where necessary.

4. To understand philosophical objections against Machiavellianism, and to evaluate for oneself the truth and/or falsity of Machiavellian business ethics as an adequate expression of human life and responsible action.

1. THE MACHIAVELLIAN BUSINESS PERSON

The mid-seventies saw a most unlikely "moral" prophet emerge as inspiration and guide to the business community. His name is Niccolò Machiavelli, the crafty, shrewd Renaissance statesman. He flourished as secretary of state to the Florentine Republic (1498–1512), but when business people read him today, they feel he is speaking to themselves. His approach to human behavior and the workings of power is dispassionate, firmly rooted in observation and experience, deadly accurate, and uncluttered by moral sentiment. In his method and outlook he is much more our own contemporary than he was of the philosophers and statesmen of his day. He was no ivory-tower philosopher. He knew whereof he spoke. Profoundly attuned to the workings of government, Niccolò Machiavelli understood the intricate internal conflicts and problems of managing both line and staff—barons and courtiers, he'd call them. And he knew the cynicism and intrigue that governs the external relations among polities— among competing corporations we'd call them. He outfitted armies. He conducted sensitive diplomatic missions to Cesare Borgia, Pope Julius II, and Louis XII among others. Only in 1512, with the advent of a new government and his ouster from power (his "disgrace," he called it), did he take to writing up the accumulated fruits of his experience. He took himself to a country villa, where he'd gossip and play cards with the ignorant peasants by day. In the evenings, he'd don his curial robes, betake himself to his study and, musing over happier times, record the insight and wisdom acquired during his glory days.

Our aim here is not to present a nuanced view of the historical Machiavelli. Rather we look to the modern Machiavellians who inhabit the corporate suites and roam the marketplace. What do *they* see in Machiavelli? How have *they* drawn inspiration from him? What are the outlines of a Machiavellian "ethic" as business people profess to live it today? What are its premises, and to what consequences does it lead? How would one critically evaluate it?

Antony Jay[3] has drawn in detail a direct parallel between the Machiavellian state and the modern corporation. Citing chapter and verse, he finds Machiavelli's literal advice directly relevant to successful business management today. Richard Buskirk,[4] sensing the same parallelism, finds Machiavelli's *method* the most fruitful stance for analyzing and dealing effectively with management problems. Then there is that unholy duo—"The Power Boys," *Time*[5] magazine called them—Robert Ringer[6] and Michael Korda.[7] The former never once mentions Machiavelli's name, but he lines up a no-nonsense philosophy (call it "ruthless" or "realistic," as you choose) for salesmen, and it parallels point for point the premises of Machiavellian thinking. What Ringer does for sales, Korda does for internal office politics and climbing up the ladder. You'll be considering some of these themes. But first, test your own Machiavellian sentiments.

VALUES-CLARIFICATION TEST

Before each of the following statements fill in a number to indicate how far you agree or disagree with the statement or with the attitude underlying the statement:

**1 = strongly disagree, 2 = disagree, 3 = not sure
4 = agree, 5 = strongly agree.**

_____ 1. George X. says of himself, "I work long, hard hours and do a good job; the lazy wheeler-dealers seem to get ahead faster than I do, but I know my good hard work will pay off in the end." Yes, George works hard, but he's dreaming.

[3]Antony Jay, *Management and Machiavelli: An Inquiry into the Politics of Corporate Life* (New York: Bantam Books, 1967).

[4]Richard H. Buskirk, *Modern Management and Machiavelli* (New York: Mentor Books, 1974).

[5]*Time* (January 19, 1976), p. 60.

[6]Robert J. Ringer, *Winning Through Intimidation* (New York: Funk and Wagnalls, 1973). Ringer in his sequel, *Looking Out For # 1* (Los Angeles Book Corp., 1977), rejects the very concept of labeling people, especially himself, or anyone allowing himself to be labeled. He does in the book make explicit and favorable mention of those apostles of self-interest, David Seabury and Ayn Rand, the latter of whom will be treated in the next chapter. In that chapter, then, it will be more appropriate to allude to Ringer's possible contributions to "business ethics," realizing full well that he would not be enamored of the phrase.

[7]Michael Korda, *Power! How to Get It. How to Use It* (New York: Ballantine Books, 1975).

_____ 2. I'd certainly try to get help and treatment for my alcoholic spouse; but an alcoholic salesman is no good for business and should be fired after a couple of warnings.

_____ 3. Of every decision that comes up in a business day I ask only one thing, "Will it make money?" If yes, I'll act; if not it's irrelevant and a waste of time.

_____ 4. In my grocery store, for one sale item each week we *raise* the price: that makes it a "special"! If you know the rules of the game, there's nothing wrong with this.

_____ 5. I wouldn't hesitate to speak in a low voice to an elderly rival to make him think he's going deaf (a ruse suggested by Michael Korda).

_____ 1a. A business person can't afford to get hung up on ideals; it's a real world out there, and reality is all that counts.

_____ 2a. Of course, I'm a morally upright parent with my children; but when I put on my business hat, I leave my morals at home.

_____ 3a. If you want the goal, you've got to take the means. The end justifies the means.

_____ 4a. The business world has its own moral game and its own rules. This is something that outsiders don't understand.

_____ 5a. A good business person is a successful business person: that's all the business ethics I care about.

Note, first, that the higher you score, the more sympathy you'll doubtless feel for Machiavellianism as a business philosophy. It's entirely possible, however, that your reasons don't coincide with his. People can come to the same conclusions from different philosophical premises.

Secondly, note that the first five statements were concrete examples of ethical decisions; the second five illustrate the Machiavellian reasoning that might underlie your answers to the first five. Match the two sets of statements. For example, the number 1a states the principle of realism over idealism; match this with corresponding statement number 1: how realistic do you think that George is? Number 2a states the principle of private morality and public expediency; match this with corresponding statement 2: would you limit to your private family life personal concern, say, for an alcoholic? Continue matching the statements in this way. Does your theory agree with your practice?

The purpose of this values-clarification test is to help you determine to what extent, if any, you already pay allegiance to Machiavellian principles. Most of the rest of this chapter will be devoted to explaining these principles. Then at the end you will be asked to reevaluate them in the light of your fuller understanding.

2. THE CORPORATION AS PRIVATE GOVERNMENT

There is a tension between two models of corporate behavior that will be discussed in some detail in a later chapter. There is the model of corporation-as-person, the *persona ficta* of corporation law. And there is the model of corporation-as-impersonal-institution, specifically an institution along the lines of private government. In this section we will outline these two views of the corporation. Corporation-as-person is the image used by civil law. Corporation-as-institution, specifically institution along the lines of "private government," underlies Machiavellian thinking about business. Having established this latter view, we will then be ready to derive principles for ethical behavior that flow from it.

Machiavellian political thinking about public government has been coopted into the service of private enterprise. The structure of public government has become a paradigm to illuminate the workings of corporations viewed as private governments. Like public governments, private governments have their own rules and rule-making procedures, personnel programs and policies, codes of conduct and performance expectations, bureaucratic staffs and field administrators, goals and strategic and tactical plans for their implementation, all of which structure and guide their relations to their own constituencies and to rival institutions like their own. Such a paradigm shift in the way of viewing corporate behavior has far-reaching implications. And indeed this is truly a shift in our typical way of viewing corporate behavior, especially in the area of ethics and social responsibility. The usual temptation is to adopt the private individual person as the model for corporate autonomy and responsibility. The corporation is, after all, legally construed as an artificial person, and private enterprise is defined precisely in opposition to enterprises undertaken on public initiative and responsibility. We will not recount here the long and enlightening story of how corporate law developed to safeguard "private" enterprise from excessive public federal regulation and of how the 14th Amendment was expanded to protect corporations as persons under the Constitution. While the law recognizes well that corporations are not flesh-and-blood citizens, still this model of corporation as person can obfuscate the institutional impact of the corporation on society and the institutional ways that corporations behave when questions of ethics and responsibility arise.

This obfuscation has confused our way of thinking about business's relation to government. Somehow the autonomy of corporations has been assimilated into our ways of thinking about the autonomy of individual citizens. We want individual citizens to enjoy the freedom to think in maverick ways, and to have the autonomy to act even in ways that the majority would judge irresponsible, provided that the public order is not unduly disturbed. The inner workings of mind and will are the individual's sacred domain. Unlike the Roman Catholic Church which views the individual's private conscience as legitimately subject to regulation, American civil law regards the inner forum of conscience as the individual's private preserve. A person's morality, religion, ideas, associations, private behavior and nondisruptive public behavior are not to be of official public concern. Even where behavior is regulated, the regulation is external. It does not touch on the internal domain. The ways in which I govern myself, arrive at decisions, do or do not hold myself accountable, are all my own affair as long as I externally obey the law.

In great part, our law to date has extended such internal "personal" inviolability to corporations. Corporation law (the internal workings of the "person") and regulatory law are external to each other. The corporation's constitution and structure is one thing, and the corporation's accountability to its external social constituencies is another thing. Consequently, regulatory law bears on the corporation's external behavior and impact. But the corporation's internal governance has thus far remained as inviolate and as sacred a preserve as has individual conscience, as far as the law is concerned. The law, and consequently our thinking, has tended in the main to stress the similarities and analogues between the rights of private enterprise and the rights of private citizens. We have tended to neglect the myriad differences between them. One virtue of Machiavellian ethics, whatever else you may come to think about it, is that it focuses clearly on the distinction between the private individual sphere and the public institutional sphere, and consequently on the need for radically different ways of evaluating the respective behaviors of each sphere. Niccolò Machiavelli effected a revolution in political philosophy. The coopting of this philosophy to the business sphere could initiate a revolution in our ways of thinking about business philosophy with the ethics that might flow from such a philosophy.

Machiavelli was not himself a political philosopher, but he put political philosophy on a new modern footing. He was, above all, practical. He took an utterly concrete approach to political problems. He had little patience or use for abstract theories. This quality alone is enough to inspire confidence in the business decision-maker that Machiavelli perhaps has something to say. Machiavelli was careful always to tune into the actual working principles of politicians. What he saw and heard was not always very pretty. Neither always are the operative principles of the business world. But a cool and honest cynicism does not blink at this. Elizabethan writers, offended by what Machiavelli claimed to see, were wont to depict him as a conspirator with tyrants. It's a common ploy that if you don't like the bad news you blame the bearer of the news. Modern-day business people who give Machiavellian reports on what they see are liable to undergo similar accusations. But they, like Machiavelli, may simply be reporting the phenomena. The phenomena may be sinister, but that doesn't make the report sinister, too. Machiavelli saw that political phenomena followed their own laws. Traditional morality was irrelevant to them. The political world is a world unto itself. And many business people reading Machiavelli felt that they knew what he was talking about. To such as these, the Common Cause spokespersons and Third-World revolutionaries have little that is realistic to say to the business sector. They inhabit different worlds.

Machiavelli well realized how radical his approach was. Read his words. They just about say it all:

> I am breaking completely new ground from those who have gone before me. But I intend to write principles which will be useful to the careful reader. So it is more effective in my view to get back to the practical truth of a topic rather than depending on my fantasies about the matter. Many people have imagined republics and states that have never to anyone's knowledge existed in reality. For between the way men *do* live and the way they *ought* to live, there is this great difference, viz., that the person who abandons "what is" for "what ought to be" is learning a lesson of self-ruin, not of self-preservation. Any person who decides in every situation to act as a good man is bound to be destroyed in the company of so many men who are not good. Wherefore, if a Prince desires to stay in power, he must learn how to be not good, and must avail himself of that ability, or not, as the occasion requires.[8]

The hardest of hard-headed business persons could scarcely take a tougher line than this. Machiavelli supplies a framework for interpreting the business sphere in an equally tough-minded and practical fashion, without the distortions brought on by wooly moralizing.

Thus, just as the laws of government operate as phenomena ruled by political necessity, untrammeled by moral posturing, so too business is ruled by economic laws whose necessity does not readily yield to moral idealism.[9]

[8] *The Prince*, Chapter 15.
[9] This is not Spencer's absolute determinism. Machiavelli's softer version of determinism or necessity will be defined below.

Antony Jay sees a parallelism in all important aspects between the small nation-states of which Machiavelli spoke and modern business corporations.[10] The state (a business) has a government (board of directors). Its purpose is to maintain and increase wealth. The beneficiaries are the landowning classes (the shareholders). It is also engaged internally with providing for the safety and prosperity of its citizens (employees), and dealing with civil rebellion (strikes). Externally, it must contend with enemy invaders (competitors), preferably by the negotiation of favorable treaties (cartels/price rings). And so it goes.

To be sure, the analogy is not perfect. Jay admits as much. Also, there is a sense in which the multinational corporation transcends the nation-state. Indeed, one day the multinational economic entity might itself become the paradigm in the image of which a multinational political entity might be fashioned. (Certainly the U.N. debating society does not promise to furnish any such paradigm!) In any case, the parallelism suggested by Jay has a more than casual heuristic value. Indeed, business people comfortably resort to political language when justifying their business behavior. Read what a G.E. executive said during the antitrust suits of the fifties: "Sure, collusion was illegal, but it wasn't unethical. It wasn't any more unethical than if the companies had a summit conference the way Russia and the West meet."

3. PRINCIPLES OF MACHIAVELLIAN "ETHICS"

We have tasted the general flavor of Machiavellian thinking and its affinity to business. Now we set down seven explicit Machiavellian principles to guide your thinking about business morality, or more precisely, to justify why business decision-making takes place in a climate of amorality. Observe the phenomena clearly, coolly and cynically, and what do you see?

(1) *"Is" takes precedence over "ought."* On the one hand, there is the world we wish existed, that ideal world of tolerance, trust, love, honesty, and justice: this is the world of "ought." Then there's the world of "is," where injustice prevails over fairness, suspicion over trust, where every man is a knave and intolerance is the rule. When I make a business decision, I'd better be guided by what *is* rather than by what I think *ought* to be. A Detroit woman who worked for the American Arbitration Association resented her boss's ban on blue jeans. She felt they "ought" to be al-

[10]Jay, *op. cit.*, Chapter 2.

lowed and wore them anyway in protest. Result: she was fired.[11] "Is" takes precedence over "ought." For a less petulant example, consider the "is" and the "ought" of international traffic in military weapons.

(2) *Expediency reigns in public life; morality is for the private sphere.* This is a very modern conception, viz., the privatization of morality (and of religion, too, for that matter). Morality today, unlike in more homogeneous societies of the past, is viewed typically as "up to the individual." We are very wary of attempts to "impose one's morality on others." To be sure, there are attempts to legislate morality, e.g., by way of regulating homosexual behavior, Sunday sales, gambling and drug usage. But such legislation gives rise to equally strong opposition in favor of maximizing freedom in morals. It's our way of making life liveable in a pluralistic society.

The flip side of this privatization of morals is the problem of how to arrive at a publically shared set of moral values. For perversely, we want this too. We want to hold both government and business ethically accountable. Our pluralistic society is plagued with the seemingly irreconcilable desire to guarantee individual moral freedom on the one hand, while avoiding moral anarchy on the other. We tend to live with this schizophrenia without resolving it. It's an unconscious cover-up.

The Machiavellian ethic exposes this ploy for what it is. You want moral norms to be a matter of private decision only? Fine, you've got it. Morality belongs to the private sphere. But in public life, be it government or business, it's expediency that prevails.[12] Business life is not immoral. It's nonmoral. Economic necessities and results are the rule for business decisions. Morality only clouds the issue.

Minimum-wage proposals are a case in point. The Carter Administration's Secretary of Labor, F. Ray Marshall, is on a moral crusade for a world-wide "living wage." This is right in line with U.S. organized labor's unending push for a higher domestic minimum wage. What could be more morally laudable than that all workers at home and abroad make a higher living wage? But business decisions about wages do not so easily yield to moral considerations, warns Machiavelli. It is perfectly feasible for me to raise from $10 to $24 my son's weekly allowance for chores done round the house, and to do so on moral rather than on economic grounds. But a global wage hike? The question immediately translates into which economic forces I wish to unleash, and in favor of expediting what goal. A

---

[11]*Wall Street Journal* (June 14, 1977), p. 1.

[12]We speak here and throughout the chapter about the modern business Machiavellians. Machiavelli himself enjoyed no such established moral pluralism as we do today. His relegation of morals to the private sphere was shocking and radical for his time. But today his time has come. Business people read him and say, yes, that's the way things are.

global living wage cannot come about through a morally motivated fiat. Garment workers in Korea make 32¢ an hour, and 41¢ in Taiwan.[13] Higher wages for them would price them out of the U.S. market, lessen competition against U.S. garment workers, and mean fewer foreign jobs. And so much for a living wage in the Far East garment districts. Similarly, the push for a higher domestic minimum wage has moral idealism written all over it. The economically necessary result would be to price young, inexperienced minority workers out of the labor market. Even Donald Slaiman, Deputy Director of the Department of Organization and Field Services of the AFL-CIO, has come to admit this and change his mind about the desirability of sizeable increases in the minimum wage. Like it or not, economic expedience, not moral fiat, determines the result of business decisions. And this brings us to the next Machiavellian "ethical" imperative.

(3) *There are no categorical imperatives in business, only hypothetical ones.* An example of a categorical imperative would be: "Every worker everywhere *should* enjoy a decent living wage." Examples of hypothetical imperatives are: "If you want to choke off competition for union jobs, you *should* raise the U.S. minimum wage," or "If you want to lower minority unemployment, you *should* abolish both welfare payments and the minimum wage."

The truth of these statements is arguable. They are offered as examples. The first "should" concerning a global living wage is a categorical imperative. It's unqualified. There's no "if" about it. This is the way it is with moral "shoulds." Principle, not expediency, is the moralist's concern.

The other two "shoulds" are hypothetical, or conditional. *If* I decide on union job security as my goal or my end, then I *should* take the expedient means of helping competing workers price themselves out of my market. *If* I choose full employment as my end, then I *should* take the expedient means of encouraging cheap labor and removing alternative sources of income. Machiavellianism gives no guidance as to which end or goal to choose: union job security or full employment. It does however advise that once the end is given, you should not let moralistic concerns distract you from taking the most expedient means.

"The Prince must learn how to be not good . . . and must avail himself of that ability or not, as the occasion requires." In the usual case, economic or social pressure forces goals on business; and the business decision focuses on the means needed to expedite the achieving of that goal. "Be honest with your customers," the categorical moralist would say; "when

[13]The facts of this example are taken from L. H. Clark, Jr., "Global Minimums," *Wall Street Journal* (June 14, 1977), p. 24.

your restaurant has no free tables at 8:00 P.M. you should so inform would-be diners who phone in." "It depends," said the Machiavellian, immediately looking to the hypothesis. "If I want customers to run up a bar tab while waiting for a table, I should tell them to come right along"; "If however I want to appeal to customers who desire secure reservations, then I'll allot my tables precisely on schedule." In business decisions, the issue is not morality, but is rather expedient means to the ends desired.

(4) *A business is a self-contained organism with its own functional laws.* In moral matters, the individual and the state are not to be assimilated to each other. The human individual is one kind of animal. A business (a nation-state, in Machiavelli's philosophy) is another. In business decisions, then, consult not your private conscience, but try rather to determine the unique laws that govern the business operation, for it has a life all its own. The question, then, is not how businesses *should* act and how their constituencies *should* respond; rather, we search for that which in actual fact makes all of these parties tick. The state, and the relations between states, Machiavelli saw, are governed by functional laws rooted in human passions and desires. The Ten Commandments will not attune a business to its consumers' passions (except perhaps in reverse!), but a marketing survey will. Once I determine the emotional forces that move my customers, then they are ripe for manipulations toward my goals. This play upon human passions is the root of business power. Once I learn and can manipulate the functional laws that actually move men to action, then I am a man of *virtù* (to use Machiavelli's term), a person of power.

(5) *"Virtù = power and effectiveness in reaching goals.* Virtue is defined in nonmoral terms. The "virtuous" person is the one who does the job. A "good" business person is a successful business person. A successful business person is one who is attuned to what Machiavelli calls the "passions" of men and women. In other words, the successful person, aware of the forces that move people to action, can manipulate them to his own ends. Consider the TV business.

As of this date, it's golf that's been the staple of sports programming for all three major networks.[14] This in spite of the fact that, compared to other sports, golf ranks almost the lowest in the Nielsen ratings; miles of cable and over a dozen cameras with the associated highly paid technicians working for days on end are needed to cover each tournament, thus mak-

---

[14]The data for this illustration are drawn from Frederick G. Klein, "Quick Now, Cut to the Kemper Open," *Wall Street Journal* (June 23, 1977), p. 20. The citation is intended to illustrate the Machiavellian definition of *virtù*. Of course, one must evaluate for oneself this definition in which the goal of action escapes moral scrutiny. This has major moral implications for a host of related issues like market segmentation, the derogation of the elderly TV market, the targeting of children, etc.

ing golf the most expensive sport to produce for TV; and to the nonaficionado, it is dull, dull, dull: how enthralled can you get watching how many putters lining up how many putts on how many greens—of necessity, greens-play monopolizes the screen time. What person of *virtù* decided that this unlikely sport with its comparatively miniscule following should with its 12 percent share of TV sports time outbid tennis (10 percent), baseball (9 percent), bowling (3 percent), and be practically on a par with basketball which accounts for 13 percent of sports programming? The "numbers" tell the tale. Fifty-eight percent more families of the total population earning $20,000 per year watch golf than watch basketball, and it is the low-income population who watch bowling. So not only are the human passions there (golfers on golf are a passionate lot), but there, too, are the dollars to indulge those passions. The luxury car, air lines, business machine, and insurance advertisers know it, and the network sellers of TV time know they know it, if they are truly persons of *virtù*.

To sum up, TV is in the business of delivering the maximum number of buyers to advertisers. Entertainment, public service, news, education, cultural uplift are all subservient to this goal. To the extent that these can tap and manipulate human desires, the person of *virtù* will use this passionate power to effect his goals. Business is a self-contained organism with its own functioning causes. Passion, not principle, is its guide, in the Machiavellian view.

(6) *You can bend but not upend the natural laws of business.* For Spencer, the business environment is inflexible: it ruthlessly roots out the unfit in favor of those adapted to survive. There is little or no play for human freedom, and consequently, little or none for morality either. Machiavelli has a softer view of determinism. Business cannot with impunity flaunt nature's laws; but business can bend and manipulate them toward its self-chosen goals. So like Spencer, Machiavelli recognizes the role of necessity (or "Fate" as he calls it) in human affairs. Political (and economic) necessity is like a rampant flood (to use Machiavelli's metaphor). The swirling waters bear down on small valleys. There is no way I can stop the flood: I am not free to suspend the operation of economic laws. I can however, build dikes and diversionary streams. I can manipulate human passions and purses to my own ends: Such is the locus of freedom operating in a context of determinism and necessity. If I *choose* an end (freedom), there are certain means I *must* use (necessity): that hypothetical imperative again!

This freedom, however, is not a moral freedom in the Machiavellian view. Only in private life do I have sufficient freedom to act out the categorical imperatives of morality. Such a luxury does not obtain in the public sphere, as we have seen. Moralists, for example, can parade in front of utility companies bearing placards urging "Clean Air Now." The business managers inside know that to obey such an injunction would close the factory down. They may be in favor of clean air as private citizens, but there is no flaunting of the natural laws of business. Private moral injunctions do not apply in the public sphere. However, there are certain amoral expedient moves a business can make, and the Machiavellian business person addresses himself to them.

In La Cygne, Kansas, some years ago, Kansas City Power and Light Company foresaw the swelling governmental pressure to alleviate air pollution. Clean-air laws are backed up with economic clout in the form of fines and penalties. It saw a local supply of coal—a dirty fuel—which would be cheaper than fuel shipped in from Wisconsin. So the economic laws of fuel supply came into play. Finally, it agonized over the installation of smokestack scrubbers—initial investment $36 million—that would enable them to use the cheaper fuel and at the same time comply with federal emission standards for sulphur dioxide and particulates. The scrubbers were installed. In due course, over the long run, K.C. Power enjoyed the payoff. Fuel was cheaper; the company was a leg up both in compliance with environmental law and in scrubber technology; only just lately have some 300 other fossil-fueled utilities begun to drag themselves into the EPA fold on clean air.[15]

So Machiavellianism has no quarrel with so-called "socially responsible" behavior in business. But the origin, implementation, and consequences of this behavior are judged on grounds of expedience, not morality. EPA regulations and fines, the cost of smokestack scrubbers, the price of local as opposed to out-of-state fuel: these economic necessities and constraints cannot be flaunted. But Kansas City Power found a way of bending this raging flood of economic determinisms toward its own goals. This was the focus of freedom, amoral but effective, and therefore "virtuous."

(7) *A man of "virtù" must be prepared to be not virtuous when required.* Lest the reader think, from considering the smokestack-scrubber case, that Machiavelli is smuggling in moral considerations under the guise of expedience, read his words:

> The Prince must appear to be filled with sympathy and trust, and seem to be humane and honest and religious, and indeed actually be so; and yet, when necessary, he must be mentally ready not to practice these virtues, ready, in a word, to do the opposite, and to do the opposite with class and skill.[16]

---

[15]George Getschow, "Coal Cleanup," *Wall Street Journal* (June 14, 1977), p. 1. This story is cited for illustrative purposes only. It is not the last word on the K. C. Power and Light situation or on this complicated environmental issue in general.

[16]*The Prince*, Chapter 18.

So our seventh and concluding Machiavellian principle is a parting shot against slipping into easy private moralism when in the public and business domains. There is nothing wrong with appearing compassionate, trustworthy and humane. In the above case, K. C. Power certainly appeared virtuous. There's nothing wrong even with being virtuous. K. C. Power actually was virtuous: they cleaned up the air. But the business person who possesses the quality of Machiavellian *virtù* must be ready skillfully to change to the opposite when so required. He must learn to use force. Braniff Airlines did, when the little upstart intrastate Southwest Airlines, free of CAB regulations undercut Braniff's intra-Texas fares. Braniff smothered Southwest with lawsuits, fired Security Couriers package pickup and delivery company when it learned the company was dealing with Southwest, and lobbied intensively against Southwest's use of airport facilities, fuel facilities, and ticket-purchase plans.[17]

A person of *virtù* must also learn when to use guile. Under the umbrella of First Amendment protection, advertisers divert children's attention on TV from product qualities by offering flashy "free" gifts, imply that beer-guzzling fosters youth and slenderness, and persuade the citizenry to poison themselves with junk masquerading as food.[18]

Finally, the Machiavellian business person must be prepared even for fraud and lies, *if* required—remember, the only imperatives are hypothetical ones. If you want to spruce up your menu and sales in the restaurant business, be prepared to lie. Call turkey salad, "chicken"; call canned soup, "homemade." Turn Pacific rockfish into "California red snapper." For "Idaho" potatoes, substitute California potatoes. Cook "fresh fish" and "fresh peas" from supplies stored months in the freezer.[19]

In sum, then, we've seen seven "ethical" principles for the Machiavellian business person. They are drawn from observation of the way that public life and business life actually work. Faithfully followed, they will produce a person of *virtù*.

We have enumerated seven "ethical" principles for business, while at the same time stating that Machiavellianism has no business ethics, that Machiavellianism is amoral. Note that we carefully put "ethics" in quotes when referring to business behavior in this chapter. Clearly, Machiavellian premises do result in a decision about ethics, viz., that ethics does not apply in public life. Machiavelli, more than other philosophers we are consid-

---

[17]Jerry Landauer, "Aerial Dogfight," *Wall Street Journal* (June 23, 1977), p. 1. Again, the example is cited as a possible illustration of Machiavellian *virtù*. The details of the case itself are more complicated and are susceptible of other interpretations than the Machiavellian one.

[18]"The FTC Broadens Its Attack on Ads," *Business Week* (June 20, 1977), pp. 27–28.

[19]See Stephen Sansweet, "The Way We Eat," *Wall Street Journal* (June 20, 1977), pp. 1 and 20.

ering, confines himself to descriptive ethics, i.e., "what *is*." For public life, at any rate, he does not take the normative step—"what *ought* to be." The normative is not relevant at the institutional level, in Machiavelli's view. "Good business is bad ethics," we say of Machiavellianism. In other words, what would be considered bad ethics if we were talking about private life (e.g., fraud, deception, force) could in some circumstances be good business. Strictly speaking, in the business world such practices are not unethical, however dubious they might be if practiced in private life. Business actions are never either moral or immoral. They are amoral. So say the Machiavellians. We now invite you to consider for yourself whether or not this is true.

4. SUMMARY AND EVALUATION

Machiavelli would not be so attractive to many modern business people if there were not at least a strong prima facie case for what he says. His doctrine could be called an essay in "descriptive ethics." It claims to be based on the phenomena—the way business people actually do behave. As we did for Spencer, now we ask Machiavelli the truth-questions. Does Machiavelli present a true picture of the business world? Are the phenomena the way Machiavelli says they are? Judge for yourself how valid his "descriptive ethics" is. Then move on to the question of normative ethics. Is this the way things *should* be in the business world? Does Machiavelli's picture of human nature lead to a valid conclusion about the role that ethics should or should not play in business decision-making?

There follows now a series of summations of Machiavellian principles. After each principle is restated, a question (Q) is presented to highlight a philosophical objection that can be raised against the principle. Then the Machiavellian answer (*A*) is briefly stated. The intent is to help the reader to view the pros and cons of Machiavellianism as a business philosophy so as to arrive at a self-evaluation of this ethics. The intent is not to endorse either Machiavellian ethics or its opposite.

(1) A *moral* action is one that is consistent with an ethical standard of what it means to be a human being. An *immoral* action is an action that has nothing to do with one's meaning and worth as a human being. Business decisions in Machiavellian thinking are amoral—they have nothing to do with my human meaning and worth. I detach myself from the person I am and the person I want to become. Expediency, and expediency alone, rules the day. At home I am the complete human being. I try to be faithful

to the intellectual, emotional, moral and spiritual sides of myself. I know and act on who I am and what I'd like to become. At work, I put this humanity aside. I look only to the goals of the job and to the expedient means to reach these goals. That full humanity of mine can only get in the way. Morality for the living room, yes; for the office, no—it is irrelevant and even harmful to the task at hand.

Q: Can a Machiavellian be a human being?

A: Not while engaged in business.

Do you agree? Why/why not?

(2) Social Darwinism in theory has no ethics, because in Social Darwinism, there is no place for freedom. The laws of natural selection are in no way amenable to human intervention. Whatever anyone may try to do, the survivors survive and the weak go under, period. But in Machiavellianism there is a place for freedom. Of course, economic necessities and laws cannot be tampered with, but I can direct these forces to my own ends and do this freely.

Q: Does this freedom bring with it moral responsibility as to what means I choose and how I direct those means?

A: No. If I want a business goal, I may take any means to the goal. Expedience in business is a good in itself. The end justifies the means.

Do you agree? Why/why not?

(3) Human beings with their passions and desires are among the chief means that business uses to attain its goals. In private life, I respect persons as ends in themselves, just as I respect myself as a moral human being. But in business, the passions, desires, and ignorance of my potential customers—including children—become fair game for me to manipulate toward my own goals.

Q: Are human beings in business rightly treated as means to an end, viz., the economic goal and other purposes of a business?

A: Yes. Ethics here is irrelevant; business is as amoral with regard to persons as it is with regard to other means.

Do you agree? Why/why not?

(4) The imperatives of business are hypothetical; if I want the goal, then any means are justified. The goals of business are pretty much given. Economic pressures (e.g., survival and a fair return on investment) and social pressures (e.g., government regulations, consumer unions and labor unions) force me to define my immediate goals narrowly:

Q: Are the goals of business then, immune from moral considerations?

*A:*Economic realities in the context of social pressures leave little scope for choice. Goals are not immune from moral evaluation. Rather, ethical considerations are irrelevant, because they can have no realistic impact on business decisions about goals and ends.

Do you agree? Why/why not?

(5) A business is a self-contained organism with its own rules. You'd never expect a soldier in battle to live by morals that are proper to his private family life. The same goes for business.

Q: Are business and family two utterly separate worlds? Do you say that the "oughts" of morality are relevant at home, but that business must deal in facts, not ideals?

A: Yes. Leave your humanity at home. There's no virtue in ignoring the amoral expedient ways that make up the real world of business. It's another world.

Do you agree? Why/why not?

(6) A corporation, while different from a human individual, is legally a person. As a person, it should enjoy all the protections and autonomy that an individual enjoys under the Constitution. This is a moral as well as a legal right. Government tampering with the internal workings of a corporation is an affront to humanity as we understand it in the Western World.

Q: Is it true that government regulation is one of the very major enemies of socially beneficial free enterprise? Should the autonomy and privacy of the internal workings of a corporation enjoy the same protections as the autonomy and privacy of individuals? Besides external regulations, should there be internal checks on the processes of business decision-making and accountability?

A: If businesses and individuals inhabit two separate worlds, it's not clear that this argument is valid. Perhaps there is a place for regulatory law to be assimilated into corporation law, even though it would be offensive to so attempt to regulate the autonomy of private individuals.

Do you agree? Why/why not?

After considering these six areas of critical evaluation, to what extent do you conclude that Machiavelli's "Good Business is Bad Ethics" provides a valid framework for business decision-making?

We have seen the "no ethics" of Spencer's automatic application of the law of natural selection to business. We have seen the "bad ethics" of Machiavelli's exclusion of morality from public life. We come finally in the next chapter to an example of what might truly be called a business ethic.

It's not your garden variety of ethical theory, however. Its principle could be stated as follows, "Love is the Root of all Evil."

DISCUSSION QUESTIONS

1. In a series on "The Business of Medicine" in the *Washington Post* (June 12, 1977), pp. A1 and A3 (copyright by *Washington Post;* reprinted with permission), staff writer Lawrence Meyer interviewed a young Washington internist who had trouble making ends meet. The doctor undertook several measures to ensure his getting "my share of the pie." He began recommending that his patients get annual physicals and sending them reminder notices.

> Reporter: But did you also become more prone to doing laboratory work?
> Doctor: Well, along with the physical tends to go laboratory work.
> Reporter: That's also an income-producing item?
> Doctor: Oh yeah, sure. Doctors have a formula that's worked out by Blue Cross/Blue Shield which allows them to charge a certain percentage of what the tests cost the doctor.
> Reporter: What is your mark-up?
> Doctor: I'm allowed 50% of cost . . . up to a point. . . .
> Reporter: Will you, as some doctors do, make a diagnosis in conjunction with the physical, so that they can attempt to collect from their insurance company for it?
> Doctor: I won't make up the diagnosis, but I'll be very general and vague about my description of the problem, such as weakness and fatigue which justifies doing an electrocardiogram. I don't do x-rays because I consider that to be a potentially dangerous procedure which I wouldn't subject my patients to every year.
> Reporter: Why do you do the other tests?
> Doctor: Because they don't harm the patient, and from time to time I do pick up some valuable information that's helpful to a patient. . . . The pie can be cut up so many ways—the pie being the fund of money to pay for professional medical care—and everybody is fighting for their share of the pie. So, do you use frugality with insurance companies . . . when everybody else is not being frugal? Then you're the guy who doesn't make it financially. . . . I mean, why should I go broke and not take my share of the pie? That's our retainer. That's what keeps us going. You gotta take care of healthy people if you want to make a living.

(1) State the hypothetical imperative that guides the doctor's treatment decisions.

(2) See number 4 in the previous section. Does the doctor have any moral alternative to operating under this imperative?

(3) Is he taking a good means to the end in a Machiavellian sense? Why? What philosophy of human person and society is he operating under?

(4) Is he taking a good means to the end in your view? Why? What philosophy underpins your answer?

> Doctor: I talked to (another internist) ... He was grossing $170,000. He claims he's only seeing 12 patients a day.... There was something going on.
>
> Reporter: What do you think it was?
>
> Doctor: I think it was x-rays. I think he was doing an enormous number of x-rays, absolutely outrageous and unnecessary x-rays.
>
> Reporter: Just to make money?
>
> Doctor: Yeah, I know another guy grossing $190,000 a year ... [because he was seeing 40 or 50 patients a day].
>
> Reporter: So he was busy.
>
> Doctor: He was busy. But how do you get to see 40 or 50 patients in an eight-hour day or even longer?
>
> ... He created the need in his patients for weekly or biweekly or monthly vitamin shots.
>
> Reporter: So in other words, he didn't have that many patients, he was seeing them frequently.
>
> Doctor: For vitamin shots.
>
> Reporter: And how much was he charging for vitamin shots?
>
> Doctor: Just his office fee. A big bottle of vitamins only cost him a buck, I mean, they're cheap, you know.... He was charging for a few minutes with his patients and the vitamin shot, $15.
>
> Reporter: Was there any medical benefit from the vitamin shots?
>
> Doctor: No.
>
> Reporter: Do you see anything improper in that?
>
> Doctor: I don't know. It depends. The whole issue in medicine now is placebos. If the patients feel better and feel that they're getting help, isn't that valid treatment? Lots of people think placebo is valid treatment. I personally can't do it. It doesn't suit my style.

Regarding the x-ray doctor and the vitamin doctor:

(1) What hypothetical imperative are they operating under?

(2) Do you consider their hypotheses amoral, in the Machiavellian sense? Explain.

(3) These doctors are simply manipulating human passions and desires to their own ends. Which doctor is the better business person, in the Machiavellian sense? In your sense? On what philosophical grounds?

2. Consider the following case:

Giles and Evelyn Chapman last year celebrated the silver jubilee of a very happy marriage. Giles owns the Chapman Chemical Company, founded by his father and developed by himself. He has worked long and hard to make it the largest employer in the small industrial town of Libertyville. As a result, the town is flourishing. In both pay and benefits John is generous with his employees. Evelyn is active in the community, contributing her services to both the consumer movement and the environmental-protection movement. She was recently designated an EPA investigator.

But Libertyville is in trouble. The town has been cited twice during the past year for exceeding air pollution limits to the point of endangering the community's health.

As if that weren't bad enough, Chapman Chemical has had some severe financial setbacks, forcing several personnel cutbacks and the threat of 100 more layoffs in the near future. In fact, in a recent nonbinding referendum, the citizens had voted that the company continue to pollute rather than shut down. In fact, Giles needs a turnaround soon, if the factory is not to fold.

Evelyn, in the course of her investigation for the EPA, discovered to her horror that Chapman Company has been secretly (and with Giles's full knowledge) by night pouring pollutants into the air. Detection of the open chimneys in the darkness is very difficult.

Evelyn is an idealist; she's no Machiavellian. But her dilemma is tearing her apart. Should she go public, thereby risking her husband's reputation and heavy fines for the troubled company? Should she keep quiet, thereby risking her own reputation, violating her official duty, and abetting the health hazard to the town? (In a court of law, she probably wouldn't have to testify against her husband.)

(1) What's the expedient course of action for her?

(2) What's the socially and morally responsible course of action for her?

(3) If these answers to the first two questions differ, what differing premises about the meaning and worth of human life and society account for the difference?

(4) State a hypothetical imperative that might show the constraints under which Giles feels he must act.

(5) Perhaps Giles feels that he is following a categorical imperative, i.e., is obeying an unconditional moral obligation. Give a possible example of such a categorical imperative.

(6) For both Giles and Evelyn, would you apply the Machiavellian distinction that morality is for private life, but in public life, expediency is the only rule? Explain.

SUGGESTED READINGS

Anglo, Sydney. *Machiavelli: A Dissection.* New York: Harcourt, Brace and World, 1969).

Buskirk, Richard. *Modern Management and Machiavelli.* New York: Mentor Books, 1975.

Jay, Antony. *Management and Machiavelli.* New York: Bantam Books, 1969.

Korda, Michael. *Male Chauvinism!* New York: Berkley Publications, 1977.

_____ . *Power! How to Get It, How to Use It.* New York: Ballantine Books, 1975.

Machiavelli, Niccolò. *The Prince.* New York: Mentor Classics, 1952.

Ringer, Robert J. *Looking Out For #1.* New York: Funk and Wagnalls, 1977.

Ringer, Robert J. *Winning Through Intimidation.* New York: Funk and Wagnalls, 1974.

Strauss, Leo. *Thoughts on Machiavelli.* Seattle: University of Washington Press, 1969.

Whyte, William F. Jr. *The Organization Man.* New York: Doubleday, 1956.

CHAPTER 4

AYN RAND'S OBJECTIVISM: RATIONAL SELF-INTEREST AS MORAL GUIDE

Today, the average man often takes "altruism" to mean simply benevolence or kindness or respect for the rights of others. But . . . that is not the term's actual philosophical meaning. Altruism—as an ethical principle—holds that man must make the welfare of others his primary moral concern and must place their interests above his own; it holds that man has no right to exist for his own sake, that service to others is the moral justification of his existence, that self-sacrifice is his foremost duty and highest virtue. It is a curious paradox of human history that this doctrine—which tells man that he is to regard himself as a sacrificial animal—has been accepted as a doctrine representing benevolence and love for mankind.

Nathaniel Branden[1]

The minimal state treats us as inviolate individuals, who may not be used in certain ways by others as means or tools or instruments or resources; it treats us as persons having individual rights with the dignity this constitutes. Treating us with respect by respecting our rights, it allows us, individually or with whom we choose, to choose our life and to realize our ends and our conception of ourselves, insofar as we can aided by the voluntary cooperation of other individuals possessing the same dignity. How *dare* any state or group of individuals do more? Or less.?

Robert Nozick[2]

[1]Nathaniel Branden, *Who Is Ayn Rand?* (New York: Random House, Paperback Library, 1962), pp. 11–12.
[2]Robert Nozick, *Anarchy, State, and Utopia* (New York: Basic Books, Inc., 1974), pp. 333–34.

65

OBJECTIVES FOR CHAPTER 4:

1. To assess one's own libertarian leanings, viz., toward the primacy of individual liberty as the basis for distributing economic goods and services;

2. To understand the philosophical underpinnings of Ayn Rand's objectivism (a form of libertarianism), specifically:

    (a) the metaphysics of objective reality;

    (b) the epistemology of productive reason;

    (c) the ethics of self-interest;

    (d) the libertarian social philosophy.

3. To understand the pitfalls of preferring benevolence to self-interest in economic affairs;

4. To evaluate for oneself the arguments for and against Rand's conceptions of value, productive reason, altruistic love, self, and society.

Self-interest is what this chapter's all about—*rational* self-interest. And when love gets in the way of rational self-interest, then love's got to go. "Love thy neighbor" does not head the list of business secrets for enhancing the bottom line. This is not accident. Anyone entering business under the banner of universal love of others is doubtless out of business by now. Test your own self-interest attitudes. The following statements approximate some of the philosophical beliefs of Ayn Rand. How closely do they approximate your own? Having determined where your sympathies lie, you will be ready to reflect on the philosophical arguments for and against your position.

VALUES-CLARIFICATION TEST

Before each of the following statements, fill in a number to indicate how far you agree or disagree with the statement or with the attitude underlying the statement:

1 = strongly disagree, 2 = disagree, 3 = not sure
4 = agree, 5 = strongly agree.

_____ 1. I'd rather have truth and personal responsibility than unconditional love and belongingness: you can't have both.

_____ 2. Someone's got to *make* money before someone else can mooch it; it's a violation of reality and the moral law to take money you have not earned.

_____ 3. Who is fit to inherit money? Only the person who doesn't need it.

_____ 4. True morality is first and foremost *self*-interested.

_____ 5. Self-sacrifice is immoral: it's making yourself a means to serve the other's purpose.

_____ 6. Your work and your devotion to it determines your worth as a human being.

_____ 7. Love must be earned; not all human beings deserve to be loved.

_____ 8. *Do you need others?* You are a parasite: you live a second-hand life. Why not live firsthand?

_____ 9. To consume more than you produce is dishonest: there's no free lunch.

_____ 10. America is not a free economy because it tries to be fair: our Constitution guarantees freedom; it does not guarantee that life should be fair.

The higher your score, the more likely you are to tune into the business philosophy of Ayn Rand. Who is Ayn Rand? You might call her a philosophical counterpart to Milton Friedman. Their theses about business are similar. Her angle is the philosopher's; his the economist's. Academic philosophers have mostly chosen to ignore Ayn Rand. But that doesn't make her go away. She's rightly called "one of the most widely discussed philosophers of our times."[3] Her works, especially her novels, have sold copies in the millions and still do. She is just as contemptuous of academicians as they are of her. But for two decades now, her countless readers have adopted as their own the philosophical message of this fiercely independent Russian-born American, Ayn Rand. Her philosophy is called "Objectivism." The reason lies in her metaphysics (translated "theory of reality"; further translation: see below).

Objectivism more than the other business philosophies we have seen so far is explicitly concerned with distributive justice. As such, it is a philosophy peculiarly apt to illuminate issues of business ethics. This becomes evident when we consider the relation of business to distributive justice. Business, you recall, is concerned with the ethical norms that should guide

[3]William F. O'Neill, *With Charity Toward None* (New York: Philosophical Library, 1971), p. 4. Her masterwork is the novel, *Atlas Shrugged*, whose hero John Galt is the living exemplar of Rand's philosophy. Outstanding among her nonfictional works are *For the New Intellectual, The Virtue of Selfishness,* and *Capitalism: The Unknown Ideal.*

the proper apportioning out of the economic burdens and benefits in this process. These norms will flow from one's philosophy of society. Hence distributive justice is a branch of social justice. In other words, your philosophical view of the individual's relation to society will guide your moral view of "who should get what." Your social philosophy provides the moral basis for distributing economic goods and services. Keep this connection in mind so that you maintain your focus on business ethics as you thread your way now through Ayn Rand's (1) metaphysics, (2) epistemology, (3) ethics, and (4) social philosophy. Issues like affirmative action, equal pay, reward for merit, and government regulation hang in the balance.

1.   "WISHING WON'T MAKE IT SO": A METAPHYSICS OF OBJECTIVE REALITY[4]

Here's that distinction again between wishful thinking and real being, between "ought-to-be" and "is": sounds like Machiavelli all over again. But there is a difference. For Machiavelli, business lives in the world of "is," the world of objective fact: ethics is relegated to the world of "ought," the never-never-land of wishful thinking and ideals. So, for Machiavelli, ethics has nothing to do with business: they live in different worlds. For Ayn Rand, like Machiavelli, business lives in the world of "is"; but for Rand, unlike Machiavelli, this world of objective fact is the basis of ethics. *Ought* is based on *is*. Rand doesn't consider the real world to be at war with ethics. The real world—objective reality—is the very life-blood of ethics. So she calls her philosophy "objectivism." Morality *means* being faithful to the objective facts of business life. The objective facts do not tolerate either the ostrich's head-in-the-sand or the dreamer's head-in-the-clouds. These latter attitudes, then, are unpraiseworthy and immoral, as we will see, precisely because they try to ignore the objective realities of business.

So objectivism rejects any attempt to base ethics on feeling. Objective reality doesn't care what you feel. I might very well feel, for example, that crime doesn't and shouldn't pay. But a recent book called *Crime Pays* lists the following tax-free annual "business salaries": shoplifter, $15,000; drug importer, $165,000; house-burglar, $25,000; pickpocket, $20,000. Objectivism, as we will see, does not condone such "businesses," but these facts remain to be dealt with objectively, however distasteful they may be to my feelings. Rand puts the matter limpidly: Reality is what is; A is A. This is square one. This is where you start.

[4]This heading, and the next three, are from Ayn Rand's own outline of her philosophy in "Introducing Objectivism," *The Objectivist Newsletter* (August 1962), p. 35.

Objectivism rejects conventional morality, viz., "common practice," or "what everybody thinks," or "knows," or does. The bag of conventional wisdom about business and economics is filled with the most wondrous contradictions: "the profit motive is evil"; "the bottom line is all that matters"; "women should have fifty percent of managerial jobs"; "merit and merit alone should determine promotions"; "consumer litigation is killing businesses"; "industry is a conspirator with government against the consumer." And the list goes on and on. Again, objective reality could care less about such nuggets of conventional wisdom. *Reason*, says Rand, is the power that each person has to discover what's real and what isn't about these conventional nuggets. The immoral majority do not use their reason. They allow themselves to be swept along by the tide of social tradition about ethics.

Religion is one version of conventional morality. God or the Bible or revelation—the religious conventions—"decide" good and evil. But mysticism is even more irrational, and so even more ethically abhorrent. Consider this issue. Each year the TV networks fly in the media critics to preview the new season's offerings. They're lodged in posh hotels, wined, dined, and entertained. Who's to say, asks the moral mystic, whether or not such red-carpet treatment is a bribe for good reviews? Is it ethically wrong for the networks to offer such emoluments? Is it ethically right for critics to accept? "Each person must decide for himself," is a typically mystical and irrational answer to questions like these. Nobody *decides* moral right from moral wrong, says Ayn Rand. "Nature does not *decide*—it merely *is*; man does not decide, in issues of knowledge, he merely *observes* that which is."[5] People won't open their eyes and look at objective reality for what it is. When you do open your eyes, what do you see?

2. "YOU CAN'T HAVE YOUR CAKE AND EAT IT TOO": AN EPISTEMOLOGY OF PRODUCTIVE REASON

"Epistemology" means theory of knowledge, theory of how the mind works. Use your mind rationally, and you will be productive and happy. Use it irrationally (in other words, don't really use it) and you'll be unproductive and unhappy. Objective reality is unforgiving. You can command it to serve you, but only *if* you observe its laws. John Galt, the hero of Rand's novel *Atlas Shrugged*, explains that only the rational man can find happiness, because only he aims at rational goals alone and takes pleasure

[5]"Intellectual Ammunition Department," *The Objectivist Newsletter* (February 1965), p. 7, as quoted by O'Neill, *op. cit.*, p. 27.

in rational actions alone.[6] The rational mind is the mind that gets fed the correct data about objective reality. It will yield productivity, value, happiness. But the irrational mind, out of touch with objective reality, brings failure and misery. It's like a computer: garbage in, garbage out. Feed it the wrong program, and with perfect logic it will spew forth the wrong answer. What, then, is the correct program?

(1) Nothing comes from nothing. Productive reason applied to real (i.e., objective material) problems gives rise to profit. Profit *is* objective value. Here lies happiness. You don't pray for happiness, dream about happiness, wish for happiness. No. What you do is work for happiness. Apply your practical productive reason. Pay the price. Earn it. Women, for example, are understanding this law. As of March 1976, 37.8 million American women were in the work force. This is the practical reason that Rand is talking about. Properly applied, it brings material reward, which is another way of saying it brings value. Value here means objective clearly definable value, the kind without which there is no human happiness.

(2) Happiness, then, is a function of achieving values. Values are defined in materialistic terms. You may quarrel with such a materialization of value, but the approach is not without merit. Earned property is tangible. By focusing on it, I can put my life firmly under my own control. As we just noted, this lesson has not been lost on women who are bent on achieving full human rights and autonomy. Control over their economic destiny is essential to control over their human destiny. Prosperity-consumption-enjoyment of life are all of a piece.[7] Their achievement is not a matter of luck or accident. Profit (or objective value) is an *effect* with a definite cause. The cause is productive reason working on material problems. Women are now practicing this Randian logic, and advertisers are long last taking note, as they zero in on the working woman. The dizzy housewife taking advice from "Mr. Clean" is fast disappearing in favor of the 46 percent of women now in the marketplace themselves producing various versions of Mr. Clean for profit, and making 60 percent of vacation-destination decisions, 50 percent of color TV brand selections, and 30 percent of new car purchases.[8]

(3) This example is meant to illustrate the straight forward character of Rand's epistemology of productive reason. Reason *causes* profit. "Profit" not arising in this way is pseudo-profit yielding pseudo-happiness—a fake. It's no wonder that women are no longer content to lead second-hand lives. There is no uncaused wealth. To live off the wealth caused by others is a futile attempt to reverse the law of causality. It is to abandon

[6]See Rand in *The Virtue of Selfishness* (New York: New American Library, 1965), p. 29.
[7]*Ibid.*, p. 84.
[8]See *Wall Street Journal* (July 5, 1977), p. 1.

reason—the very essence of your humanness. It is replacing your mind by seizing the products of other minds.[9] This is the bitter price exacted by immoral behavior. There are no miracles. Don't we all know this? No. A recent survey revealed that most Americans want the Post Office to increase services sharply while drastically cutting the cost of postage. Ayn Rand's epistemology of productive reason—however self-evident she may think it to be—is still far from becoming accepted wisdom. We still believe in miracles. We close our eyes to what *is*.

3. WHAT ONE "IS" DETERMINES WHAT ONE "OUGHT" TO DO: AN ETHICS OF SELF-INTEREST

We've just seen in outline "what one is," i.e., Rand's philosophy of human nature. Ethics is simply a corollary: "act accordingly." *Is* determines *ought*. To put it philosophically, Rand's metaphysics is normative. Reality defines the norm by which you tell moral good from evil. An ethical life is simply productive reason in action. This is the path to objective value and happiness.

Ayn Rand is not original in her deriving of "ought" from "is." Consciously or unconsciously, a theory of reality underlies every theory of ethics, as we have seen. Such a view could be open to the objection that it falls into what is called "the naturalistic fallacy." This is the fallacy of claiming that ethics mirrors nature or reality. The fallacy lies in the wrongheaded view that just because something is natural or real, that makes it morally good. It may be natural, i.e., just "human nature," to cheat a competitor; but to argue that this natural behavior is thereby ethical, is to fall into the naturalistic fallacy. There's no way out of this problem if ethics is claimed to be merely the mirror of nature with all its flaws and evils.

Such, however, is not Rand's claim. She does not fall into the naturalistic fallacy. Her metaphysics endeavors to give not a picture of nature with all its flaws, but a "true" picture of the way nature is supposed to work when its real laws are allowed to operate. Ayn Rand's "reason" is not a passive mirror but a creative instrument interacting productively with nature. Her theory of reality is an account of this productive interaction and its laws. In this sense, the theory of "what is" will yield rules for what one ought ethically to do. It is those whom Rand attacks who fall

[9]A perfect vignette of this mindless second-class living is given by the National Republican Congressional Committee's pamphlet of advice to candidates' wives: "When your husband is speaking, watch him proudly . . . Never appear bored, even if you've heard the same speech repeatedly." Quoted by *Ms.* (July 1977), 50.

into the naturalistic fallacy. Most people live in a world of wishful thinking, of "something for nothing"—the attitude that one can receive without producing. It would indeed be a fallacy to call this "natural" way of thinking ethical. It is a fallacy that Rand rejects.

So happiness is the reward of a morally good life, and it's all in my own hands. No one can die for me. No one can live for me either. It's my life. It's a private and individual affair. To put the burden of moral responsibility on the individual, however, does not turn this into a subjective morality. *What* is right, and *what* is wrong is not up to the individual. The "what" is objective:

(1) Value (happiness) is caused by effective behavior.

(2) Effective behavior is caused by true knowledge.

(3) True knowledge is caused by right reason (i.e., by a clear-eyed view of "what is": see previous sections).

(4) So right reason causes, and is basically synonymous with, value.

The truth of these propositions is not "up to the individual." What is up to me the individual is to take my life in hand and live by these truths.

Morality is no luxury. "Is" determines "ought." Moral *good* = survival by the use of right reason and productive work; do this, and your life is on the firm stable ground of nature—the way things are. Moral *evil* = survival by parasitism—living off the productive reason of others. It is an inhuman, and therefore, an evil way to live. Such people—the "moochers," Rand calls them—choose to survive by theft, by force, by brutality, or quite simply, by default; they surrender their survival into the hands of others. The result is misery, anxiety, and ultimately, self-destruction. The penalty of immorality is that my fate is determined by the whims of others.

Ethics, then, is a matter of rational self-interest. On a desert island it is not the stringing of beads or the mumbling of prayers that keeps you alive. You survive by identifying the objective facts and living by them. Morally speaking, we are all on desert islands. Each person's life is in his/her hands. To surrender this autonomy is self-renunciation. It is the end of happiness because it is the rejection of the conditions of happiness (i.e., right reason actively involved with objective reality). A morality of self-renunciation makes death its standard, not life. Such a morality tells you to close your eyes to the principles of life, viz., objective reality that yields objective value.

Two things above all can seduce us away from the life-ethic toward death: excessive government and the blandishments of altruistic ethics. These are two ways of saying: "I am my brother's keeper," or worse, "I am your brother/sister, you are my keeper." We'll examine these seductions in the next two sections.

4. "GIVE ME LIBERTY OR GIVE ME DEATH": A LIBERTARIAN SOCIAL PHILOSOPHY

Like the Social Darwinists, Ayn Rand advocates a hands-off, laissez-faire relationship of government to business. But whereas Spencer spoke for determinism, Rand is speaking for freedom. Spencer condemned government's attempts to interfere with the necessary workings of natural selection. Rand's problem is with a government that stifles human initiative, autonomy and freedom. Rand's political philosophy is the flip side of her philosophy of human nature. Government exists to protect the basic natural rights of the individual. Underline *individual*. There are no *group* rights, only individual rights. Groups have to make it on their own, whether you're talking about an airlines industry, a steel company, or a consumers' union, as we'll see. Groups are as good as their individual members. It's the individuals who possess the rights. And their basic natural right is the freedom to live according to productive reason dealing with objective reality. You can break this down into the traditional rights to *life* (to ascertain and act upon the facts that foster survival), *liberty* (to do this autonomously and without interference by others), and *the pursuit of happiness* (thereby achieving those objective property values on which happiness is based, and keeping these values as your own).

The purpose of government, then, is a very limited one.[10] Government exists only to protect you from those who would try to hinder you from living your own life and pursuing your own happiness in freedom. Your life remains yours to live. Only a repressive tyrannical government (which all present governments are to some degree) tries to live for you, decide for you, protect you from yourself, and take from you the results of your work. Such abusive use of governmental power deprives you of the aforementioned rights to life, liberty, and the pursuit of happiness. A limited government, respectful of individuals, protects you from those who would do violence to you rather than itself joining in the violence against you (e.g., via confiscatory taxes and regulations about hiring and firing). A limited government would protect you from criminals and enemies, from those who would defraud you and those who would initiate physical force against you. Finally, since even among rational persons disagreements can arise, a government rightly provides a court system to mediate such disputes. And that's it. For the rest, we should be free. Further extension of

---

[10]See Nozick's brilliant articulation, *op. cit.*, of the contemporary libertarian argument in favor of the "minimal state." Later on we will outline the present debate between Nozick and Rawls on the legitimacy of the state and on the implications for distributive justice of this debate between Nozick and Rawls and between them and the utilitarians.

government power is an affront to individual liberty, a violation of objective reality and of its unforgiving laws.

The conclusion is that the state should stay out of the business of economics. Complete laissez-faire capitalism is the only moral form of government because it alone does not prevent individuals from freely and rationally dealing with objective reality. Capitalism allows the rational person to reap the reward of his merits. It thereby encourages individual rational action with its resultant profit, property and happiness. Without such economic freedom, talk of human rights is a sham. The two go hand in hand. Unfortunately, just to describe such a free society is to make it clear how far away we are from enjoying one. What we have instead is what Ayn Rand calls a "cannibal" society. The law of causality is denied: people act as if profits drop from the clear sky. Productive reason is scorned in favor of the moochers who devour the products of mind. People become the property of the state instead of the state's protecting the right of people to enjoy the property they've earned. The average American worker annually turns over to the government the amount of his total earnings from January 1 to mid-May. Did the medieval lord and master confiscate much more than this from the serfs that tilled their land? Altruism (call it socialism, call it love) is a sweet name for the violence that punishes virtue (i.e., punishes the use of productive reason) and rewards vice (by awarding the products of reason to the parasites who never earned it). Laissez-faire has never been tried.

Objectivism's utopia would be a society founded on merit and on freedom to enjoy the fruits of merit. Rand enunciates the direction in which society should move in the long run. The totally free society cannot be achieved overnight. It would be a society where taxation was purely voluntary. I'd pay only for those government services that I want, and these would be limited to noncommercial areas like police and military protection, and courts for rational litigation. The Post Office would be privately owned and paid for by those who choose to use the same and bear the freight. Similarly, roads and sanitation would be managed by the rational dictates of the private sector; they'd cease to be plums dispensed by the cannibal chefs without regard for merit. Above all, the schools would be returned to free private individuals who would own them, run them, decide where their children will go and what they will learn. It would be a society with no unemployment. Each person's labor would find its own market value when the government no longer robbed hard-working Peter to pay Paul for not working. It would be a society without governmentally established monopolies protecting energy group interests, steel group interests, garment-worker group interests from local and foreign competition. There are no group rights, only individual rights.

Group rights pit special interests against opposing groups who presumably do not enjoy those same rights. It creates arbitrary divisions between equally free and rational human individuals. Rand rejects such arbitrary meddling. She opposes, for example, the idea of "consumer rights." Consumers should no more have rights over against producers than should whites enjoy rights not shared by blacks. There are laws against violence and fraud that apply to all, consumer and producer alike. And this is legitimate. The abomination is for the government to go beyond such laws and tell the producer what he may produce and the consumer what to consume. As a consumer, for example, I have the right to pay less for a shoddy lawnmower and use the money saved for recreation, if I so choose. I have the right not to be forced to pay for idiot-proof safety devices on appliances if I choose not to have my money spent insuring idiots against their foolery. As a producer I have the right to market clothing that will fall apart after the first washing. I may calculate that my business will survive the consequent diminished reputation; in other words, I may calculate that there is a market for customers who choose to pay less to get less. So, for billion-dollar Big-Brotherism, Rand would substitute the kind of regulation achieved by interactions of individuals each acting in his/her own self-interest. Such is a partial picture of that totally free society that has never been tried. Why never tried?

5. LOVE IS THE ROOT OF ALL EVIL: OBJECTIVE EGOISM

Love kills. What is this "love" that kills? Clearly, it is a perverse love. Such love is the enemy of rational self-interest, the enemy of objective reality, i.e., of what *is*. Love is unhealthy because it flies in the face of reality, the reality of that self-respect upon which one's existence and survival depend. Every person is an end in him/her self. Never should I allow myself to be a tool, to become a mere means to the ends of others. We raise animals to be the means to the ends of human beings. So we eat chickens and pigs and cows. But to submit other people to my ends and purposes or to let others use me for their ends is cannibalism. It's a figurative, if not a literal, devouring of the self. To urge such self-surrender in the name of love is rank sentimentalism. Rational self-interest refuses to squander the objective value of one's person to this kind of suicide.

Objective egoism, therefore, is utterly opposed to empty "self-sacrificial" sentimentality. How could love be rational when it asks the self to abandon the objective facts of the way people live and survive? To sacrifice the objective value of the self is therefore immoral. Morality is concerned with achieving and building up the self the only way that this can be done, viz., through the use of productive reason. Such self-respect, Rand insists, must never be surrendered to sentimental nonvalues, nor would the objectivist ever demand such self-destructive surrender on the part of others. The ironic fact is that such so-called altruism, whether exercised person to person or through government programs, results precisely in the destruction of that self-respect in the very persons who are allegedly supposed to be helped. Here's why.

Altruism is often presented as love in its highest and ideal form. It is offered absolutely and without condition. It says, "I love you as a human being no matter what you do or who you are; the mere fact that you are a fellow human entitles you to my concern, my help, my goods." Such altruistic sentiment underlies both the "welfare ethics" and the "true friendship" trap. This love is unrealistic, irrational, and pathological, says Rand. As a pathology, it is destructive of those whom it would help. Note how blind it is (yes, "love is blind," they say). This pathological love refuses to evaluate others on the basis of objective self-esteem. It pretends that the laws of objective reality are suspended for the "loved" ones. "No one so poor as a rich man's son," Bob Dylan used to sing. Showered with "love," he's never learned to use his practical reason to ascertain the laws of objective reality and use them on his own behalf.

Objectivism does honor genuine love that is real and rationally based. In other words, it honors a love that is earned. If you deserve love, you get love. Like everything else, love is caused. It is not unconditional, as altruism pretends to be. It is *conditioned* by actual behavior. Psychologist Eric Fromm distinguishes mother-love and father-love. Mother-love is extended to children unconditionally. Children are loved just for existing: mother-love need not be earned or deserved. It's there without conditions, period. This uncritical pouring out of self to others Rand rejects as irrational and destructive. Father-love, on the other hand, looks not simply to what the child *is*, but to what the child can become. It's conditioned on performance. If the child measures up, earns it, the love is there. It respects and encourages the child who operates according to reality's objective laws. Such a model of father-love Rand would accept as realistic, rational and genuine. I love you best when I help you to learn how the laws of reality function in your life. I love you best by letting you go, encouraging you to strike out on your own and make your own way.

These models of parent-child love illustrate Rand's evaluation of state-citizen and state-business relationships. A "maternalistic" state (mother-love model) is hatred in the guise of love. It's anti-life because it's anti-objective. It's a false kindness to turn whole groups and generations of people into helpless dependents, who know how to survive only by becoming parasites on the productive labor of others. This so-called love is the root of all evil. This is the reason that the capitalism that is respectful of the objective power and autonomy of individuals has never been tried. A healthy business and a healthy economy is one which is firmly based on objective reality. Artificial transfusions of government aid only postpone the day when such health can come to pass.

In view of all this, the resounding failure of throwing public money at problems is not surprising. Do you want to help "the poor"? Well, pick out a deserving poor person. Give help if you can which will lead that person to autonomy rather than to dependence. Help in a way that the person can make a return to you for the help you've given. Is there a deserving business in need of aid? Well, invest in it if you can, in a way that will make it independent of your infusions; the test of a *deserving* business is one which will yield a value-for-value return on your investment. Value-for-value charity is rational, objective and genuine. Something-for-nothing charity, public or private, destroys both giver and receiver. Such selfless behavior is evil precisely because it is antihuman, antiself (self*less*). If I don't respect myself first, and others as myself, love is a charade. Love is not an alms but a moral tribute, if it is genuine. This tribute is moral precisely because it is based upon objective facts, those conditions of existence that make all other values possible. *Is* determines *ought*. This is the ethics of objectivism.

William F. O'Neill[11] has made a clever thumbnail sketch of the picture of human nature that emerges from Ayn Rand's philosophical premises:

Value is wealth.
Wealth is caused by productive rational action in the realm of property relationships.
Wealth signifies productive rational action in the area of practical property relationships and therefore serves as a visible sign of a personal merit.
In any given instance, then, it necessarily holds that (1) the wealthy are virtuous; (2) the poor are depraved; and (3) everyone is either virtuous or depraved.
This being true, it stands to reason that coerced humanitarianism in the guise of such things as unemployment relief-assistance or free medical care for the aged is bad for two reasons: 1) Unearned wealth will ultimately work against and slowly destroy those who receive it; 2) The confiscation of wealth from the virtuous can only eventuate in a curtailment of true labor by the productive (virtuous) and therefore can only

[11]O'Neill, *op. cit.*, p. 226.

terminate in a decrease in the amount of real wealth (and therefore of real virtue) available within the culture at large. "The small minority of adults who are *unable*, rather than unwilling to work, has to rely on voluntary charity; misfortune is not a claim to slave labor."

You may find this picture of human nature simplistic, even revolting. But an unpleasant picture need not mean an untrue picture.

6. HOW OBJECTIVE IS OBJECTIVISM?

Objective reality is called objective because wishing that it would go away will not make it go away. It operates independently of my subjective whims, desires, and even ignorance. We've seen Ayn Rand's account of this objective reality, from which she deduces her ethics of individual rational self-interest. Now comes the time to ask how accurate and coherent is the picture she paints. The business ethics here stands or fails by the philosophy of human nature that underpins it. As we examine these business philosophies in turn, we ask you to evaluate how true is the picture of reality, how accurate and complete is the meaning of "human" in society, and hence how adequate are the ethical norms that follow from these premises. I assume that by now you've thought of dozens of possible objections to the Randian picture of reality. We suggest here only five criticisms to consider as you come to your personal evaluation of objectivism as a business ethic. We briefly probe the adequacy of Rand's conceptions of (1) value, (2) productive reason, (3) altruistic love, (4) self, (5) society.

In each case we will restate Rand's conception in summary form. After each restatement, a question (*Q*) is presented to highlight a philosophical objection that can be raised against Rand's conception. Then Rand's answer (*A*) is briefly stated. The intent is to help the reader to view the pros and cons of objectivism as a business philosophy so as to arrive at a self-evaluation of this ethics. The intent is not to endorse either Objectivist ethics or its opposite.

(1) *Value*

Value is tangible and objective. It consists in control over actual property rationally produced and acquired. Herein consists human satisfaction and happiness. These latter are subjective responses, to be sure. But the tangible results of labor remain the necessary objective considerations for true human happiness.

Q: Granted, attachment to possessions can make me happy. Is not *detachment* another path to human freedom and satisfaction? If, for example, I have no desire to own a boat, am I not humanly more free and happy than the person who owns an outboard, but yearns for a yacht?

A: No. Economic power is the condition for human autonomy and worth. A person actively working for a yacht is more productive and virtuous than, say, a monk who stifles his productive desires and hence his productive powers.

Do you agree with Rand's materialization of value and human worth? Why/why not?

(2) *Productive Reason*

All people are endowed with reason by which they can produce the wealth that brings happiness. The moochers choose not to use this productive reason to earn their way. In choosing to be parasites they are anti-human because they abdicate productive reason whose exercise is the highest sign of genuine humanity.

Q: Don't we need environment and other people to educate and develop this productive reason? I'm dependent on society for the chance to learn how to earn my way. Am I to be called depraved just because I was born and raised in a deprived environment?

A: True, others teach you material facts. But no one gives you the power to think and use your head. Either you take your life in hand and use the powers you have or you don't. That part's up to you, and your decision here makes you either virtuous or depraved.

Do you agree that the unproductive adult is morally blameworthy? Why/why not?

(3) *Altruistic Love*

Altruism is a pretty name for masochism. To spend myself on another without tangible return is perverse. For government to take my goods and allocate them to others who haven't earned them is perversity writ large. It makes the idlers still more unproductive and punishes the virtuous for their work.

Q: Granted, masochism is perverse. Is it really always destructive to give unconditionally without hope of return? Is not the joy of giving a sign of genuine altruistic love?

A: Not genuine. You forget how you harm the receiver of your "love." You deceive the recipient into thinking that wealth and happiness come free. You thereby show hate, not love. You destroy the other, if not yourself.

Do you agree that love is a charade if it is not based upon value for value exchange? Why/why not?

(4) *Self*

A person is an end, not a means. Never allow yourself to be used as a tool for others. Other people's misfortunes give them no right to appropriate for themselves the products of your labor.

Q: I am an end in myself; so are other people ends in themselves. This is the basis for rejecting unconditional altruistic love. On this basis, too, it is said that conditioned love is the only genuine love; value is received for value given. Isn't such conditioned love a form of using people for my own ends? Am I not calculating, what can the other person do for me? What has the other person done for me lately?

A: No. Conditioned love is rather a respect for the other as an autonomous rational productive human being with too much dignity and objectivity to take the fruits of another's energy without putting forth energy of his own.

Do you agree that love "with strings attached" is *not* a "using" type relationship? Why/why not?

(5) *Society*

Society is a mere collection of individuals. Hence, the best government is laissez-faire: it leaves individuals as free as possible to make their own way. And capitalism is the most humane economy: it trusts that the interplay of individual rational self-interest will optimize the distribution of goods and services.

Q: Is not society at least equally as real as individuals? Society bestows on me an identity, a culture, an ability to grow and develop my individual powers. Should not governmental and economic structures, then, ensure that individuals contribute to the society which formed them?

A: No. Society is the product of individual productive minds, not the other way around. Therefore, to deprive individuals of the products of their minds only diminishes the culture as a whole.

Do you agree that in an ideal economy and government, productive individuals take first place, and society is an abstraction? Why/why not?

CASE FOR DISCUSSION

In a lake area on the U.S.–Canadian border, the residents in the American town of Pineburg had for years watched tourists every summer heading past their homes into the developed Canadian vacationlands some 60–70 miles away over the border. A group of local business leaders were contacted by out-of-town investors about redeveloping the Pineburg area so as to intercept some of this vacation traffic. They bought up as much lakefront land as they could and initiated drainage projects, aerial spraying against insects, especially mosquitoes, and started to build campgrounds, motels, and boating and bathing facilities. Before the project was even completed, tourism and employment were on the upswing. There took place, however, a bitter reaction by many of the Pineburg natives against the despoiling of the natural beauty of the local lake and wooded area. They were equally concerned about the proven buildup of pesticide concentrations in fish and fowl, and the petty vandalism and nuisances created by the crowds of tourists. They formed a Native Residents' Union, and called for a halt to further development and for a concentrated effort to devise measures to reverse the pollution and environmental deterioration. They urged, too, a program for more effective control over irresponsible tourist behavior. Mayor Callaway called a meeting with Hiram Haskell, the president of the Native Residents' Union, and Robert Kroc, the out-of-town investor who was heading up the vacation-development program.

DISCUSSION QUESTIONS

1. (a) Suppose Ayn Rand were in attendance at this meeting called by Mayor Callaway. Essentially, a conflict of *values* is splitting the town. Recall Rand's definition of value. What values would Rand say are at issue in this case? What would be a logical recommendation according to R-ethics? Note in this and subsequent answers that Rand's principles could very well lead to differing and even opposing concrete recommendations. This exercise in philosophical criticism aims at a heightened appreciation of the philosophical values underlying concrete decisions more than at the concrete decisions themselves.

(b) Do you see other values at issue, besides those in the R-world? If so, what different assumptions from Rand's account for your values?

2. (a) Recall Rand's philosophy of *self*: from the interplay of individual self-interest, the best and most rational solutions will emerge. If Haskell, Kroc, and Callaway each pursues his own rational self-interest, what course of action might each logically pursue?

(b) In the Canadian vacationlands over the border, there are no native environmental groups stirring up trouble. Can the American parties safely ignore the Canadian scene as they pursue their individual goals? How do you evaluate Rand's individualistic theory of the "self"?

3. (a) Hiram Haskell, the president of the Native Residents' Union, argues that Pineburg has a duty to preserve an environmental heritage for

future generations. Do future generations enter into the moral calculus of Rand's world-view?

(b) Do future generations enter into your moral calculus? Review Rand's philosophy of *society*. Does yours differ? How? If you were in Kroc's shoes, how would you argue your case?

4. (a) For at least part of each year, at least 24 percent of Pinesburg's residents have to go on welfare. They are poor, without economic clout, and politically apathetic. No one represents their interests at the mayor's meeting. If you offered this lack of representation as an objection, what would Rand reply?

(b) Would your view of the rights of the poor differ from Rand's? If so, what in your social philosophy accounts for this? To what extent do you agree and disagree with Rand's philosophy of *productive reason*?

5. (a) Love must be earned; it's not to be given away free, Rand argues. Many of Pineburg's senior citizens have little to offer anyone physically, economically, or emotionally; their lives are spent. Would Rand consider them possible objects of love? Why?

(b) In your view, do these senior citizens merit any special concern at the mayor's meeting? How do you evaluate Rand's philosophy of *altruistic love*?

6. Return now to the Values-Clarification Test at the beginning of the chapter. Answer the questions again. Have any of your answers changed? Why? Do you understand the implications of any one question more clearly than before? Which one? Why? Compare your answers with the answers others gave.

SUGGESTED READINGS

Branden, Nathaniel. *Who Is Ayn Rand?* New York: Random House, Paperback Library, 1962.

Friedman, Milton. *Capitalism and Freedom.* Chicago: University of Chicago Press, 1962.

Hayek, F. A. *The Constitution of Liberty.* Chicago: University of Chicago Press, 1960.

Locke, John. *Two Treatises of Government,* ed. by Peter Laslett. Cambridge: Cambridge University Press, 1967, second edition.

Nozick, Robert. *Anarchy, State and Utopia.* New York: Basic Books, Inc., 1974.

O'Neill, William F. *With Charity Toward None: An Analysis of Ayn Rand's Philosophy.* New York: Philosophical Library, 1971.

Rand, Ayn. *Atlas Shrugged.* New York: Random House, 1957.

————. *Capitalism: The Unknown Ideal.* New York: The New American Library, 1966.

————. *The Virtue of Selfishness.* New York: The New American Library, 1965.

Rawls, John. *A Theory of Justice.* Cambridge: The Belknap Press of the Harvard University Press, 1971.

CHAPTER 5

ETHICAL RELATIVISM IN BUSINESS: "WHEN IN ROME..."

Rollins, Inc. . . . for the last several years . . . has paid off a number of local and municipal government officials in the Republic of Mexico. About $127,000 was paid out over a period of five years. . . . It is Mr. Rollins's contention that such low-level bribery is the "legitimate way" of doing business in Mexico. "You do those things because some fellow says this is how it's done around here," says Rollins.[1]

Accepted Practices. . . . too often unethical practices become a routine part of doing business. To determine just how routine, we asked: "In every industry there are some generally accepted business practices. In your industry, are there practices which you regard as unethical?"
. . .[t]wo thirds of the responding executives in 1976 indicate that such practices exist, compared with nearly four-fifths who so responded in 1961.[2]

OBJECTIVES FOR CHAPTER 5:

1. To understand the meaning of conventional morality (abbreviated "C.M.") and the problems it gives rise to both cross-culturally and within the same culture;

[1] *Wall Street Journal* (October 1, 1976), p. 8.
[2] Steven N. Brenner and Earl A. Molander, "Is the Ethics of Business Changing?" *Harvard Business Review* (January-February 1977), 60.

2. To become aware of one's own present leanings toward this ethics of "When in Rome do as the Romans do";

3. To see how C.M. contrasts with the ego-centered philosophies we have treated so far;

4. To give the arguments in favor of social approbation and disapprobation as a norm of ethics;

5. To explain the role that reason plays in making a decision based on C.M.;

6. To evaluate for oneself the pros and cons of C.M.'s philosophical adequacy, especially in view of the ethical relativism that it implies.

1. THE "LEGITIMATE WAY" OF DOING BUSINESS

Thus far, business ethics has been treated pretty much as an individual affair in the Spencerian, Machiavellian and Objectivist philosophies that we have examined. Equipped with the rationale and ethical "M.O." of one of these philosophies, business people can in good conscience make the necessary and realistic decisions that their goals require. Such has been the assumption. But we've found it necessary to question the social philosophies of Social Darwinism, Machiavellianism, and Objectivism. Each is strong on individualism, to be sure. And as such, these philosophies are appealing to business people. For, more than most other segments of our population, business people prize individual assertiveness, aggressiveness, and competition. These qualities make for success, and the philosophies that we have seen so far legitimate these qualities. They become the central moral values enshrining the best in human nature. Individual survival, the expedient use of power, rational self-interest—these have been singled out as cardinal virtues. But the nagging critical question of social sensitivity remains. Do these individualistic philosophies sufficiently attend to the repercussions on society of business decisions?

The question of social impact is a philosophical question, to be sure. We want an adequate and accurate picture of society's relation to the individual and vice versa. But this philosophical question is eminently practical. Involved is not only the impact on society of business decisions, but the repercussions of society on business. Businesses do not act in a socioethical vacuum, and a business philosophy and ethic that ignores this is seriously deficient. There is a moral penalty for trying to operate on the basis of a deficient philosophy. The penalty is not hellfire, but hell on earth: the philosophy won't work. The ethical environment of business demands to be incorporated into the operative business philosophy. One main avenue toward achieving this is to pay attention to the conventional morality that surrounds a given business operation. Our focus now swings from individual to society. To the question, "What is the ethically correct thing to do?" we now consider the conventional answer: "When in Rome, do as the Romans do." We are ready to examine the type of business ethics that looks to society for its norms.

Conventional morality is the kind of thing one is not tempted to examine unless and until it becomes a problem. The conventional, after all, is the accepted, the "obvious," the taken-for-granted. I take for granted the homely but necessary advantages of toilet paper; I might be challenged to question this in Bombay if I were to encounter Indians sniggering at this filthy European t.p. habit, since it is "obvious" to them that river water strategically applied with the left hand is the civilized and sanitary way to deal with such functions. When my complacently accepted conventions abruptly clash with conventions that are different from my own, then instead of norms and guidelines the conventions become problems.

The quotations at the head of this chapter illustrate two such problem areas that force us to examine the conventional moral claims made on business people. First, nation clashes with nation, and culture with culture, in their conventional expectations about business behavior. The resultant ethical conflicts are what plague the multinational businesses. A second broad problem area of conventional morality can occur within the boundaries of a single nation and culture. A business can clash with an employee, or a corporation can clash with the public, regarding "accepted practice" in the way of doing business. What is *accepted* in one group may not always be *acceptable* to another. Notwithstanding such conflicts among various conventions about ethical behavior, the appeal to the group for a norm of morality remains a persistent philosophical rationale for ethical business decision-making.

The word "corrupt" springs easily to the lips when one culture evaluates the ethical practices of another. In America, the prevailing ethos is meritocratic. This accounts for the moral revulsion that many feel, say, against affirmative-action programs that favor certain individuals on grounds other than merit. Recent federal legislation forbidding discrimination against the handicapped and urging quantitative goals (quotas?) for hiring the handicapped is a case in point. Questionnaires are beginning to appear that inquire whether paraplegia, facial disfigurement, alcoholism, or drug addiction exists in the job applicant. Such qualities entitle their happy possessors to consideration not afforded to applicants who present themselves on purely meritocratic grounds. The meritarian will characterize such policy as bizarre and morally corrupt. It offends his conventional ethics that the absence of drug addiction, for example, should tip the scales against him.

There is, however, an opposite conventionality to the meritocratic one. It regards the handicapped and deprived as "special," and for this reason, privileged. By no means do all or even most of the handicapped share this assumption (which could be regarded as patronizing). In any case, for this opposing conventional morality, deprivation means entitlement. This paradoxical principle was appealed to in July 1977 when New York City suffered an extended electrical power failure. Throughout the long night of darkness, looting was rampant. When the sun rose over the ruins, spokesmen for the looters readily consented to interviews. They declared to be "corrupt" a system that kept significant segments of the population in economic deprivation. *Deprivation means entitlement.* The looting was not looting at all. It was "Christmas." It was a brief reprieve during which the truly just society prevailed; for a few short hours, the poor could appropriate goods necessary and desirable.

More commonly, the label "corrupt" is assigned by one nation to practices that prevail in another nation and culture. Anything remotely smacking of nepotism, for example, offends the moral conventions of a meritocracy. S. Dillon Ripley, Secretary to the Smithsonian Institute, was recently rapped for giving a favorable review in *Smithsonian* magazine to a book on Panamanian birds written by his son-in-law.[3] According to the American conventional ethic, he should have disqualified himself as a reviewer, or at least have admitted his kinship to the author. But in more traditional societies of the Southern Hemisphere, what counts for "nepotism" in the American convention becomes "familial duty" there. In such societies, it is morally "obvious" that one's primary duty is to one's family rather than to an impersonal institution. When a favored member of the family achieves a key governmental or business post, he is expected to use that position to support and enhance his extended family in every possible way. He has received the highly coveted key that unlocks the impersonal institutional treasury, and he is expected to use that key in favor of the family which looks to him for support, and expects that support in no uncertain terms. "Corrupt" behavior for such a person would be to ignore the conventional familial demands on his loyalty. Extortion and bribery may well be misnomers for transactions conducted in a conventional moral context like this one, however much those same labels might be aptly applied to certain under-the-table conduct by congressmen and business people on the American conventional scene.

We have outlined in anecdotal fashion some of the conflicts that make conventional morality a problem for business. It might be tempting at this point to launch into an examination of this particular version of C.M.

---

[3]"Mighty Museum," *Wall Street Journal* (July 18, 1977), pp. 1 and 17.

compared to that particular version. For example, is a meritocratic conventional system of hiring and firing superior to a conventional system in which nepotism is the socially approved principle? If your ethics is based on something other than convention, you'll want to tackle questions such as this. But that would be to miss the point of C.M. For C.M., social approval and disapproval is self-validating; it is the ultimate determinant of right and wrong. The fact that something is the socially approved way of acting becomes by that very fact the morally good way of acting. If the merit system is socially approved, then a business meritocracy is the ethical way of doing business; if nepotism is the social rule, then this makes nepotism morally right. We need now to examine the arguments in favor of a business ethics based on social convention. Such an appeal to conventionality is a frequent one. It is the "When in Rome . . ." philosophy, if you're talking about multinationals. More generally, it is the "commonly accepted practice" argument used to justify both domestic and foreign business behavior. Before moving on, test first your own attitudes toward conventional morality. If you shy away from Social Darwinism, Machiavellianism, and Objectivism as philosophies which are excessively individualistic, to what extent are you willing to look to the group for ethical norms?

VALUES-CLARIFICATION TEST

Before each of the following statements, fill in a number.

**1 = strongly disagree 2 = disagree 3 = not sure
4 = agree 5 = strongly agree**

Your final decision in each case will depend on all the circumstances. But indicate how far you agree with the attitude and orientation underlying these statements. Are they basically wrong-headed, naive, and unrealistic, or do they indicate a tough-minded, sensible, and ethically correct direction for business to take?

_____ 1. Business's responsibility extends beyond the letter of the law and the economic bottom line; it is more than "give in order to get"; it cares about the people it affects, and should respond to the expectations that society has of it. For example, a bank should assist a deteriorating neighborhood rather than red-lining it, or itself closing down thereby hastening the deterioration.

_____ 2. When self-interests are in conflict, look to society to decide. Consider, for example, a U.S.-owned tourist hotel in the Bahamas. Should it be staffed with highly qualified U.S. help or with less-qualified local help? Let the Bahamanians decide.

_____ 3. A U.S.-based company need not enforce the same occupational safety standards on its foreign subsidiaries as it does on its U.S. operations. Rather, local working conditions should be the norm.

_____ 4. Even at the risk of losing a one-shot sale, I would not lead an unsuspecting customer to believe the truth of the exaggerated marketing claims of the computer software he is intending to buy from me.

_____ 5. An engineering director lost a contract by informing a buyer that the scheduled delivery dates could not be met. As his superior, I should reassure him that his intention was good and that he did the right thing.

_____ 6. A corporation planning manager from Maryland acquires an Ecuadorian company which uses two sets of books to evade income taxes. He plans to continue the tax evasion on the grounds that this is a local standard practice.

_____ 7. I'm a salesman earning about $25,000 per year. I pad my expense account by about $2,000. My boss knows this and says nothing, so I feel morally justified.

_____ 8. My company has discovered a revolutionary and secret film-developing process in the highly competitive photography industry. Our chief rival offered to hire me and the secret at double my present salary. I'm accepting. Money's the name of the game, and both companies know this.

Interpretation of test answers. Statements 1 and 2 test whether you give primacy to self or to group in ethical attitude orientation. Conventional morality looks to the immediate functional group for its ethical guidelines. Following this principle, statement 3 is an application of "When in Rome..." It eschews moral idealism—higher U.S. standards need not be exported around the world. Conventional morality is a position midway between self-interested egoism and moral idealism.

Though rejecting idealism, the conventional moralist is not myopic in his ethical vision. He is able to take the role of the other. In statement 4, he is able to put himself in the customer's shoes and act accordingly. And so, for the conventional moralist, the bottom-line consequences are not the whole story. Good intentions do count. See statement 5.

The final three statements test the "When in Rome..." principle again, whether it be "Rome," Ecuador (statement 6), or "Rome," America (statements 7 and 8).

All in all, the higher you scored in this test, the more attuned you are to that cluster of ethical attitudes that typifies the conventional orientation to moral norms.

General characteristics of conventional morality. Conventional morality is indeed a genuine morality like that of objectivism. In this it is unlike the so-called "ethics" proposed by Social Darwinism and Machiavellianism. Social Darwinism, you will recall, is based upon the blind, implacable determinism of natural selection. There is little or no place for the kind of freedom where moral responsibility could make a difference. And as you remember, Machiavellianism gives up completely on the relevance or morality for public life: deliberate amoral expedience is the only rule. But objectivism is a genuine attempt to ground a business ethics, as also is C.M. Both of these philosophies are looking for a norm to guide ethical decisions. Both appeal to conscience. Both distinguish good from evil. Both assign a role to reason and to feeling in the moral life.

C.M. introduces a radical shift in focus away from that of Objectivism. There is a movement away from the individualistic preoccupation with self-interest toward concern for the group. Not here applicable are Ayn Rand's strictures against an altruism that puts the interests of others ahead of one's own. C.M. sees individual identity as bound up with the group's, and further, even as determined by the group's definition of the criteria for belonging. A conventionally oriented business is not some isolated transient that drops into a social setting to make a killing, and stays ready to pull up stakes when the pickings become slim. A conventionally oriented business sees itself not only as having a stake in the community, but as being shaped, structured, and guided by the aspirations and expectations of the groups with whom it interacts. In other words, the very identity of the business is a function of the socio-moral climate in which its operations are carried on.

The psychological mind-set of C.M., then, is not one of self-preservation and self-aggrandizement. Rather, a socially responsible business person, oriented in the framework of C.M., will cultivate his role-taking capacities. He'll be most ethically responsible when he can confidently stand in the shoes of his constituencies and walk the paths that they walk. Be they customers, stockholders, suppliers, directors, employees—he will be sensitive to their expectations and will look to these groups for norms and guidelines of ethically responsible behavior. Often, the moral directions pointed out to him will involve pain to himself, as well as effort and the sacrifice for his company. But he has cast his lot with the groups that make up his identity as an individual; he views his company's strength, character, and identity as coming from the same source, and so he pays the price of ethical sensitivity to C.M.'s demands.

Hence the definition of moral good lies not with self-interest over against the community, but rather in conformity to the community's responsible expectations. Altruism is not the bad word that it is for the objectivists for whom it signifies a self-destructive squandering of oneself and one's resources. But conventions need not be altruistic. Social groups may indeed expect and approve altruistic behavior (e.g., concern for product safety, neighborhood enhancement, minority hiring); or these groups may expect and approve in the name of other values behavior in some ways socially harmful (e.g., approving jobs over clean environment, profit incentive over welfare incentives, cheaper products over safer products). But in either case, C.M. orients business toward the social environment. What business spends on its social environment is by that very fact an investment in itself, because business *is* the groups with which it interacts. Such is the philosophy of human nature implied by C.M. Moral good means acting in conformity with this picture of the way things are. To flaunt the expectations of your socio-ethical environment is moral evil. The penalty is ostracism—withdrawal of support by the groups which confer identity in the first place. That identity comes at a price, the price of observing the canons of C.M.

Moral conscience is that faculty by which one arrives at responsible decisions. Objectivism's ethics of rational self-interest gave a high place to reason in this process. It was suspicious of sentiment and feeling. For these latter threaten to betray the self's best interests. Feeling is much more important for C.M., though reason is not without its role to play as well. Let's look at one way C.M. spells out this interplay of reason and feeling. British empirical philosopher David Hume (1711–1776) gives classical expression to this approach to morality. We'll briefly outline what he has to say.[4]

Of course, Hume's problematic is not ours today. We will not try here

[4]What follows is nothing but a skimpy outline of one possible construction of Hume's theory of morals. My purpose is not to provide an adequate and faithful account of Hume's views but to suggest a framework for discussing the relation of moral conventions to business ethics. See Hume, *A Treatise on Human Nature*, Part III, and *An Enquiry Concerning the Principles of Morals*. For a careful analysis of this aspect of Hume's thought in all its complexity, see Jonathan Harrison, *Hume's Moral Epistemology* (Oxford: Clarendon Press, 1976).

The modern reader will find many unresolved ambivalences in Hume. We have to become sensitive today to many issues that were not acute in eighteenth-century England. For example, it is important for us today to distinguish what arouses moral approval and disapproval in *me* individually from what arouses approval or not in mankind in general. To Hume, this didn't seem to make much difference since he probably thought that humans everywhere were roughly alike in essential moral matters. Nor did Hume make a clear distinction between subjectivity and objectivity in moral approval, viz., Do I approve or not of an action because of something in me or because of some quality objectively in the action? In the face of such ambivalences, I have rather arbitrarily made one plausible reconstruction of Hume with the pedagogical purpose of helping the reader evaluate C.M. as it appears in the business world today.

to recapture the eighteenth-century philosophical climate that shaped the moral teaching of Hume. Rather, as before with Machiavelli so now with Hume, we will outline typical Humean themes as these find expression in current business thinking about ethics. Few or no business people are conscious disciples of Hume, but his accent is often detectable in their moralizing. The emphasis on moral good sense as opposed to abstract reasoning about ethics, the need for viewing ourselves objectively as others see us ("how would my behavior look in the headlines?"), and stress on the need to be sensitive to the social expectations of business on the part of business's constituencies—such contemporary themes are echoed in the moral philosophy of Hume. So we give now one simplified interpretation of Hume's complex moral thinking. It is presented, not as an exercise in history, but as a foil against which the reader can judge and evaluate C.M. as it appears in the business world today.

2. ETHICS AS SOCIAL APPROVAL

Logic—abstract reason alone—does not move people to action. There is the illusion, doubtless fostered by the scientific and technological climate in which we live, that cool, detached, objective logic is the ideal guide for human behavior. John Galt, the hero of Ayn Rand's *Atlas Shrugged*, was a man of reason and logic. He allowed no sentimental fellow-feelings to cloud his calculating analysis of the demands of objective reality. This is all very nice in the ideal order. But any parent interested in directing a child along the straight and narrow quickly learns the futility of sitting down with the kid and "reasoning together," say, about the virtues of keeping dirty clothes off the floor or the dangers of too much TV viewing. You've got to hook into the kid's feelings. Let him bask in your praise and approval of his tidy room or play a fun game instead of watching television. By his hooking into your feelings of approval and disapproval, he becomes socialized into the family and guides his behavior accordingly. "Good" behavior is behavior approved by the family group.

If feelings rather than logic are what characterize a child's path to socialization, then this is one area in which we are all children. For example, the campaign waged by women for equal treatment in business has not been an affair of sweet, cool reason. It has involved intensive "consciousness-raising," first of all among women themselves. Behavioristically, i.e., if you look at what's actually going on, "consciousness-raising" translates as "emotion-changing," or even "attitude-manipulation." The goal of this manipulation is practical. When my feeling-set changes, my behavior follows suit. One does not revolutionize the ethics of sexual equality in business without revolutionizing feelings about equality of treatment in business. Polemical books, rallies, sensitivity groups, advertising, legal threats, lobbying—all of these "consciousness-raising" tactics are not exercises in abstract logic, but are attitude-manipulation ploys. Their aim is to socialize women into full participation in the business world. Many behavior patterns both of women and of the business establishment have been changed in these ways and will have to continue to change if this goal is to be fully attained. This is another way of saying that the feelings about this revolution of sexual roles must change. When these changes take place, then sexual equality in business becomes the socially approved pattern. Then this becomes the ethically good way to behave just as truly as 30 years ago it was a moral "no-no" (i.e., socially disapproved) for a woman to "abandon" her children and family for a career.[5]

David Hume pointed out this split between abstract reason and experimental attitudes in moral matters. Reason, he said, deals in universal principles. Mathematics, for example, operates on reason alone. All the feelings in the world are not going to change the totals spewed forth by the supermarket cash register. And logic operates on reason alone.

"All humans are equal as persons; women are human; therefore, women are equal as persons." Very logical. Well, what are you going to do about it? "Ho-hum" logic doesn't lead to action.

"Endangered species should be protected; Northern Fur Seals are an endangered species; therefore, Northern Fur Seals should be protected." Sounds logical. I can't quarrel with it. What else is new? Logic doesn't lead to action.

Morality, says Hume, deals with matters of fact, existential beliefs, feelings about behavior. Ethics is primarily a matter of "passion." Logical principles about the preservation of endangered species have little effect on passion. But show me movies of wide-eyed unsuspecting baby seals being

[5]Several themes are interwoven here. Intuition or moral sense takes priority over precise reasoning. This intuition, socially formed, reflects the cultural milieu. Moral education, relative to the culture, results then in an ethical relativism. To the extent that the resultant ethical norms are culturally linked and in that sense are arbitrary and nonobjective, they are a form of subjectivism—social subjectivism. Now, moral intuitionism, ethical relativism, and social subjectivism do not form a logically necessary package. Any one of them could exist without the others. But together, do they describe adequately the way ethics actually does (though not logically must) operate in the business world? And if so, does it do justice to our moral experience as human beings? Is C.M. a valid and true ethical philosophy? This is the question.

The matter is further complicated by the coexistence within the same person of several, often conflicting, conventional codes. The individual executive, for example, gives allegiance to a religious code (perhaps), to a family code, a corporate code, a legal code, etc., applying now one, now another. See Chester I. Barnard's classical treatment of such "private codes" in *The Functions of the Executive* (Cambridge, Ma., 1938), especially Chapter XVII, "The Nature of Executive Responsibility" (also available in paperback in the new 30th-anniversary edition, 1968).

bludgeoned to death by grown men; take me on a U.S.-sponsored tour bus to the killing grounds on St. Paul's Island to view the "harvest." Now you're not dealing with logic, but with experience. These are facts. They arouse passion. They hook into feelings. They stimulate my approval and disapproval. I begin to talk about the wrongness of killing seals.

I listen to the hunters of the seals. I'm introduced into their meagre households. I see their children subsisting on bare necessities. I learn that the seal trade is their only source of income. And I begin to talk about the rightness of killing seals. It's not logic but feeling that tips the scales.

What we have here is the opposite of Ayn Rand's objectivism. C.M. is a subjectivism. Feelings and attitudes are, after all, subjective. But we're not talking about individual whims. We're talking about behavior sanctioned by groups. We're talking about socially established norms that knit society together so that people can live and grow in harmony. Ethics, then, is no luxury. It is the glue that binds us together. A morally sound society is a strong society. Undermine morality and you undermine society itself, in the view of Hume's C.M.

Of course, there is a philosophy of human nature implied here. Humans are not viewed as plunged into a battle with each other in a Darwinistic struggle for survival. No. Hume sees sympathy as the basic moral passion. It is sympathy or fellow-feeling that causes humans to band into groups. The truly human norm is best manifested in societies, not in individuals locked in cutthroat competition. What type of ethics flows from Hume's philosophy of human nature? Feelings of approbation held in common establish the ethical code.

Reasons can and do exist for these commonly held feelings. But reasons are not enough. Without the feelings, morality doesn't enter the picture. There is a Zen story that illustrates this. Suppose I'm rowing down the river peacefully alone in my little boat. Another rowboat, empty, swept by the current, bumps into mine. What do I do? Startled, I turn and see the other boat. I either gently push it away, or tie it to my own and tow. Now change the scenario. I'm rowing peacefully along as before. Again, another rowboat bumps into my own. Again, startled, I turn. But this time there's a man in the other boat. I yell at him to look where he's going, condemn his carelessness, and inform him that his type are a menace to boaters everywhere. In both cases the physical event was identical: one boat bumped into another boat. The first was morally neutral. Feelings didn't enter in. The second event aroused passions of disapproval, and my mouth was filled with moral condemnations. Similarly, a tornado could destroy my business, and I would not consider it a moral matter; but let vandals accomplish the identical damage, and words could not express my moral indignation.

Hume is ambiguous about how widely shared these moral feelings are. At minimum, they represent a consensus of one's own group, one's own society. The behaviors that are prized by the group are by that fact morally good. Do there exist moral sentiments that are shared not merely by this or that group, but by all of human kind? At times, Hume speaks in such universalistic terms:

> ...the affections of humanity are the foundation of morals, the basis upon which moral praise or censure is established. There is a kind of universality in sentiments, for what one person cherishes is cherished by the group, since "the humanity of one man is the humanity of every one."[6]

Even today we experience this tension between the obvious moral pluralism that exists from group to group and culture to culture on the one hand, and on the other, the search for common moral sentiments like honesty, justice, peace, and freedom in which all humans might share. The "When In Rome..." principle expresses the narrower view of C.M. in which justice, for example, might be said to be concerned with "Roman rights." The more universal view would look to "human rights" and conventions that are approved by all peoples.

Our treatment has emphasized the narrower understanding of C.M. that begets the ethical pluralism giving rise to the kinds of business conflicts discussed at the beginning of the chapter. In any case, however subjective and emotive C.M. may be, it does rule out merely personal likes and dislikes as a norm of morality. The basic moral passion is that fellow-feeling, loyalty and conformity in essentials are the basis of society. Consider this plaque that used to hang in many F.B.I. field offices:

> If you work for a man, in heaven's name work for him! If he pays you wages that supply you your bread and butter, work for him—speak well of him, think well of him, stand by him and by the institution he represents.[7]

Such loyalty, though in a much looser sense, is the kind of moral demand that society at large puts on its members. The subjectivism is a *social* subjectivism. "X is right" doesn't mean, "*I* happen to like X." No. It means, "*We* approve of X." Such socially shared benevolent sentiments are good and virtuous. Contrary feelings are evil.

[6]William S. Sahakian, *Ethics* (New York: Harper and Row, 1974), p. 194, in which Sahakian is expanding on the phrase in quotation marks from Hume's *Enquiry Concerning the Principles of Morals.*
[7]Timothy Schellhardt, "The Next FBI Chief," *Wall Street Journal* (July 15, 1977), p. 8.

To put it another way, selfishness is the root of evil. Selfish feelings are those not shared by the group. They are thereby antisocial and antimoral. The unethical individual goes his own tyrannical and arrogant way. His behavior undermines the group, is disapproved of by the group. When I see that my personal feelings are socially condemned, that is the clue that I am on an unethical path. This perception of social disapproval is a warning of conscience.

To be perfectly logical we should understand "benevolence" and "selfishness" in the loosest sense possible. Hence, "benevolence" would mean that I share the sentiments of my group, even when the group recommends individualistic egotism; "selfishness" in the broad sense means that I ignore or reject the group's sentiments even when the group rejects altruism. For example, anthropologist Colin Turnbull describes in his book *The Mountain People* a displaced African tribe called the IK. The tribe had been herded from their hunting lands into a barren mountain area; this action reduced them to a culture built around food—or rather the lack of food—and starvation. In this extremity, an ethical code arose that put a premium on any individual action, however brutal or cruel, taken in the name of survival (e.g., stealing food, or leaving untended the sick and dying). Among the IK, altruistic acts are ridiculed and scorned. Deviants, whose misplaced generosity led to their death, were considered to deserve their fate. Under these harsh moral conventions, it was "selfish" to show pity, and it was "benevolent" to live by the necessarily harsh code of the group. This limited case is bizarre and was certainly not envisioned by Hume, but it highlights the precise thrust of C.M., viz., not "be kind to society," but "be guided by society." Discerning this social guidance is not always easy. Important is the role of reason which we now describe.

It is reason that protects me from the dangers of individual subjectivism, i.e., from selfishness or evil. Reason works in a guiding or advising capacity to moral passion and emotion. True, C.M. is a social *subjectivism*. But reason helps me to be objective in correctly reading the moral imperatives expressed by these subjective conventions. My reason helps me step outside my immediate situation so that I can view it as a *disinterested observer*. I become like an innocent bystander looking at myself, at the ethical decision I am contemplating, and at the sentiments of the group. As an innocent bystander disassociated from the scene, I try to discern how my sentiments correspond to those of the group. For it is this social approbation that is the touchstone of morality. Society's shared sentiment is the seal of ethical good housekeeping. Thus, the disinterested observer in me, i.e., reason, can easily distinguish good from evil, right from wrong, and I can guide my behavior accordingly. The actions themselves are morally neutral until the group views them positively as socially enhancing, or neg-

atively as socially destructive. Reason clues me in to this social sentiment
that is C.M.'s norm of good and evil.

Last year an oil executive gave out to his employees a marvelously
practical directive to guide and ensure ethically responsible decision-making. It expressed perfectly the relation of reason, the disinterested spectator
to the sentiments of the group. The executive's memo stated, "If you have
any doubt about the ethical propriety of a prospective action, ask yourself
how it would look in tomorrow's front-page headlines." Imagine the headlines and you are using reason as a disinterested spectator. And what the
headline story says will tell you the social sentiment about how ethical
your course of action is. A recent *Harvard Business Review* questionnaire
to executives came up with much the same kind of norm:

> It seems to us that our respondents are saying that managers facing ethi-
> cal dilemmas should refer to the familiar maxim: "Would I want my
> family, friends, and employers to see this decision and its consequences
> on television?" If the answer is yes, then go ahead. If the answer is no,
> then additional thought should be given to finding a more satisfactory
> decision.[8]

So there again the little maxim capsulizes the approach to business ethics
that rests on conventional morality.

Summary. In philosophical terms, we have called C.M. a *social subjectivism.* It is a *subjectivism* in that it first and foremost stresses the role of
feeling in moral decision-making. In calling the subjectivism *social*, we are
pointing to the role that *reason* must play in distinguishing genuine moral
feeling from whimsical selfish feelings. We'll briefly summarize in turn
these two sides of conventional morality.

First, the subjective side of C.M. clearly distinguishes it from the ra-
tionalistic ethics of Ayn Rand's Objectivism. C.M. is subjective in three
ways.

To begin with, subjectivity means that feelings come first in moral
matters. In the moral education of children, your appeal must be more to
the heart than to the mind. And the same holds true for adults. Various
moral revolutions are undertaken in the name of consciousness-raising.
These, however, are more involved with attitude manipulation than with
logical exercises.

Secondly, C.M. has a firm grip on the need for concrete results in ethics. It has little patience for moral theories or for the dreamers who spin
out such theories. And whether you are out to save an endangered species

[8]Brenner, *op. cit.*, p. 71.

or to galvanize a nation for war, you need action. It's the appeal to feelings that gives rise to action. In this, mere logic is sterile.

Thirdly, ethical feeling is the glue that holds society together. We need to know where people are at and to predict in some minimal fashion how they will behave. So society's moral conventions canonize its expectations of its members. Ethics becomes the foundation of social order.

We turn now to the *social* side of social subjectivism. C.M. may be subjective, but it's not arbitrary. We showed this in three ways.

First, while C.M. downplays logic, it does not allow individuals to fly off in any direction they want to. The collective wisdom of society stands as the norm. Morality may be nonlogical, but it's not chaotic.

Secondly, while abstract reasoning is sterile for ethics, reason does have a very important role to play in helping to discern good from evil. In moral matters, it's easy to deceive oneself. Through the use of reason, we can look at our moral decisions objectively, i.e., see ourselves as others see us. Would others approve or disapprove if they saw our actual decision? By asking this question, reason keeps us honest.

Finally, the sociality of C.M. highlights what's best and most central to human nature, viz., the benevolence and fellow-feeling that draw us together. C.M. is the enemy of selfishness. The arrogant individual pursuit of power is at odds with that sociality that most properly defines a human being. Hence selfishness is another name for moral evil.

Such then is the argument in favor of conventional morality in business.

3. WHOSE "SOCIAL APPROVAL"?

C.M. thus rests upon a philosophy of human nature with two strong pillars. First, it realizes the crucial impact that feeling has on human beings. And second, it has a clear-eyed view of society's stake in human behavior and of the immense pressures that society, if it is to survive, must put on individual persons and businesses. Now, to a critical evaluation. How true a picture of human nature does this philosophy paint? How adequate is C.M. as a method of handling conflicts faced in the business world? How do you evaluate for yourself the pluses and minuses of social subjectivism as a business philosophy? We'll consider in turn possible criticisms against five of C.M.'s major themes: 1. the primacy of feeling in ethics; 2. the sterility of logic as a guide for responsible action; 3. social approval as a moral norm; 4. the role of reason as disinterested observer; 5. the stress on benevolence over selfishness.

In each case, we will restate the C.M. theme in summary form. After each restatement, a question (Q) is presented to highlight a philosophical objection that could be raised against that theme. Then an answer from the point of view of C.M. is briefly stated. You will note that most of the objections center around the problem of ethical *relativism*. The intent is to help the reader to view the pros and cons of C.M. as a business philosophy so as to arrive at a self-evaluation of this ethics. The intent is not to endorse either C.M. or its opposite.

1. *The primacy of feeling in ethics.* An ethical code, if it is to have any effective force, must be the expression of society's gut feelings of approval and disapproval. Anything less, however seemingly reasonable, is a mere abstraction.

Q: Doesn't this lead to the absurd conclusion that *any* action could be morally condoned, provided only that society approved of it? Corruption is corruption in no matter what country it takes place; if the society approves, then the society is corrupt.

A: Actions can't be judged in a vacuum. It's the social context that gives moral meaning to the action. Ten dollars given to a headwaiter is a "tip"; $10 given to a customs official is a "bribe"—the transactions are identical. Why the difference? The first payment is socially approved of and therefore moral; the second is socially disapproved of and therefore immoral: the context of social feeling makes the difference. Similarly, feelings about ways of doing business will vary from culture to culture, and your moral judgments should follow suit.

2. *The sterility of logic as a guide for responsible action.* Abstract reason can justify anything. But a stable economy must be able to anticipate that certain common practices and understandings will be observed. Morality means conformity to these very concrete social expectations and not to logical word games.

Q: Once reason is removed from the picture as a way of determining what is right and what is wrong, doesn't morality become self-contradictory? All ethical principles, and even contradictory ones, can become defensible. We say that price-fixing, for example, is morally wrong. You say that your cartel approves of price-fixing, which makes it morally right. On C.M.'s grounds, I have to agree with the one who contradicts me. We are both right. Price-fixing is at the same time morally wrong and not morally wrong. A is not-A. A giraffe is not a giraffe. This whole approach is self-contradictory.

A: The objection must be conceded on the level of abstract logic. But, unfortunately, societies don't operate on such antiseptic logical rules. C.M. agrees with the person who said that consistency is the hobgoblin of little minds. Society demands stable business arrangements; it does not demand that these arrangements be identical the world over. To require a universal ethical standard of pricing is just as irrational as is the alleged self-contradiction of leaving it to societies to decide what their own ethical arrangements will be. To demand that ethical standards be universally consistent is just as irrational as to allow them to be contradictory and inconsistent.

3. *Social approval as a moral norm.* However much C.M. may stress feeling, it is not a prescription for anarchy. It does not approve of individuals running amok; just because an individual feels something is right doesn't make it right. We are social animals. It is our responsiveness to society that makes us responsible as individuals. So in business decisions, I ask myself: "How would my decision look on TV? . . . does society approve?"—this is the norm of morality.

Q: C.M. rightly sees the dangers of the irrationality that it so cheerfully espoused in the previous answer. Once ethics is admitted to be irrational, then, "anything goes." C.M. appeals to "social approval" as a way of avoiding such anarchy. But the cure is as bad as the disease. What we have here is morality based on head count. It's the tyranny of the majority. Individual convictions mean nothing. Are there no minority rights? C.M. claims the majority to be right, just because it is the majority.

A: The minorities enjoy all the rights that the majority in a society feels can be safely tolerated. In America, for example, minorities have been accorded rights that even work *against* the majority, e.g., in "affirmative-action" programs. Individuals and groups can work to change established conventions using whatever methods of bringing pressure to bear that operate in a given society (e.g., using politics, communications, boycotts, strikes, etc.). But C.M. recognizes that there is no society without certain essential conformity. If every business and every business practice is a law unto itself, then the economic community comes tumbling down. If "head count" ethics is the only alternative to moral anarchy in business, so be it.

4. *The role of reason as disinterested observer.* The person who wants to be his own lawyer has a fool for a client, the saying goes. No one is a judge in his own case. C.M. is not as irrational as opponents make out. Reason is essential to moral decision-making. I must use my mind to step out of my situation and see myself as others see me. Business and business persons, like any other human beings, are all too prone to neglect the wider picture in the name of their own selfish interests. This use of reason is the necessary safeguard.

Q: It is praiseworthy that C.M. attempts to take the role of other disinterested parties, and to thereby achieve some emotional detachment in ethical decisions. Unfortunately, the attempt to do this quickly reveals one of the major problems with this approach to morality. Most ethical dilemmas involve *conflicts between opposite conventions*! How can convention decide, if the conventions themselves are in conflict? The National Organization of Women would morally approve my leapfrogging of women up the managerial ladder. Male candidates with seniority disapprove. The government, through the courts, arrives at conflicting decisions, establishing a legal precedent for each opposing side. So my reason as a disinterested observer takes the role of society. I see myself as others see me, as I come to make an ethical decision about a promotion policy. What does this disinterested reason of mine see? It sees conflicting groups with conflicting conventions, each with firm emotional moral commitments to ethical policies on a collision course. True, reason helps me avoid individual selfish subjectivism: I look to society for guidance. But what do I find? Not merely social subjectivism, but social subjectivism*s*. I avoid the moral anarchy of individuals. But I'm confronted with moral anarchy among groups espousing conflicting conventions, and I have no way to decide among them. If I imagine my decision appearing on television, some of the viewers would approve, whatever I do, and others disapprove. Social approval and social disapproval—does that make me right or wrong?

A: It is hard to devise an answer to this difficulty if one stays within the framework of a narrow definition of "society" and "group" and "convention." Here is where we are driven to look to moral sentiments that are not limited to this or that nation or culture but to sentiments that are shared by the human community itself. Are there implanted in human nature at least some moral sentiments which transcend national boundaries and narrow group concerns? If I could discover such universal human sentiments, then I could use them to adjudicate the conflicting moralities established by narrower conventions. Subsequent chapters in this book will be a search in this direction.

5. *The stress on benevolence over selfishness.* C.M. appreciates this impulse to look for ever more universally applicable conventions. It sees this as a confirmation of the priority that C.M. gives to the group over the individual. Indeed, a universal community would be the most desirable group of all upon which to base a morality. We have more to fear from the individual than from the group. Individual selfishness, whether it exists at the level of the person or of the corporation, is the enemy of society and the enemy of morality. Narrow, self-centered individualism is the root of moral evil. When you're talking about moral progress in business, C.M. is a quantum leap over narrower philosophies of self-interest like Objectivism.

Q: We can concede that selfish individualism is the enemy of morality. But the selfish individual is not the same as the autonomous individual. This is a distinction that C.M. overlooks completely. The nonconforming individual as such need not be the enemy of society. I can be nonconforming like a criminal and tear society down. Or I can be nonconforming like a reformer and lead society above and beyond its established conventional ways. Both the criminal and the reformer reject C.M. So social subjectivism condemns both. It has to. Group approval is the norm. Those who offend the group are wrong. C.M. has no place for the reformer who would offend the group in order to help it to grow.

A: Granted, individual selfishness is not the same as individual autonomy. But more often than not the selfish individual masquerades as a reformer. Saints are rare, especially in business. How many leaders of consumer unions, labor unions, business unions are out for themselves under the guise of improving the common welfare? An individual who claims to be a reformer of the unselfish variety must have earned his spurs. If he has traveled the path of conventional morality, striven to live up to the norms which society exacts, faced the agonizing conflicts that arise when one tries to conform to society the way it exists in the actual real world, then maybe then, and only maybe, has he earned the right *not* to conform in the name of some higher morality. It is cheap and easy to condemn conventional norms. Diatribes against business's conventional practices come easy to any college sophomore's lips. Let him try to abide by those conventions for 10 or 30 years, and then maybe he'll have earned the right to talk of individual moral autonomy and reform, if indeed he is still so inclined to do so. Conventional morality is an easy out mainly for those who've never submitted themselves rigorously to its demands. Society has high expectations of business. No business that achieves "social approval," the norm of C.M., needs to be ashamed.

CASE FOR DISCUSSION

Headquartered in Atlanta is Rollins, Inc., a pest-control and communications firm. Chief executive and chairman of this $200-million business is O. Wayne Rollins. During the last five years, the company's outdoor advertising subsidiary has paid bribes in the Republic of Mexico amounting in total to about $127-thousand. Approximately a dozen local and municipal government officials received payoffs last year. The bribery was for a wide variety of things, including licenses to put up billboards, nights on the town, and people to watch company cars—whether or not the cars needed watching. It is Mr. Rollins's contention that such low-level bribery is the "legitimate way" of doing business in Mexico. You do these things "be-

cause some fellow says this is how it's done around here," says Rollins.[9]
The money wasn't deducted for income-tax purposes, nor did it come from
any slush fund or other secret account.

(1) Were these legal payments also moral? Why or why not?

(2) Does conventional morality—"When in Mexico, do as the Mexi-
cans do"—provide an adequate guide for an ethically correct decision in
this case? Explain.

Last March, Rollins decided to disclose publicly that his company
was making these payments. More than that, he asserted that such payments would continue "when no reasonable alternative is available." He
said it would be hypocritical for his company to say that it would, or
could, conduct business in Mexico without such payments. "We thought
we were being simon-pure," he said.

(3) Was Rollins morally right to inform the investors, the two governments, its customers, and the general public of its practice of bribery
and its reasons why?

(4) If this was a morally good decision, was it also a good business
decision?

Neither Rollins's customers nor its investors seemed particularly concerned with the disclosures. Rollins received only a few letters from shareholders, and all of these supported him. Three major billboard customers—R. J. Reynolds, American Brands, and Philip Morris—all said that
they hadn't heard about the Mexican matter, and felt that it really wasn't
any of their business.

Stop here before going on. Think, discuss, and arrive at your own conclusions so far before proceeding.

The Mexican government was not so indifferent. "We find Rollins's
statement absurd and insulting," said one high-ranking government official based in Washington. "Companies from around the world do business
in Mexico. Certainly all of them do not bribe our officials."

The Security and Exchange Commission said that officially it would
allow such payments to go on as long as they were fully disclosed.

The Federal Communications Commission became involved because
Rollins, Inc., owns a string of 11 radio and TV stations. The FCC threat-
ened to use pressure on the company to get it to discontinue its payments.
"We should regard bribery of foreign officials the same way we do the
bribery of U.S. officials," said an FCC spokesman.

(5) How do you evaluate the ethical principles underlying each of
these three reactions?

[9]The Rollins story is quoted and abstracted from *Wall Street Journal* (October 1, 1976),
p. 10: "Rollins Payoffs: Perils of Candor."

(6) Do ethical norms cross cultural and conventional borders, as the FCC spokesman implies?

Reaction from the Mexican government was so adverse that on April 27, less than two months later, Rollins directors voted unanimously to rescind the payments policy. This reversal is in line with A. H. Sterne, Rollins's friend and business associate. "Any way you slice it, it's a bribe." Sterne went on to say that if he were doing business in Mexico, "I'd try to do it without bribing, and I believe I'd succeed."

Mr. Rollins now wonders why he ever made the original disclosure. "All we had to do was say nothing and we wouldn't have had a problem," he says. "We made a mistake when we made our disclosure."

Bill Paul, WSJ reporter, comments: "The moral of the story is when in doubt, keep your mouth shut. It appears that by trying to abide by the law and his own conscience, Mr. Rollins got his company into a pickle."

(7) Is Sterne morally right?

(8) Do you agree with Bill Paul that conscience should have given way to business in this case?

(9) Do you agree with Rollins's hindsight-assessment of this whole saga? Is the business really worse off now, or better off, as Sterne might say?

SUGGESTED READINGS

Barnard, Chester I. *The Functions of the Executive.* Cambridge, Ma.: Harvard University Press, 1938, and in a new 1968 edition, also available in paperback.

Benedict, Ruth Fulton. "Anthropology and the Abnormal," *Journal of General Psychology* (10), 1934.

Conklin, John E. *"Illegal But Not Criminal": Business Crime in America.* Englewood Cliffs, N.J.: Prentice-Hall, 1977.

Harrison, Jonathan. *Hume's Moral Epistemology.* Oxford: Clarendon Press, 1976.

Hume, David. *An Enquiry Concerning the Principles of Morals,* 1751. Section I and Appendix I.

———. *A Treatise on Human Nature,* 1740. Especially Book III, Part I, Sections 1 and 2.

Ladd, John. *Ethical Relativism.* Belmont, Ca.: Wadsworth, 1973.

Smith, Adam. *The Theory of Moral Sentiments,* 1959.

Sumner, William Graham. *Folkways.* New York: New American Library, 1960.

CHAPTER 6

LEGALISTIC ETHICS: THE LETTER OF THE LAW

> If you want to know the law and nothing else, you must look at it as a bad man, who cares only for the material consequences which such knowledge enables him to predict, not as a good one, who finds his reasons for conduct, whether inside the law or outside of it, in the vaguer sanctions of conscience. . . . I often doubt whether it would not be a gain if every word of moral significance could be banished from the law altogether, and other words adopted which should convey legal ideas uncoloured by anything outside the law.
>
> Oliver Wendell Holmes, Jr.[1]

> The law reflects the thought prevailing in the community, including its moral values, and thus it becomes a basis of business ethics.
>
> Carl Fulda[2]

OBJECTIVES FOR CHAPTER 6:

1. To understand the philosophical *questions* raised by law as a form of social control of business, and by the law's relation to ethics;

2. To become aware of one's own inclination to divorce law from ethics or, conversely, to see law as determinative of ethics;

3. To understand two legal philosophies that focus on the letter of the law:

[1]Oliver Wendell Holmes, Jr., *Collected Legal Papers* (New York: Harcourt, Brace and Co., 1920). pp. 171, 175.

[2]Carl Fulda, "The Legal Basis of Ethics," as quoted in Alvin O. Elbing, Jr. *et al., The Value Issue of Business* (New York, McGraw-Hill Book Co., 1967), pp. 42–43.

(a) the reasons for pure legalism in business which divorces law from ethics;

(b) the premises and consequences of moral legalism that completely equate ethics with the observance of law;

4. To evaluate for oneself the adequacy of these two contrary philosophical ways of viewing the letter of the law.

Introduction. Whereas Social Darwinism, Machiavellianism, and objectivism might be classified as egocentric philosophies of human morality, Conventional Morality is other-centered. Concern for others, rather than preoccupation with self, takes center stage. C.M. bids business to look for moral guidance in the expectations of its various constituencies, as we have seen. While C.M. is not the last word in moral maturity, it does constitute an advance over self-aggrandizement and expedience as moral norms. Conventional demands are relatively altruistic.

This heteronomous, or other-centered, morality can remain informal and unspecified. In the previous chapter we examined this informal version of moral conventionality as expressed by appeals to "common practice"—in an uncodified loyalty to the expectations of business's relevant constituencies. More common, perhaps, is the formalized version of C.M. as expressed by appeals to law, i.e., to conventions as formally and legally codified. Whence, this chapter is devoted to legalistic ethics. Legalistic ethics looks to the letter of the law for guidance. The next chapter will continue our examination of law as the basis for ethics, but law considered more broadly, viz., the spirit of the law. Then, having dealt with these heteronomous moralities, the final chapters will review autonomous business philosophies that search for a basis of ethics which transcends any given set of laws or conventions.

1. ISSUES OF MORALITY AND SOCIAL CONTROL OF BUSINESS

Social control is the usual context in which issues of business responsibility have been discussed. Social control is a fact of business life. As long as business operates in a social environment, that environment's impact will be in a greater or lesser degree controlling. Only at peril to its own survival and well-being does business ignore this social input. These *de facto* controlling pressures show themselves on many levels. There is, for example, the economic leverage exercised by consumers. Also to be contended with are the force of public opinion mustered by the media, backroom political arm-twisting, employee strikes and threats of strikes, stockholder rebellions, as well as the lobbying of minority unions, women's groups, and Third World and other liberation fronts. All such business constituencies are component forces of social control.

Mores as controlling. More pervasive is the impact of community mores on business decisions. Such conventional ethical guidelines were the subject of the last chapter. This moral pressure is informal, for the most part unconscious, but not for that the less powerful. As we saw, these moral pressures become problematic, and therefore conscious, once they become a source of ethical conflict. When the mores of one society conflict with those of another, the business person, caught in between, is forced to examine the roots of his own conventional morality. It is precisely here that issues of social control part ways with issues of philosophical ethics.

At issue: not the fact of controls, but their legitimacy. Economics, psychology, sociology, and political science study and describe the extent and the workings of the various dimensions of the social control of business. These sciences can evolve tactics of effective control—economic, political, psychological, etc.—to be utilized in favor of various business strategies. Public opinion, moral suasion, and economic pressure are facts of life to manipulate and be manipulated. But the last chapter was not primarily concerned with the de facto impact of social mores on business decisions. The focus was rather on their legitimacy, their philosophical validity. Our quest is philosophical rather than scientific, de jure rather than de facto. We are less concerned with *what* established business philosophy guides business decisions. We are more concerned with the de jure question: *by what right* does a given business philosophy guide business decisions? Do the presuppositions and the consequences of the philosophy prove its adequacy as a basis for business ethics? So in the last chapter we were less concerned with *what* the conventions of business ethics are, and more concerned with how adequate conventional morality is as a foundation for business ethics.

Law as controlling. It is precisely the inadequacies of conventional morality that push us to examine in this chapter another all-pervasive social control of business, a control that more than any other is an irritant to the business community and a control whose legitimacy the business community constantly questions. I am talking about the control of business that issues from government in the shape of laws and agency regulations. This raises the deeper questions (1) of the whole philosophical relationship of business to government, and (2) of how far the law should function as the basis for business ethics. Note the philosophical turn of the latter question. It is the de jure question that we are asking, viz., how far *should* the law impinge on ethics? At issue here is your philosophy of law. Are ethics and law two ways of saying the same thing? Or are they completely dis-

tinct? Or do law and morality have some nuanced and overlapping relationship to each other? What are the consequences of each philosophy for
the ethics of business decisions?

At issue: legitimacy of law as ethical norm. The social control exercised by the moral pressures of conventional morality functions informally
and rather arbitrarily from society to society, as we have seen. It thus lacks
clearly defined sanctions. As the arbitrary and subjective expression of society's collective feelings about behavior, conventional morality is fundamentally irrational. This leads to ethical dilemmas when moral conventions clash. And conventional morality does not supply a method for
resolving the dilemmas that it raises. These inadequacies of conventional
morality lead many business people to look to *law* for more clear-cut, rational, and manageable ethical guidelines. Law as a basis for business ethics certainly has its problems, as we will see, but at least you know what
you're up against. Compared to the morass of conventional norms, the legal norm is relatively clear-cut, and there is a feeling that when a business
has succeeded in complying with law, its moral hands are clean. Social responsibility may always push for more in the way of philanthropic ideals,
but when the law has been met, the ethical accounts are fundamentally in
order. Law can mediate the conflicts of conventional *mores*; law has its
own rationale; and law clearly defines for the responsible business person
the extent and limits of duty.

Of course, not every business person appreciates these wonderful "advantages" of law as an ethical norm. Business's relation to government,
and especially to law, is a source of bitter controversy. At one extreme is
the antinomian position that views every government intervention in the
business process as an unjustifiable and basically immoral intrusion which
violates that freedom both of business initiative and of market forces—the
very freedoms best designed to serve human economic needs. At the other
extreme is the view of business as an anarchical, antihuman, irresponsible,
and regressive force that must be tied and bound, brought kicking and
screaming by law to show the most minimal social or moral concern.

The antinomian forces can point to the rising tide of litigation that
threatens to engulf many small businesses, and which paralyzes even the
larger ones. The prevailing litigious climate in America backs up their
claim, as do the proliferation of legislation and the widening of the pool of
those who have "standing" to bring suit. The resultant horror stories fill
the daily papers. When the Passamequoddy and Penobascot Indians were
suing to take over much of the state of Maine, this didn't do much for the
local municipal bond market. G.M. has been a subject for a class action for
several trillion dollars, a suit leveled for pollution on behalf of all future
generations. Suits brought by environmental groups have stalled power

projects, and for years on end. Conversely, the suits aren't all antibusiness: the big four oil companies have successfully appealed to the National Environmental Policy Act to have a federal court block antitrust suits against them. Again, litigation delayed the Alaska pipeline for five years until Congress broke the legal roadblock. But Congress doesn't always come to the rescue. I.B.M. and Justice are currently entering their second decade of that antimonoply suit. Whether the legislation is used by business against its constituencies or by the latter against business, the effect is the same— paralysis of economic activities, skyrocketing court costs, the impending breakdown of the legal system and of respect for law as a social institution. Law is no longer seen to be a source of social order and justice. It seems to have become an instrument of disorder and of irrational chaos. In such a climate, to be antinomian (literally, "antilaw") appears to be the only human, sane and moral philosophical stance to adopt.

The other side of the coin is the claim that business has brought this upon itself. Stanley Marcus, Chairman of Nieman-Marcus of Dallas, a person whose business credentials are impeccable, states this position eloquently:

> Americans still believe in the free-enterprise system. They have no quarrel with profit-making. But they do have a quarrel with unethical and questionable business practices conducted at the public expense.
>
> They do have a quarrel with companies which pollute our water and air and are apparently indifferent to the hazards of pollution until the Government intervenes.
>
> They do have a quarrel with that majority of businessmen who have fought and obstructed and delayed every piece of progressive legislation enacted during this century.
>
> Who among the business community today would seriously propose that Congress repeal our child-labor laws—or the Sherman Antitrust Act? The Federal Reserve Act, the Securities Exchange Act? Or workman's compensation? Or Social Security? Or minimum wage? Or Medicare? Or Civil Rights legislation?
>
> All of us today recognize that such legislation is an integral part of our system; that it has made us a stronger, more prosperous nation— and, in the long run, has been good for business. But we can take precious little credit for any of the social legislation now on the books, for business vigorously opposed most of this legislation.
>
> I wonder sometimes if we really believe in the free-enterprise system. When those who have the greatest stake in it often turn out to be its greatest enemies, I wonder if free enterprise can survive.
>
> Can it survive when some of its greatest proponents seem determined to strangle the life force of the system—competition—with such practices as collusive bid-rigging and price-fixing?

Can free enterprise survive inaccurate, misleading, or "unexplained" financial reporting? Or auditors who violate their code of ethics to help companies falsify financial statements and perpetrate massive swindles, running into the hundreds of millions of dollars, that involve inflated assets, sales and earnings, fraudulent insurance policies, nonexistent securities, and the collection of death benefits on coverage that never existed?

What are we to think—not just of the executives behind the fraud and the auditors who helped them—but of the dozens of employees who knew about the fraud but did nothing, and the powerful investors who benefited from the inside information?[3]

We will try to put into perspective this divisive controversy over the proper role of law in business. At heart, the issue is philosophical. How is law meant to function in society? Is obedience to law a matter of ethics? If so, why? Or are laws more like the rules of a game—a matter of practical constraints, to be sure, but hardly raising human and moral issues? What human philosophy underlies this and other alternative versions of the relation that should obtain between law and morality?

2. ALTERNATIVE MORALITIES CONCERNING SOCIAL CONTROL

Before we get into specific legal philosophies, take a quick test of where your own philosophical proclivities lie on this controversial interface between law and ethics. Is obedience to the law a moral matter or, rather, is the legal system a game, a hurdle to be got around, but not itself a matter of ethical concern? Your answers to the first two cases (A-1 and A-2) will help you determine where you stand on this view of law as an amoral game (pure legalism). Your answers to the second two cases (B-1 and B-2) will underline the extent to which you see law as determinative of ethical right and wrong (moral legalism).

VALUES-CLARIFICATION TEST

Below are described two pairs of business decisions. In front of each decision, write a number which expresses the extent to which you agree

[3]From a speech by Stanley Marcus, by permission of Stanley Marcus; copyright 1975 by the New York Times Company: reprinted by permission. *New York Times* (December 15, 1975). "*Op-ed*," p. 31.

with it. Then, if your answer to the second decision of the pair differs from your answer concerning the first, state your reason why.

**1 = strongly disagree 2 = disagree 3 = not sure
4 = agree 5 = strongly agree**

_____ A-1: A manufacturer of cattle feed includes as an ingredient the synthetic female hormone DES (diethylstilbestrol) which fosters growth in cattle and sheep. Men preparing the feed have experienced sexual impotence and severe breast enlargement. Worker complaints have evoked no response on the part of the company. The company points out that OSHA inspectors have not found any legally defective working conditions. The decision was made to continue production as usual.

_____ A-2: Imagine a similar situation, where the workers are unaware of the hazards of DES. The company's doctors point out to management the hazard of sexual disorders in men handling the artificial hormone. The company decides to keep this information from workers and to use every legal loophole to maintain unchanged present manufacturing procedures and working conditions. The men need the jobs and are well paid, and an overhaul of the production process is not economically justified. For any fines and penalties that could result from this decision would be relatively small.

Did you change your agreement or not from A-1 to A-2 If so, why?

_____ B-1: At a Southern bank, the bank president, his wife, relatives, friends, and other bank officers habitually and substantially overdraw their accounts. As a matter of policy, the bank charges no interest on these overdrafts. There is criticism that the bank is being run for the benefit of insiders, and that the policy on overdrafts is an unsafe and unsound banking practice. The bank president defends himself on the grounds that this specific practice is not illegal and is, in fact, quite common.

_____ B-2: The same bank president admits that the policy of "courtesy" overdrafts is on the borderline as regards unsafe practices. If the Comptroller of the Currency, Administrator of National Banks, orders an end to this practice, he will have it stopped. But not otherwise. It is the law, and nothing else, which defines ethical duty. Did you change your agreement or not from B-1 to B-2? If so, why?

In A-1 and B-1 the law did not enter into that picture. The decision was made on nonlegal grounds. What determined your answer in these cases? To what ethical norm of right and wrong did you appeal? In A-2 and B-2, law is introduced into the picture. Did the introduction of *legal* considerations have any *ethical* impact on your decision? Is the impact amoral and without added ethical obligation (see A-2), or does the law give added weight to ethical obligation (see B-2)?

Let's examine now the arguments that underlie, first, the pure legalist position, and then the moral legalist position in business ethics, in order that you can critically assess your own legal philosophy. These two business philosophies focus on the letter of the law, the first with a view to contravening it, and the second with a view to fulfilling the law's letter.

Outline. First, there is "pure legalism." See the quotation from Holmes at the head of this chapter. Pure legalism looks at law the way a bad man looks at it. It's not true that the bad man has no respect for law. On the contrary, he will consider very carefully what the law is likely to do to him, and guide his decisions accordingly. Did you ever park your car in a "no-parking" area where it was sure to be tagged? "The $5 fine is well worth the convenience of parking here," you tell yourself. Justice Holmes would agree wholeheartedly with your reasoning. You're thinking like a bad man. This is the correct way to understand the import of law. By the way, how did you evaluate the decision in A-2 above? Do you lean toward pure legalism?

The second philosophy of law that we'll consider is legal moralism. As Carl Fulda puts it, "The law reflects [the community's] moral values, and thus it becomes a basis of business ethics."[4] Legal moralism holds that when you're talking ethics, you're talking law, and vice versa. In business, morality is simply and completely a matter of obeying the law. How did you evaluate the decision in B-2? Do you lean toward the legal-moralist sentiment expressed there?

In the next chapter, we'll examine two business philosophies which focus on the spirit of the law. These third and fourth alternative legal philosophies I call the "social-responsibility" model of the relation of business ethics to law and the "social-accountability" model. In the latter, the law endeavors to ensure that its spirit will be followed: business is rendered legally accountable. The social-responsibility model, on the other hand, assumes that business on its own can and will fulfill the law's spirit. But now we turn to the first two models, which focus on the letter of the law. The first takes law completely out of the realm of ethics, and the second places law at the heart of whatever ethics may exist in the business world.

3. ALTERNATIVE ONE: PURE LEGALISM—NO CONTROL AS NORM

The pure legalist views law as a perfectly arbitrary game. The rules are hurdles. Get over them, under them, around them, or avoid them alto-

[4]Fulda, *op. cit.*

gether, if you can get away with it. Obedience, or not, to the law is a matter of tactics, rather than ethics. At times the law may perchance forbid what your conscience also forbids. This is mere happenstance. The law, precisely as law, does not bind in conscience. Law is not morality. To confuse the two does a service to neither. If you want to understand the import of law, you must keep this distinction firmly in mind.

You may feel bound to do what a law happens to command, but you don't feel bound *because* the law commands it. For example, the law forbids "bait-and-switch" advertising. The pure legalist might avoid "bait-and-switch" advertising because of his own good business or ethical reasons, but not precisely because of the law. The law, as such, has no moral impact. Its impact is nonmoral: it is an obstacle to overcome when it stands in the way of decisions that are extralegally arrived at. In the name of ethics or of profit, one might decide to bribe or not to bribe, to pipe in Muzak to workers or not to—whatever the law says or fails to say on these matters.

Well, if the law, as such, doesn't define an ethical obligation for me, what does it do? Former Supreme Court Justice Oliver Wendell Holmes (1902–1932) explains the legalist view.[5] Law, says Holmes, is a matter of prediction. Lawyers are in the prophecy-making business. When you pay a lawyer, you're not interested in moral exhortations or legal theories. You are interested in the public clout (e.g., fines and imprisonment) and in how likely the courts are to visit that clout upon you, if you engage in a given activity. *That* is what you want lawyers to predict for you, and it's what you pay them for. Holmes goes so far as to say: "The prophecies of what the courts will do, in fact, and nothing more pretentious, is what I mean by law." The pure legalist who is running a movie house, for example, is not interested in the moral impact of his shows on the viewing public. He will, however, ask a lawyer to predict his chances of being fined or closed down if he shows a particularly violent or pornographic film.

This becomes clearer, says Holmes, if you look at the way that a bad man views the law. Good people and bad alike are anxious to stay out of jail and avoid paying fines. Now, the good person will usually avoid jail and fines for many reasons which have nothing to do with the law. Conscience, morality, social convention all operate to keep him on the straight and narrow. These considerations don't hold for the bad person. So, if you want to know what the law means in itself, the bad person is a particularly good instructor. For *his* focus is completely on the law, i.e., on correctly predicting the likelihood of legal sanction for a given activity.

Law is suffused with the language of morality: "rights," "duties," "malice," "intent," "negligence." Such language, says Holmes, seduces us

[5]Holmes, *op. cit.*, pp. 167–202.

into the incorrect belief that the law is best understood in moralistic terms. Of course, law and morality often overlap. Embezzlement is immoral, as well as illegal. But if you would understand the precise *legal* import of your action, consult the bad man. He will predict which usages of funds will land you in jail, and which usages escape legal sanctions. The good man, introducing ethical considerations, may well proscribe activities that the law does not touch on or touches on only in a borderline way. The bad man will predict what legal fines certain acts entail and ponder whether these acts are worth the price. The good man may well proscribe these same acts on moral grounds alone. The law, for example, may enjoin an industry to stop polluting or be fined. To the bad man, the issue is purely legal. Predict the likelihood and the amount of the fine. Decide whether it is more profitable to pollute and pay, or to clean up and avoid paying. To him, the law defines no moral duty. The fine is construed as no more than a tax randomly levied, a possible cost of doing business. The good man might view pollution as an ethical issue and the fine as an inducement to develop a responsible environmental policy.

During the past century, Anglo-American jurisprudence has tended to view the law in this positivistic way. So, it is not surprising that many in the business community operate under a philosophy of pure legalism vis-à-vis the law. Nor has this attitude been discouraged by the ever-swelling flood of legislation that has engulfed business during the last decade. Businesses drowning in litigation are not inspired to look to the law to keep them ethically afloat. Clean Air amendments, Consumer Credit Protection amendments, OSHA regulations, Consumer Product Safety laws, Equal Employment Opportunity laws, Water Pollution Control amendments, Anti-Trust Procedures and Penalties, Age Discrimination and Retirement Income Security laws, Equal Credit Opportunity amendments—and many others, all passed since 1970—have generated this explosion of lawsuits, skyrocketing costs, and interminable delays. Ten Commandments can point out a path to moral and ethical responsibility. But Ten *Thousand* Commandments? It's no wonder that multiplication of laws diminishes respect for law as a source of moral guidance or inspiration.

The caseloads and number of appeals threaten a breakdown of the legal system. In the area of antitrust, there is real doubt whether the courts can begin to cope with the sheer physical volume of documents, depositions, and data. This casts further doubt on appeals to law as an instrument of moral justice and ethics in business. IBM, AT&T, and the government are still fighting issues that were first raised 30 years ago, and there is no end in sight. In the IBM case, for example, the government is faced with sorting through 27 million documents, with no index (it was destroyed). In the AT&T case, the government has all but thrown in the towel. AT&T, meanwhile, collects $1 billion in annual profits, which is not excessive, given its asset base; but on this economic scale, a $2 million annual antitrust legal bill appears as a minor cost of doing business. In scenarios like these, law is experienced as having little to do with business ethics or moral responsibility. The philosophy that we have called pure legalism seems to describe the only realistic way to proceed.

Finally, a pervasive social acceptance of lawlessness is another aggravating factor that impels business in the direction of pure legalism. Law as touching on business is predominantly concerned with white-collar crime. If the law equals prediction of what the courts will do, then the prediction about white-collar crime is that the courts will not do much. As a matter of fact, they will not (can not?) do much about any kind of crime. This leads to the suggestion that the lines between the legal offender, the normal individual and the convicted offender are not as sharp as we'd like to think either in business or in any other area. Consider the following questions and propositions offered by sociologist Joseph Rogers.[6]

> How many of us have never departed in any way from observance of the law? Is occasional legal deviance perhaps the norm rather than the exception? In other words, is the legal offender the norm? Are not moral holidays, sporadic defiance of authority, and legal shortcuts well-nigh universal human traits?

Philip Slater goes so far as to suggest:[7]

> In the hard reality of everyday life, however, the incorruptible man is at best an inconvenience, an obstacle to the smooth functioning of a vast institutional machinery. Management leaders, for example, tend to prefer corrupt union leaders—"people you can do business with"—to those who might introduce questions and attitudes lying outside the rules of a monetary game. The man who can not be bought tends to be mistrusted as a fanatic.

You may not want to go so far, but consider. In the year 1975, limiting ourselves only to the F.B.I.'s eight "index" offenses, police were aware of 11 *million* violations. Only *half* a million persons are incarcerated at any one time. Even allowing for repeaters, that's an awful lot of offenders walking around. Now, to those 11 million "index" crime offenses, add all

---

[6]Joseph W. Rogers, *Why Are You Not A Criminal?* (Englewood-Cliffs, N.J.: Prentice-Hall, Inc., 1977), pp. 115ff. Rogers offers these ideas as food for thought rather than as fully substantiated claims.

[7]Philip Slater, *The Pursuit of Loneliness: American Culture at the Breaking Point* (Boston, Ma.: The Beacon Press, 1970), p. 17.

the narcotics violations, arsons, forgeries, embezzlements, tax evasions, and dozens of other crimes, white collar and other, and you come up with millions more offenses, only to give a context to this discussion of law's relationship to morality. Clearly, crime does pay. Crime is almost common enough to be considered a human trait. In this context, pure legalism, which completely separates law from morality, appears as a plausible philosophy.

In summary, then, three considerations caution us against adopting an overly righteous or moralistic tone against business's violations of law, and toward business's tendency to view law as a bothersome hurdle, rather than a moral guide. First, the sheer volume of laws and regulations on business encourages a calculating nonmoral approach to law. Second, the resultant flood of litigation and overload of the court system, with the consequent capricious enforcement, makes it only sensible to view law in a purely penal way: it is the likelihood of penalty, rather than the substance of the law itself, that concerns me. Third, the wide public acceptance of many forms of lawlessness provides a "C.M." type of legitimation for separating law and morality. Underlying all of these considerations is the "bad man's" view of law as nothing more than the consequences likely to follow from its infringement. Observance of ethics separates the good man from the bad; observance of law is something else again, according to the pure legalist philosophy.

4. ALTERNATIVE TWO: MORAL LEGALISM—LEGAL REGULATION AS A NORM

Pure legalism is neither our last word nor necessarily the prevailing view of business's ethical obligation to obey the law. To divorce law from morality is to divorce law from human nature. As opposed to such *pure* legalism, *moral* legalism sees law as having something to say about human nature, and hence about morally responsible behavior. Carl Fulda succinctly describes this approach:[8]

> The law reflects the thought prevailing in the community, including
> its moral values, and thus it becomes a basis of business ethics.

Law is not some arbitrary and perverse game whose rules are to be stretched, twisted, or evaded altogether. No. Law, rather, commands our moral respect. Obedience to law is bound up with our worth and meaning as human beings. Business's concern for law, then, is a matter of ethics. To

[8]Fulda, *op. cit.*

the moral legalist, law completely defines the ethical obligations of a business person and a business. Socially responsible behavior means legally correct behavior and nothing else. Law equals morality. Morality equals law. Business ethics is a matter of operating within the law. Obey the law, and your conscience is clear. Nothing further is required.

As in the case of other business philosophies, a very definite philosophy of person and society underpins moral legalism. And, as we have seen before, the adequacy of the ethics depends on the validity of the underlying philosophy. Anarchy is what the moral legalist sees when he looks at human nature. Civilization is but a thin veneer covering and restraining the basic lawlessness that lies just below the surface. At heart, the business world is a cutthroat jungle. British philosopher Thomas Hobbes was the most eloquent spokesman for this view of humankind. There's a war on—the war of everyone against everyone else. Make no mistake about it. Businesses are self-contained units pitted against one another. Business failure is the one great evil to avoid. To this end, the overweening goal must be the unlimited pursuit of profits and power. Consider, for example, this comment made by the chief executive of a well-known mouthwash company. The firm was accused of using a cheap form of alcohol in the formula. There was a possible danger to users' health. In defense of this, he said:[9]

> We broke no law. We're in a highly competitive industry. If we're going to stay in business, we have to look for profit wherever the law permits. We don't make the laws. We obey them. Then why do we have to put up with this "holier than thou" talk about ethics? It's sheer hypocrisy. We're not in business to promote ethics. Look at the cigarette companies, for God's sake! If the ethics aren't embodied in their laws by the men who made them, you can't expect businessmen to fill the lack. Why a sudden submission to Christian ethics by businessmen would bring about the greatest economic upheaval in history!

[9]Recounted by Albert Z. Carr in "Is Business Bluffing Ethical?" *Harvard Business Review* (January-February 1968), copyright __ 1967 by the President and Fellows of Harvard College; all rights reserved, p. 148.

The reader might find it interesting to discuss this alleged incompatibility of Christianity and competitive Capitalism. Would loving concern for others, beyond what is legally mandated, drive a business into bankruptcy? Can business people live realistically by Christian ideals when their competitors do not? Is Christianity only possible in a world without sinners? Does Christianity urge mindless altruism, or can love be intelligent and realistic? Can a business person be a genuine Christian while living and acting in a very imperfect world?

Daniel Bell tackles this question at a more generalized level in *The Cultural Contradictions of Capitalism* (New York: Basic Books, Inc., paperbound edition, 1978). He sees the origins of capitalism in the impulses of human acquisitiveness and Christian asceticism. Originally, the latter served the former. Today asceticism has given way to hedonism, yielding an unreconciled tension between Christian culture and modern capitalism.

Note that, except for law, no restraints are recognized by this executive. This illustrates the anarchical side of human nature that Hobbes recognized so well.

Now, Hobbes saw that it is intolerable for human beings to live in a state of pure anarchy. If businesses have no other concern in the pursuit of their own survival but to destroy competitors and trample on consumers, then civilization and, indeed, the business process itself, become impossible. There is a paradox here. On the one hand, the natural élan of the marketplace must be to engage in an all-out war. The market for goods and services is not unlimited. Survival, then, involves a ruthless struggle for this necessarily limited piece of the action. On the other hand, this condition of natural anarchy—"the state of nature," Hobbes calls it—puts an end to business.[10]

> In such condition, there is no place for Industry; because the fruit thereof is uncertain; and consequently no Culture of the Earth; no Navigation nor use of the commodities that may be imported by Sea; no commodious Building; no Instruments of moving and removing such things as require much force; no Knowledge of the face of the Earth; no account of Time; no Arts; no Letters; no Society; and which is worst of all, continuall feare, and danger of violent death; and the life of man, solitary, poore, nasty, brutish, and short.

Business life becomes a jungle of cutthroat s.o.b.'s doing unto others before others do unto them, until it all comes tumbling down.

Now, says Hobbes, this is an intolerable way to live. Humankind's natural anarchy cannot be allowed to go unchecked. Good sense—"the dictates of reason" is Hobbes's phrase—tells us this. Reason or conscience dictates that there must be some ground rules so that business be not conducted in an atmosphere of unbridled anarchy. If life is to be tolerable, we must live by at least these three commandments:

1. Don't do unto others what you would not have them do unto you.
2. Give up your right to make your own rules to the extent that others do, too.
3. Keep your agreements, under penalty of relapsing into that intolerable state of natural anarchy.

Next Question. If the human beast is basically an all-out aggressive and competitive animal, as Hobbes claims, then how can I trust the other fellow to live by these reasonable dictates? This is where law comes in. The internal forum of conscience is not enough. It's got to be backed up in the external forum by legal enforcement. So, businesses in society operate un-

---

[10]Hobbes, *Leviathan*, Chapter 13.

der an implied social contract. The right to unfettered pursuit of power and profit, each surrenders to the state to the extent that others do, too. The state thereby holds the common power of all. This common power, in the form of police, prisons, and fines, forces businesses to live by the rules. Society, then, is born of fear—fear of that machinery of governmental power which will be visited on those who break the law, i.e., who violate those rules that keep us from falling back into unchecked anarchy. Whatever semblance of order there is in the natural business jungle is due to fear of the law backed up by state power. This is true of business and of society as a whole. To the extent that this fear is effective, it keeps businesses from destroying each other, their customers, and their employees. It is only the external coercion of law that tames the natural inner beast, and makes possible the veneer called civilization and the fragile appurtenances of social concern and cooperation.

The world-view of business and society has the following consequences for ethics. First, where the law is silent, anything goes. There are no natural intrinsic bonds among human beings. Nature shows the opposite. Man is intrinsically aggressive and competitive. So business has the perfect moral right to exercise this aggressive competitive freedom as it pleases. The only ties binding human beings together are those externally coerced by law. A business, then, owes customers, employees, stockholders, and the general public only what the law says it owes. So, when it comes time to make an ethically responsible business decision, there is only one question to ask: "Is it legal?" Ethics is synonymous with law. And absolute moral freedom is the rule where the law has nothing to say.

Secondly, this ethics is voluntaristic. It is the will of the state as expressed through law that creates society. Humans are not naturally social. There are no rationally perceived natural ties. Hence the legal ties that join human beings together are not the rational reflection of human nature. No. The law is not a matter of reason. It is a matter of will—the will of the sovereign power. It follows that you do not ask whether a law is reasonable. There is no natural basis for answering such a question. You only ask, is it law? The *will* of the government is the necessary and sufficient basis of law. Laws regulating business may often seem arbitrary, whimsical, irrational. So be it. Law is the only thing that stands between us and natural anarchy. For that reason I obey it, and not because it somehow makes rational sense in itself. And if this is not enough, then fear of punishment keeps me in line.

Finally, since the law and nothing else defines the ethical duties of business, there is no basis for conscientiously objecting to a law as unfair. Fair is what the law says is fair, period. This year, you kick off from the 40-yard line. Next year, you're supposed to kick off from the 35-yard line.

A 40-yard line kickoff is legal and therefore fair one year and illegal and therefore unfair the next. Why? Because football's sovereign powers have so decreed. And that's the end of it. The same goes for the laws governing business and society. If you send 22 players onto a field and tell them to play ball without giving them rules and making the rules stick, you won't have a game; you'll have chaos.

To sum up, then, it's law or anarchy. This and nothing else is the basis for the business ethics that flows from a Hobbesian view of human nature. Business people left in their natural state would be driven to unbridled and ultimately destructive all-out competition. Good sense, or conscience, dictates that some ground rules are necessary if the business process is to proceed successfully. But such rules, to be effective, need external sanction. Whence the state comes into being as the ultimate enforcer that makes business (and, indeed, all civilization) possible. The state's laws backed by the state's power become the only source of moral restraint. Where the law is silent, people are morally free to express their natural competitive instincts as they wish. The law's *fiat* creates good and evil. There's no higher law by which civil law can be judged. The legal, precisely as such, is also ethical.

5. SUMMARY AND EVALUATION

We have been examining the much vexed question of government's regulation of business, and of the ethical stances that businesses adopt in the face of such regulation. One response is to focus narrowly on the law and its provisions. We have examined two legal philosophies that might underlie a response like this. The first was the philosophy of the pure legalist. To him, the law has nothing to do with ethics; it's a purely practical hurdle to be gotten over. The second was the philosophy of the moral legalist. To him, the law has everything to do with ethics: the only ethical obligations of business are those that are legally defined. There are no others. In the next chapter we'll examine two other philosophies that have a broader conception of business's ethical obligations vis-à-vis the law.

Now, we suggest some questions that might be raised against the philosophical underpinnings first of pure legalism (abbreviated PL), and then of moral legalism (abbreviated ML). Recall the criterion by which we judge philosophical adequacy and ethical truth, viz., how comprehensively and consistently does the philosophy in question reflect and describe the realities of what it means to be a human being in society? How complete and accurate a picture does the philosophy paint? Does it leave out any aspect of human nature, or blur it over? We will restate the arguments for

PL and for ML in summary form. After each restatement, a question (*Q*) is presented to highlight an objection that could be raised against the argument. Then, an answer (*A*) from the point of view of PL or ML, as the case may be, is briefly stated. The intent is to assist the reader's own evaluation; it is not to endorse either PL or ML, or their opposites.

I. *Pure Legalism*

(1) *Law is not morality*. This is PL's fundamental assumption. Law predicts the probability of court sanctions against certain conduct. The bad man can give you the best advice about what to do in order to keep the courts off your back. Morality recommends conduct worthy of a good human being. To use this moral standard in interpreting legal obligations only confuses the issue.

Q: PL here confuses *obligation* with *meaning*. Perhaps the "bad man" can best describe the law's meaning and the limits of legal liability. Now once the meaning is clear, why can't I ask myself whether it is morally incumbent upon me to obey this law? Isn't there, then, an overlap of law and morality?

A: I may, indeed, be morally obliged to obey a law, but only on *moral* grounds, not legal. Embezzlement, for example, violates a moral injunction against stealing. The fact that embezzlement also happens to be illegal adds nothing to the force of its moral proscription.

What do you think?

(2) *The litigation explosion*. Ever proliferating governmental regulation of business has engulfed the business process in a morass of mindless and often contradictory regulations. However noble the law's intent, the actual result is confusion and irrationality. Business's interface with law as it actually exists breeds cynicism and deviousness, not ethical responsibility.

Q: Regulation is intended to protect society from economic abuse by business and to maximize economic benefit for all. At issue is not an arbitrary legal game, but human values of health, safety, honesty, and fairness. To the extent that law concretely enshrines these values, is it rightly divorced from business ethics?

A: Rational consistency is a human value. Irrational and inconsistent regulations can make no human moral claim. The viability of the economic process is also a fundamental human value and, indeed, human necessity. Regulations that obstruct and overwhelm this process are to that extent inhuman, and so do not deserve ethical allegiance. In business, law and morality are separate realms.

Which, do you think, is the more accurate understanding of law?

(3) *Public acceptance of lawlessness.* Law does not operate in a vacuum. The law's practical meaning and import is a function of the public's will to obey and enforce it. A law is not effectively a law just because it is on the books. From this point of view, most white-collar crime is not crime at all. How many people can honestly say that they've never broken a law and justified it to themselves? Personal ethics is one thing. Observance of law is another.

Q: True, the books are filled with anachronistic laws that have lost all legal and ethical force. But most business violations—white-collar crimes—do not fall under this category. True, chiselling on income tax and on unemployment insurance are common. But "common" does not mean "condoned." People recognize the human social import of the laws they violate. They do not divorce the good person from the good citizen.

A: Figures give the lie to this objection. Legal offenders in the U.S. number in the tens of millions. Imprisoned convicts at any one time number one-half million. What government tells me to do, and how I choose to live, are different matters. The latter involves my moral integrity. The former has nothing to do with it.

Which, do you think, is the true view?

II. *Moral Legalism*

(1) *The state of nature.* The business person and the business enterprise, untrammelled by artifical outside restraints, are naturally driven to unlimited competition. Resources and markets are limited. But self-preservation dictates that each maximizes his own market share, his own corner on resources. Whence the law of nature is unbridled destructive cutthroat competition; the only restraint on this intolerable condition is civil law backed up by civil force. So, law defines morality: intolerable anarchy is the only alternative. Where the law is silent, the natural right to self-preservation comes to the fore.

Q: Law is the only basis of ethics if, indeed, human beings are essentially atomic, competitive and hostile. But this is not the whole story about human nature. Do not humans possess cooperative impulses as well as competitive hostile impulses? If humans are naturally social, as well as naturally individual, then respect for human sociality provides a nonlegal basis for business ethics. A business would have duties to others even where the law is silent.

A: This view of human sociality is naive. See how humans behave in time of war and natural disaster when the rule of law breaks down: anarchy is the order of the day. What masquerades as fellow-feeling is really motivated by the law's sanctions. Would the most public-spirited business give to charity the amount of money now collected by taxes if taxes were abolished? What business enterprise would ever say "Enough" to security and profits? Sociality is the state's creation: law is its only guarantee. Naturally, humans are at war.

What do you think?

(2) *Ineffectiveness of conscience.* There is a schizophrenia between business's chafing at government regulation, on the one hand and, on the other, the uncertainty and insecurity born of unbridled competition. Business hankers after self-regulation: let conscience be the guide. But who can trust the conscience of the competitor? So law becomes a necessary evil— the only effective basis of ethics.

Q: At issue, again, is the natural sociality of human beings. Business people and business enterprises show honesty, fairness, responsibility, and restraint in a thousand ways not mandated by law. Hobbes's view of human nature would require a policeman over the shoulder of every individual if society were to be possible. But isn't conscience based on natural human sociality sufficient to make us cooperate in many ways, independently of legal force? Isn't conscience often operative in the business world even where the law isn't?

A: The dictates of reason might impel sporadic, occasional socially responsible behavior. But the rule of conscience is not sufficient to protect business people of good will from being trampled upon by their less scrupulous competitors, especially when survival is at stake. At heart, businesses and people are pitted against each other in a world where there is not sufficiency for all.

Which, do you think, is the truer picture of human nature?

(3) *Legal voluntarism.* The state of anarchy without the rule of law is so intolerable that any law is better than none. True, one would prefer laws that are "reasonable," i.e., that foster the ends of one's own business. One may work within the legal system to bring this about. But one may not set oneself up as the individual judge of law. There is no higher law by which to judge the law of the state. What is legal is by that very fact just and right. The will of the sovereign makes it so, because the alternative is intolerable anarchy, which puts an end to the very possibility of carrying on the business process.

Q: If human nature is as Hobbes says it is, then business and society are impossible without law. Law is absolute. But if humans are naturally social, then can I not use my reason to judge a just law from an unjust law, a law which is in harmony with man's social nature from one which is antihuman? Law, then, would not be absolute, because the alternative to law would not be anarchy. Law would not be self-justifying but would have to pass the bar of reason.

A: The philosophical lines are drawn. Do you look at the business world and see *natural* sociality and cooperation? Hobbes and the moral legalist do not.

DISCUSSION QUESTIONS

1. Mrs. Cabot teaches history to freshmen and sophomores in college. Three months ago, she became the mother of her first child, Charlotte. Charlotte has been weaned and is now a happy, healthy, three-month-old baby. Mrs. Cabot is ready to resume her fulltime college teaching this semester, which is about to begin. She hires Rita, a recent high-school graduate, to babysit an eight-hour day, five days a week, at minimum wage. Mrs. Cabot tells Rita that she'll be paid in cash. Rita is perfectly happy to operate on a cash basis, thereby avoiding traceable income and evading income tax and social security. Mrs. Cabot is happy to avoid paying the employer share of social security and wading through the paperwork that government regulation imposes on employers. Also, Mrs. Cabot, operating outside the law, will not have to pay Rita overtime for weekend work; nor will she have to give Rita the mandated two weeks annual paid vacation.

    (a) Is Mrs. Cabot's behavior illegal? It is unethical? On what grounds?

    (b) Is Rita's behavior illegal? Is it unethical? On what grounds?

    (c) Who, if anyone, is getting cheated by Mrs. Cabot's actions?

    (d) Who, if anyone, is getting cheated by Rita's actions?

    (e) Is the law governing employer-employee relations a just law on Hobbesian grounds? Why?

    (f) If Mrs. Cabot thinks the law is silly, should she obey it? What if everyone decided to pick and choose which laws to obey?

Would you change your answer if you learned that a friend of Rita's who had been hired under a similar arrangement got her employer into legal trouble? It seems that this friend was fired for incompetence and sued her employer for unpaid overtime wages. Rita, of course, knows about this. She tells Mrs. Cabot that she would never cause any trouble, but one can never be sure.

    (g) Does the danger of getting caught affect the *ethical* side of the decision?

    (h) Is obedience to the law a matter of ethics at all?

2. The most influential business lobby in Washington today is the U.S. Chamber of Commerce. It includes 2,500 local affiliates; 1,300 professional and trade associations; and 68,000 corporations which, together, can mobilize 7 million people at the grass-roots level. Mr. Maquire, a director of a small corporation, regularly deducts his grass-roots lobbying costs as a business expense. This practice is not condoned by the U.S. Chamber of Commerce. It is expressly forbidden both by Congress and by declarations of the I.R.S. Maquire defends this practice by pointing out (correctly) that hundreds of corporations do the same. He's taking a calculated risk, has never been caught or penalized, and sees no ethical problem in thus contravening the law.

   (a) Do you agree with Maquire's position? Explain.
   (b) Suppose the law to be unclear in the matter, do you see any ethical impropriety in the public's financing (by way of business deduction) special business interests?
   (c) Does the danger of getting caught affect the ethical obligation at issue here?
   (d) Should the practice of other corporations affect the ethics of your decision?
   (e) Would you change your answer if you learned that the zealous chairman of a House subcommittee was investigating this particular practice?
   (f) Would you change your answer again if you were invited to attend a $100-a-head annual fund-raising cocktail party hosted by the Congressman in question?

3. Rick is a part-time undergraduate marketing-management major working fulltime for an import-export company at the World Trade Center in New York City. His boss, Rutherford Koberg, wants to transfer him to the company office at Kennedy Airport. Rick's apartment and school are near the World Trade Center, and the transfer would involve a lot of time and energy wasted in commuting to the new job location. Rick doesn't want this hassle even though the only alternative to the transfer is losing his job. Mr. Koberg is sorry to see Rick go, as he was a good worker and they got along well, Koberg, however, agreed formally to "fire" Rick rather than have him quit, so that Rick would be eligible for unemployment insurance. Rick was pleased with this arrangement and began to collect the insurance, saying nothing, of course, about the perfectly good job he turned down.

   (a) Rick's behavior is illegal. Is it unethical? Why?
   (b) Was it ethical of Koberg to "fire" Rick under these circumstances? Why?

    (c) Who gets hurt by Koberg's and Rick's arrangement? Is this ethically fair? Explain.

    (d) Do you see any danger of undermining the social system (see Hobbes's anarchy in the state of nature) if people systematically subvert the law as Koberg and Rick conspired to do in this case? Explain.

    4. During the Great Depression of the 1930's, many Pennsylvania coal miners were thrown out of work by the closing of the mines. More and more coal companies were deciding to keep the coal in the ground at the prevailing depressed prices. They would resume mining operations only when the price of coal began to rise again. Miners and their families plummeted into great poverty and distress. Gradually, the miners began to dig the coal on their own. They used the coal to heat their homes, and they also sold it. Permission to mine the coal was neither sought for nor given by the companies. Local police were well aware of what was going on, but they did nothing.

    (a) Was the miners' behavior legal? Was it ethical? Explain.

    (b) Was the attitude of the local police legally correct? Was it ethically correct? Explain.

    (c) Was the coal companies' policy legally sound?

    (d) Did the coal companies meet their ethical responsibilities?

SUGGESTED READINGS

Bell, Daniel. *The Cultural Contradictions of Capitalism.* New York: Basic Books, Inc., paperbound edition, 1978.

Carr, Albert Z. "Is Business Bluffing Ethical?" *Harvard Business Review* (January-February 1968).

Conklin, John E. *Illegal But Not Criminal: Business Crime In America.* Englewood Cliffs, N.J.: Prentice-Hall, Inc., 1977.

Fulda, Carl. "The Legal Basis of Ethics," in Robert Bartels (ed.), *Ethics in Business.* Colombia, Ohio: The Ohio State University Bureau of Business Research, College of Commerce and Administration, 1963.

Hobbes, Thomas. *The Leviathan.* especially, Part I, Chapter 13.

Holmes, Oliver Wendell, Jr.: *Collected Legal Papers.* New York: Harcourt, Brace and Co., 1920.

Rogers, Joseph W. *Why Are You Not a Criminal?* Englewood Cliffs, N.J.: Prentice-Hall, Inc., 1977.

CHAPTER 7
RESPONSIBILITY MODEL vs. ACCOUNTABILITY MODEL: THE SPIRIT OF THE LAW

The operational difference between legal obligation and social responsibility is that business determines its legal obligations by asking lawyers what the law requires, whereas business determines its social responsibility by asking experts what society needs and then consulting its conscience as to how it can best help to meet the needs of society.[1]

Since the corporation can act only through the agency of its officers and, apart from their agency, cannot act at all, such authority as they have has been delegated by themselves. In spite of all theory to the contrary, they are in fact responsible only to themselves. Which is to say they are irresponsible and their power is arbitrary.

They are irresponsible and their power is arbitrary quite independently of the motives which guide them in their performances . . . Any power is arbitrary, however benevolently it is used, if its uses fall beyond

[1] Lee Loevinger, "Social Responsibility in a Democratic Society: Government and Business Have the Same Public," *Vital Speeches of the Day* (April 15, 1973), 386. This speech was delivered at the Key Issue Lecture Series at N.Y.U. by Loevinger, member of the law firm of Hogan and Hartson.

The first half of this chapter appears in slightly altered form as an essay, "Is It Enough for Business to be Socially Responsible?" in James B. Wilbur (ed), *Human Values and Economic Activity*, Proceedings of the 1978 Conference on Value Inquiry (Geneseo, N.Y.: State University College at Geneseo, 1978), pp. 320–28.

the controls of law. Any actor is licentious, however benignant his intentions, if, being accountable to no higher authority, he is judge in his own cause.[2]

OBJECTIVES FOR CHAPTER 7:

1. To understand the debate about how business ethics should be institutionalized, specifically, to compare the social responsibility model of business ethics with the social accountability model;

2. To understand the underlying premise of the social-responsibility model, viz., that the corporation legally is a person and enjoys personal qualities, to wit:
   (a) a conscience;
   (b) a right to privacy;
   (c) a right to be free from internal regulation while being socially controlled by external sanctions only;

3. To understand how the social-accountability model differs from the social responsibility model regarding the role of government;

4. To see an example of how business conscience can be institutionalized;

5. To understand and evaluate the main shortcoming of each model.

1. THE SPIRIT OF THE LAW

The two legal philosophies examined in the last chapter assumed an adversary relationship between business and society. To the PL, law is a hurdle to be got around. To the ML, law expresses society's legitimate demands on business and defines the extent of business's moral duty to society at large. Loevinger and Taylor, quoted at the head of the chapter, move beyond this narrow conception of law. To the ethical business person, the law's spirit is more important than the letter of the law. The law's spirit is the focus of the two legal philosophies that we turn to now. These philosophies or models by which businesses today understand their relation toward the larger society we'll call the social-responsibility model (abbreviated SR) and the social-accountability model (abbreviated SA). These conceive society's relation to society and government in positive terms. Business does not operate in a vacuum. The good of business involves the good of the social environment and business's duty to enhance the environ-

---

[2]John F. A. Taylor, "Is the Corporation Beyond the Law?" *Harvard Business Review* (March-April 1975), 128, Copyright © 1965 by the President and Fellows of Harvard College; all rights reserved.

ment. The law, letter and spirit, can serve as a moral guide to the directions of such enhancement. The law is emphasized as a positive moral and educational force encouraging business, like the good citizen, to respond beyond the mere letter of the law.

The distinction between SR and SA points up a tension that underlies every effort to deal with business ethics, i.e., the tension between the individual and the institution. When I move from my personal life and ethics at home to the life and ethics of the business institution where I work, do the rules of the moral game change? The SR model answers in the negative; no new rules are required; the conscience of the corporate person is as good as the consciences of the people who work there. The SA model answers in the affirmative; there's a difference in kind between the behavior of people in institutions and their behavior in their personal lives; therefore, the conscience of the corporation must be institutionalized in the form of legally mandated decision-making procedures. An ethically healthy business climate cannot be left to vagaries of the personal consciences of individual business people or to the private initiatives of business institutions.

The main focus in this book has been and will continue to be ethics on the level of the individual rather than the institution. The SR model is still the dominant one under which the readers of this book must function. The ethical climate of a business is still very much a function of the participants, and especially of the policy-makers in that business. The morally upright individual can at best count upon the support of other individuals in the business; failing this, there are usually no institutional ethical supports to fall back on. The SA model suggests what such institutional supports might look like, and how a formally institutionalized corporate conscience might operate.

To illustrate the distinction between the SR model and the SA model, consider the following dispute. Which position would you take?

1. A ·major network wants to introduce a sex farce into prime time TV. Nothing will be sacred—neither family, motherhood, nor religion. The network president is determined to act responsibily. "Not only law, but conscience and the social good will be the rule," he says. Network executives, operating under the constraints of ratings, advertisers, and conscience are in the best position to make an informed, conscientious business decision in this matter.

2. The PTA and the National Citizens Committee for Broadcasting are lobbying for a law mandating effective citizen input into decisions about the content of TV programming. This flies in the face of the National Association of Broadcasters Code Board. The Board asserts that

citizen input is important but not decisive. Actual decisions, according to the Board, belong to broadcasters and not to inexperienced pressure groups. The PTA and NCCB, to the contrary, contend that the media should be legally accountable to the public.

Position one illustrates the SR model. The network's conscience is embodied in the consciences of the individual business decision-makers. The corporate person, just like individual persons, should enjoy the liberty to make ethical decisions without decisive outside interference. The law that is being lobbied for in position two illustrates the SA approach to corporate conscience; network responsibility needs to be assured through legally mandated accountability procedures in the decision-making process: the behavior of the corporate person cannot safely be left to individuals who happen to work there at any given time. Note that SR and SA both agree in their appreciation of business's duties toward society. But they differ markedly in their ways of conceiving and defining these duties.

The key to the radical differences between SR and SA lies in the opposite answers each gives to the following question: Does the process of corporate decision-making roughly reflect that of ethical decision-making by individuals? Yes, is the answer of the SR model; corporate ethical decisions and individual ethical decisions can be conceived of roughly in the same way. No, is the answer of the SA model. Corporate decisions are a different kind of animal from those made by individual business people. Put the same question another way: Is the ethics of a corporation roughly equivalent to the sum of the ethics of the corporate decision-makers? Yes, says the SR model; if you know the moral character of the individual people in a corporation, you could roughly predict the standards of conduct upheld by the business as a whole. No, says the SA model; institutional decision-making procedures could yield an entirely different ethical result than you might expect from the personal ethics of the individuals who carry out those procedures.

This chapter, along with the previous two, examines conventionality and law as moral norms. Subsequent chapters will treat more autonomous approaches to ethics. The SA model will provide a transition from heteronomous ethics to autonomy. On the one hand, SA looks to law (heteronomy) to provide a responsible framework for corporate decisions, but its aim is to leave corporations free to act autonomously within this responsible framework. But first to SR. In the next four sections we describe the SR model and point out some of its assumptions. Then in Sections 6 through 8, we suggest serious shortcomings of the SR approach. These point us toward an SA model, which will be the subject of the final part of the chapter.

2. ALTERNATIVE THREE: SR MODEL—LAW PLUS CONSCIENCE

PL and ML were preoccupied with the letter of the law. SR is a third alternative philosophy that avoids a narrow legalism. To orient the discussion of SR, right off we state its main assumptions in syllogistic form:

1) Persons have consciences;
   @ the corporation is a person;
   =. the corporation has a conscience.

2) Persons enjoy the right to internal privacy in their decision-making processes;
   @ the corporation is a person;
   =. the corporation enjoys the right to internal privacy in its decision-making processes.

3) Bad persons can be controlled by penalties of the law for their bad external actions;
   @ the corporation is a person;
   =. the corporation can be controlled by the penalties of the law for its external bad actions.

Let's examine these assumptions about the corporation.

3. CORPORATION AS PERSON

Note the fundamental premise of the SR model: the facile equation of businesses with individuals. Businesses are hypostatized into persons. True, the law creates the fictitious corporate person with legal agency. This *persona ficta* can accomplish many actions that flesh-and-blood persons also perform. It can sue and be sued; it can acquire property and alienate it; it can marry (enter into legal union with another *persona*) for money. The corporation, like individuals, can make contracts, produce goods and market them, pay and avoid taxes, fight with the government, prosper, and go bankrupt. So it is probably not surprising that the legal fiction is extended by attributing to corporations other, extralegal qualities possessed by individual humans. Whence come the assumptions about the corporation "consulting its conscience" as it exercises "freedom for individual action," about the corporation's right to privacy and about its effective punishability—alleged personal qualities of the corporation that we now come to examine. The corporation seems to have acquired a metaphysical as well as a legal existence! Are such philosophical assumptions about the corporate *persona*, in fact, the case?

4. THE CORPORATE PERSONA POSSESSES A CONSCIENCE

Beyond strictly legal obligation, says Loevinger, business in a democratic society has a wide range of discretion in deciding conduct and courses of action vis-à-vis its social environment.[3] Law limits itself for the most part to proscribing what society considers intolerable conduct. Business is left free to determine for itself what manner of socially desirable conduct it will undertake. First, then, we consider the SR model's appeal to the corporation's conscience.

> The major difference between a democratic and an authoritarian society is that democracy leaves the maximum range of freedom for *individual* (my emphasis) action, establishing legal requirements only as deemed necessary to protect and preserve society.[4]

Note the implied parallelism between the corporate actor and the free "individual."

> Business determines its social responsibility by asking experts what society needs and then consulting *its conscience* (my emphasis) as to how it can best help to meet the needs of society.[5]

Note, that, like the individual, the corporate actor is assumed to have "its conscience." Corporations, like individuals, are to be guided by conscience where the law falls short. The formula in this model is law plus conscience. It would be oppressive in the extreme for the law to prescribe the citizen's every action. A democracy presupposes a social climate of civility, trust and cooperation. Conscience, and not the policeman's billyclub, governs most of our responsible dealings with others. For the most part, I tell the truth, refrain from stealing and murder, and try not to be a litterbug because my conscience so bids, whatever the law may or may not say about such activities. Police action is reserved for the exceptional conduct that tests the limits of deviance. The general rule is each person's conscience serving as his/her own police officer. And in the SR model, the

---

[3]Loevinger, *op. cit.*, p. 392. It is interesting to note that in May 1978 the Supreme Court extended the rights of the corporate *persona* to "First-Amendment free speech rights." In the name of this "free speech," corporations may now legally pay for advertisements to influence the outcome of ballot propositions or referenda.

[4]*Ibid.*, p. 392.

[5]*Ibid.* Robert Hay and Ed Gray in "Social Responsibilities of Business Managers," *Academy of Management Journal* (March 1974), 135-43, trace the stages in the development of a business concept of SR beginning with the minimalist view of stage one, "profit-maximizing management."

As businesses became more sensitive to and aware of their wider social constituencies, there was progress to stage two, "trusteeship management," and stage three, "quality of life management." Loevinger, in opposing the minimalist approach, is concerned with SR in the wider sense of these latter two stages.

story is the same with business. In a democratic society, business, too, must and does assume social responsibilities beyond the pale of the law. Democracy can only flourish in a climate of voluntary compliance with law and of voluntary assumption of SR where the law is silent: such are the twin pillars of the SR model of business ethics.

5. INCORPORATION LAW vs. REMEDIAL REGULATORY LAW

Now we turn to the second assumption of the SR model, that of business's right to privacy in its decision-making processes. As early as 1878, the courts began to construe that a corporation's privacy, like the individual citizen's, enjoys equal protection under the 14th Amendment. Consequently, corporate law (or, more exactly, "incorporation law" governing the chartering and structure of corporations) began to develop in a very different direction from business regulatory law aimed at remedying the socially harmful effects of corporate decisions. The former tended to leave corporations free to conduct business in any way they chose to. Corporate law has been very hesitant to tamper with the internal workings of this *persona ficta* that is the corporation. A corporation's internal governance and constitution have come to be construed as inviolable on the analogy of the flesh-and-blood person's privacy. For example, I as an individual need fear no legal interference with the process by which I come to moral decisions. I can use my head, confer with my spouse, consult Scripture or an astrological chart: the law cares not. Similarly, the law is scrupulous about the inviolability of the internal governance of the corporate *persona*. With few exceptions, its decision-making methods are left to "its conscience." Such is the hands-off policy of incorporation law. And in the SR model, this is how it should be. This assumption is currently under fire by those who would reform corporate law toward what I call a fourth model, the SA model business's relation to society. The SA model would involve federal chartering of corporations with provisions to ensure accountability in their decision-making processes. But the business community at large stands firm in the conviction that SR is enough, that the corporation's internal governance should remain inviolable.

6. CORPORATE PERSONA CONTROLLED BY REGULATORY LAW AND PENALTIES

A final assumption of SR is that "bad" corporations can be controlled like bad individuals are: by punishment for external violations. The law controls corporations as it controls individual humans—externally. It focuses on external acts and consequences rather than on internal procedures. Such is the nature of regulatory (as opposed to corporate) law. Whether I, as an individual, evade taxes because of religious objections or calculated greed, the law cares not. That's my private affair. But the act of tax evasion is what society, through the law, seeks to regulate. Similarly for corporations, society is absolutely intolerant of some acts, e.g., price-fixing. Of others, society is relatively intolerant, e.g., actions like pollution or the production of hazardous products. Acts such as these are the object of regulatory law.

Regulatory law, with its focus on disapproved acts, usually comes into operation after the fact. The damage is done. Regulatory law, for example, tries to determine who polluted, where the liability lies, and what penalties are to be assessed. Corporation law, on the other hand, operates before the fact. It focuses on the institutions, i.e., on the structure of the corporate *persona* who performs the act. Originally, corporate characters were tightly circumscribed by law. They were limited as to amount of capital, purposes they could pursue, and as to length of life. For various reasons we can't go into here, and with exceptions, such restrictions on corporate structure gradually faded away.

Such exceptions as exist bear almost solely on management-shareholder relationships, such as the election and removal of directors, the compelling of dividends, and the method of dissolving the corporation. Such activities had no legal precedent in the private sphere. But regarding the corporation's relation to the consumer and to the general public, corporation law has little to say. Corporations in these latter areas are like individual humans, who can also pollute, and cheat, and cause personal harm. In such matters, the law views corporations as Big Persons, and tries to deal with them on these terms.

True, the Interstate Commerce Act (1887), the Sherman Antitrust Act (1890), and the Federal Trade Commission (1914) attempted to fill the void left by the leniency of incorporation laws passed by individual States. But meanwhile the States were vying with one another to attract to their borders these lucrative Big Persons. "Charter-mongering" became the rule. "We won't tie your hands," became the cry. And the Federal commissions continued to view the problems of "Big Business" as problems caused by Big Persons and dealt with them accordingly. Corporation law leaves these Big Persons almost entirely without internal restraints. Isn't this anarchy? No, says the SR model. Corporations, like individuals, should and will follow their consciences where the law is silent. Where corporations, or individuals, act unscrupulously, there is a body of regulatory law to step in and punish the miscreants.

But proponents of the SR model remain confident that good corporations will behave like good individuals. They will act responsibly without legal compulsion. Clearly, this situation of relative internal immunity, together with external liability of corporations, puts a very heavy burden on this "conscience" that corporations are supposed to have. A schizophrenia sets in between, on the one hand, what legal and economic necessity compels a business to do and, on the other, what a business does out of "conscience" with voluntary sacrifice to the corporate purse without legal compulsion. Make a profit within the restraints of law: that's good business. Sacrifice profit voluntarily for the common good: that's SR. To comply with product-safety statutes after every legal remedy has been exhausted is good business. To initiate product-safety measures at cost of competitive advantage is SR. To comply with minimum hiring standards, which the EEOC can effectively impose upon you, is good business. To assume the financial risks, unlike your competitors, of a broadbased program to hire ex-cons and disadvantaged minorities is SR. In each case, "conscience" seems to fly in the face of the business instinct to stay within the law while striving to allocate its economic resources as productively as possible. SR and voluntary "conscience" seem to be opposed to good business and economic soundness. Loevinger puts well this understanding of SR:

> The economist begins by defining socially responsible corporate action as voluntary action for which the marginal returns are less than the returns available from some alternative expenditure and which is undertaken for altruistic or ethical reasons.[6]

On the face of it, this sounds like SR means: to misallocate corporate funds for ethical reasons.

Once good business and good conscience have been so opposed, then the advocates of conscience have the burden of showing how SR "really" makes for good business. The strategies for healing this schizophrenia between good business and good ethics are familiar enough and won't be developed here. Basically, they involve the "long run" argument, and the "government-will-make-you-if-you-don't-do-it-freely" argument.[7]

---

[6]Loevinger, *op. cit.*, p. 389. Milton Friedman, of course, as an advocate of the minimalist view, would deny the validity of such a distinction. There can be no conflict, he'd say, between sound economic decisions and SR because to allow the free operation of competitive forces in the market is by that very fact to maximize the common good. To divert corporate funds to other goals will in the long run hurt the public interest (see, for example, Friedman, "The Social Responsibility of Business Is to Increase Profits," *New York Times Sunday Magazine* [September 13, 1970] p. 146). Friedman's model for SR is an alternative to Loevinger's, which deserves examination, but not here.

[7]Keith Davis in "The Case For and Against Business Assumption of Social Responsibility," *Academy of Management Journal* (June 1973), 312–22, outlines in addition to these main arguments other considerations urging that good business is compatible with SR. Among other things, he suggests that forestalling social problems can be easier than curing them, that an SR public image can only help a business, and that problems innovatively handled can often be turned into profits.

The "long run" argument admits that conscientious SR can have an immediate adverse effect upon the corporate economic picture. But not only does commitment to the public good redound to a favorable PR image, but a stronger and stabler community can only feed back favorably in the long run to the business that operates in that environment. Also, most corporate markets are diversified, and so are shareholder holdings. What is not immediately profitable to a corporation at one point in the market can, in the long run, benefit it at another point, or benefit a stockholder in some other part of his/her portfolio.

More persuasive, perhaps, because more immediately self-interested, is the other argument: SR is not opposed to good business, because if you don't act voluntarily out of conscience, then more government regulation will force you to do what you wouldn't do willingly. And government policing measures are more likely to be arbitrary, onerous and misinformed than freely adopted self-policing measures. The mountain of regulatory law adopted under pressure from environmentalists, consumerists, and civil-rights activitists, and the spectre of more to come, lends credence to this argument.

Such considerations mitigate the schizophrenia of the SR model, but do they make it disappear? Fundamentally, SR still seems extraneous to the business decision-making process itself. It comes in through the back door. It tries to persuade that SR will be good medicine in the long run, though it makes business sick in the short run. SR, then, is a matter of pragmatic evaluation of consequences. Should I adopt SR decisions that no right-thinking business person would ever make except for the fact that government might force even worse decisions on me? The SR model comes down to a pragmatic accommodation where business and ethics enter into an uneasy partnership in the hope of long-range good.

7. THE CORPORATE PERSONA IS BEYOND EFFECTIVE LEGAL SANCTION

How does the SR model deal with corporations that do *not* take this long-range view? There may be a pragmatic philosopher-king at the top, but middle managers, divison leaders and field persons are under heavy pressures to perform in the short run, and the philosopher-kings are unable and often unwilling to hear about the grubby goings-on down below. The SR model readily allows that corporations, just like humans, make irresponsible decisions. And in such cases it recommends that penalties be levied on corporations, just as individual human offenders are punished. Note again the third assumption that the corporation is a Big Person and that it should be punished like a person when it does wrong. We now ask whether corporations and individuals respond in the same way to legal sanction. Will the penalties that control one also control the other?

Business lawyer Christopher Stone says no. The penalties for violations of regulatory law that would work against individuals are ineffective against corporations. Stone cites Ford Motor Company as an example. In 1972, lightning struck Ford. Lightning is a favorite business metaphor for government lawsuits, aptly signifying the random enforcement of regulatory laws. The lightning bolt in this case was a record $7-million fine for an EPA violation. Compare this with the $250 million that Ford lost on the Edsel and with the $350 million netted on the Mustang. When the executives sit down to discuss the numbers, which do you think tops the agenda, sales or EPA fines? You and I rightly fear fines. To the corporate *persona*, they are a minor and random cost of doing business.

Note further that it is the corporation that pays the fine, not the individual human business person who violated the regulatory law. The corporate *persona* is the primary legally liable agent; the individual persons are, at best, accessories.[8] These accessories, operating in the field and at the local district level often, under great stress of quotas and competition, are the effective day-to-day decision-makers who are pressured to stretch and even overstep the law. Whatever penalties the slow wheels of justice may eventually grind out, do not fall on these offenders. The corporate *persona*, the primary agent, pays. Indeed, the actual offenders may have long since been promoted, transferred or died. The reality of legal penalties is not part of the experiential work-world of such decision-makers. And even when, on rare occasions, the law is able to pinpoint blame on one of these accessories to the corporation's primary agency, it is notoriously unwilling to come down hard on the white-collar offender.

A final reason why the law is reluctant to visit severe penalties on corporations, even for serious offenses, is the suffering thereby inflicted upon the innocent. Christopher Stone alludes to the flagrant violation by Richard-Merrell Pharmaceutical Company, which, by falsifying and fabricating animal tests, succeeded in getting FDA approval to market MER/29, a chloresterol-reducing drug. One of the "side effects" of this drug was that it caused blindness. The Company grossed a quick $7 million from the sale of this drug the first year alone. After two years, it was removed from the

---

[8]Note that the reason that corporations were invented in the first place was to protect individuals from the liabilities and risks associated with major economic enterprises needed to benefit the public good. And typically of institutions, roles and decisions are diffused; the result is to discourage individual accountability, and often to encourage individual irresponsibility. For this twofold reason, it is hard to devise effective legal sanctions against individuals in corporations. The corporation, as an instrument for protecting individuals from undue liability makes very difficult the pinpointing of responsibility.

market when it became apparent that it was MER/29 that was responsible for "disturbing" symptoms like glaucoma and cataracts. Judge Henry Friendly admitted that the Company's liability had been proven, yet he refused the imposition of punitive awards for hundreds of plaintiffs (some 400,000 people had taken the drug):

> A sufficiently egregious error as to one product can end the business life of a concern that has wrought much good in the past and might otherwise have continued to do so in the future, with many innocent stockholders suffering extinction of their investment for a single management sin.[9]

So the cost of doing business in this multimillion-dollar deliberate sale of a blindness-producing drug was augmented by an $80-thousand fine for lying to the FDA and by the cost of proven injuries from the drug, but by no punitive damages. It is simply not the case that abuses of SR by the corporate offender can be effectively punished in the same way that individual human offenders can.

8. THE CORPORATE PERSONA IS BEYOND THE LAW ITSELF

Now, for a final nail in the coffin of the myth that the corporate *persona* is simply a Big Person, like you and I, who are not so big. The root of the radical difference between corporations and people is that for people responsibility is attached to decision-making, whereas for corporations, responsibility is divorced from decision-making. It was not always thus. Originally, the manager-owner was the primary legal agent in transactions with suppliers, customers, and employees. He cared: he had a stake in the business. And he was visible: you knew whom to blame. But as businesses' capital needs increased, ownership became divorced from management. Owners became anonymous, and managers had no direct stake in the company's fortunes.

This prepares the way for the final blow to the SR model for business ethics, viz., the divorce of responsibility from power. As pointed out above, the individual human decision-makers, for example, the directors, wield

---

[9]As reported by brilliant corporate lawyer Christopher Stone in his classic work, *Where the Law Ends: The Social Control of Corporate Behavior* (New York: Harper and Row, 1975), p. 56. The book explores in depth the question that we are only superficially outlining here, and proposes some detailed solutions. Along the same lines, see the case for the federal chartering of corporations powerfully presented by Ralph Nader, Mark Green, and Joe Seligman in *Taming the Giant Corporation* (New York: W. W. Norton and Co., Inc., 1976) .

the power. But the responsibility lies with the primary agent, the legally created person of the corporation. Well, at least the corporation, through the directors, is an agency of trust accountable to the shareholders, isn't it? Effectively accountable, no. Incumbent managers can legally use corporate funds to wage their election campaigns; would-be challengers must finance their direct-mail campaigns from private funds. The result is that of the 7,000 corporations under the SEC's jurisdiction, the incumbents have won 99.9 percent of the time in recent years.

But worse, consider the following scenario suggested by John F. A. Taylor. Suppose a corporation, by accumulating sufficient earnings, decided to buy back all its stocks, so that in effect it owned itself. Its fiduciary character would be exposed for what it is, an accident of history, and in no way part of its essential nature. This legally created *persona* could continue to carry on all its accustomed activities, hiring and firing, making contracts, marketing goods. And in its performance of these tasks it would no longer be executing a trust. Owning itself, it would have no interests but its own. However unlikely the scenario, it would be perfectly within the law:

> It would move powerful but untouchable in society, society's unjailable civilian, legally armed with a soulless, immortal privacy which no mere mortal could ever equal, with an unpopular independence which no mere state would ever risk.[10]

The fictitious corporate entity shields all the actual wielders of power who are mere accessories and delegates of the primarily liable corporate agent. But this fictitious agent can only act through these accessories who, in fact, therefore delegate power to themselves. This, says Taylor, is another way of saying that power so exercised is arbitrary and irresponsible. This is not a matter of imputing bad will to business decision-makers. They may be men and women good and true, impelled by the highest ideals. They may subscribe 100 percent to Loevinger's SR model for governing decisions that fall beyond the pale of law. But:

> Any power is arbitrary, however benevolently it is used, if its uses fall beyond the control of law. Any actor is licentious, however benevolent his intentions, if, being accountable to no higher authority, he is a judge in his own cause.[11]

---

[10]Taylor, *op. cit.*, p. 127.

[11]*Ibid.*, p. 128. To this lack of accountability in business's exercise of social power, responses have taken two directions. Christopher Stone urges measures for legally enforcing social accountability. At the opposite extreme is the minimalist argument that businesses should get out of the SR picture altogether and stick to what they do best—profit-maximiza-

Law plus economic self-interest plus conscience is an SR model that might serve to socialize flesh-and-blood individuals into society and to protect society from flesh-and-blood miscreants, but the model fails when applied to the SR of business corporate institutions. Flesh-and-blood persons have consciences and are accountable in multitudinous ways. Corporate persons have no consciences and are, to a great extent, immune from accountability in their decision-making processes. Regulatory law attempts, futilely for the most part, to enforce accountability after the fact. So, while the SR model might work for the moral decisions of human persons, it is a mistake to carry over this model to corporate persons.

What is the answer? As long as we remain in the SR framework, we can only hope that business people will resolve on the basis of their own individual philosophies the conflicts arising between the dynamics of the economic enterprise, on the one hand, and on the other the external moral and social interests that resist this dynamic. Except for this chapter, we have focused more on individual than on institutional business ethics. But can this tension be resolved *institutionally*? What are the conditions of possibility for an institutionally sound business ethic? In the SR model, responsible decisions are not institutionally assured. In fact, the institutional bias often works against SR. The corporate *persona* exists in a kind of Hobbesian state of nature, restrained mainly by the dictates of reason operating in the internal forum of the consciences of individual business people. The problems of business ethics in the SR model can be answered by an interdisciplinary metaethical enterprise establishing the institutional conditions of possibility for a corporate (as opposed to an individual) business ethic. This would involve lawyers, sociologists, political scientists, and philosophers working toward bringing the corporate decision-making process into the external forum of law. When the dictates of reason find legal sanction, then we will have what I call a "Social Accountability" model of corporate decision-making, the outlines of which we now proceed to briefly sketch.

First, we want to emphasize (Sections 9 and 10) that SA is not just a proposal for more government regulation. Then we will outline what an institutional conscience for business might look like (Section 11). It might, for example, involve reshaping the board of directors, instituting departments of social concern, and publishing social audits of the nonfinancial

---

tion. Davis, *op. cit.*, outlines some arguments for this latter position. Business is powerful enough, he says, without intervening in the wider society; government is accountable while business is not, so let government handle society's problems; SR only distracts business from its main purpose, and business lacks social skills anyway: economic productivity and not altruism is the name of its game.

side of company activities. Finally, we will consider business's major objection to the SA model (Section 12).

9. ALTERNATIVE FOUR: SA MODEL—CONSCIENCE LEGALLY ACCOUNTABLE AS NORM

This SA model sees an element of anarchy in the first three alternative views of business's relation to law. Pure legalism is willing to use law even to defeat the purposes of law. Moral legalism sees business as morally free to do as it pleases in those areas where the law has nothing to say. And even the SR model suffers from an element of anarchy. True, it appeals to conscience as well as to law. But it leaves business people to be judges in their own case, even in decisions that have deep and, often, society-wide ramifications. Business people allegedly "know best" what is good for society. According to the SA model, however, a responsible conscience must needs be an accountable conscience.

Pressures for more accountability are even now in motion. For example, the Carter Administration's SEC Chairman, Harold Williams, stated in no uncertain terms:

> Much of state corporate law is protective and revenue-producing, rather than oriented toward corporate accountability. It is not in keeping with shareholder protection.[12]

Note, however, that accountability here is assumed to be accountability to shareholders and to them only. In criticizing the SR model above, we saw the weakness of relying for social control on business's fiduciary relationship to shareholders. The SA model we will suggest is much broader in scope. Shareholders, as we've noted, are an anonymous, often very fluid, group of investors, who have little direct interest in actual corporate decisions. It is on consumers and the general public that such decisions often have greatest direct impact. They are business's most directly affected constituencies. The question is how to make business accountable to them as well as to shareholders.

10. ACTION, NOT REACTION

Note right off that the SA model is not a plea for more government regulation of business. It sets out to reverse the trend during the past dec-

---

[12]As quoted by Joel Seligman in "SEC Asks Who's Minding the Store for Stockholders," *Buffalo Evening News* (October 8, 1977), p. C4.

ade of ever increasing governmental intervention in business. In the good old pre-Nader days, government regulation was mainly concerned with proscriptions—outlawing disapproved behavior. During the past decade, governmental regulation has been more and more directed toward prescriptions—spelling out actions and standards that businesses must follow. The locus of business decision-making has shifted in larger part than ever before from the executive suite to Capitol Hill. Businesses have lost much of the discretionary power they used to have over what to do and what not to do about clean air, consumer credit, occupational safety and health, product safety, clean water, hiring policy, and the list goes on. Government has become the conscience of business, not only in the negative sense of forbidding disapproved conduct, but also in the positive sense of mandating responsible and desirable conduct. Business is thereby put in a reactive posture. From an institutional point of view, in matters of social responsibility, decisions do not emanate from the initiatives of the autonomously functioning corporate *persona*. Rather, these decisions are *faits accomplis*. This origin is alien to the internal workings of a business. Business is treated in these matters like a child who, with little moral autonomy of his own, is reduced to reacting to the commands of the parent's conscience, a parent perceived as often capricious, if not tyrannical. The SA model situates moral autonomy and responsibility at the heart of the business decision-making process itself. The only "regulation" involved is to build *self-regulation* procedures into corporate charter requirements and structure. The SA model switches the locus of responsible decision-making away from Capitol Hill and back to the executive suite. This will involve changes in law, of course, not in more regulatory laws to police business, however, but changes in corporate law to ensure business's policing itself. SA looks forward to action on the part of business, rather than reaction in matters of social responsibility.

11. RESTRUCTURING FOR ACCOUNTABILITY

General public director. Many proposals are forthcoming as to how business can be made more accountable. Here we will enumerate and comment upon some of the suggestions made by Christopher Stone in order to convey some idea of what an SA model might look like. His first reform I would judge to be the most essential, but also the most controversial, viz., the appointment of a general public director. If ever an SA model were to become a reality, doubtless this reform would be the last piece to fall in place. This general public director would sit on the board and function as a kind of superego for the corporation. The GPD would enjoy independence from the corporation, but would be accountable to the public. Paid as a civil servant, he could "blow the whistle" on unethical practice without danger of committing career suicide.[13] But if he does his job well, there'll be no need for whistle-blowing. For the GPD is to have clout as well as independence. SA seeks to forestall ethical and legal irregularity before it happens. To this end, the GPD would be armed with a clear job definition, adequate staff, a voice in employee promotions, and a right to any and all information about company business. In turn, he would be personally liable and responsible for corporate "superego" functions *and malfunctions.* By monitoring fundamental internal systems, by an ongoing legal audit of corporate procedures and activities, by maintaining a confidential hotline for possible "whistle-blowing" at every level, the GPD's mandate would be to forestall lawsuits, ensure self-policing, and halt unethical practices before they get off the ground. His office would prepare human and social-impact studies to complement economic-impact studies, and would serve as an information interface with the corporation's environments and as its liaison with the legislative process. A thousand questions about the GPD remain to be explained: his qualifications, his commitment to and understanding of the company interest, as well as the public interest, and the methods he would use to ensure a workable integration of the company's superego concerns with its economic concerns.[14]

Although, clearly, the concept of GPD won't catch fire overnight, the idea of the corporate conscience's being institutionalized in a particular office and person is not an entirely new one. GE and GM have each on their own initiative instituted "public responsibility" committees on their boards. Businessman and ethician Theodore Purcell has urged that one director sit on the board whose exclusive function would be to serve as ethics specialist and advocate.[15] Such private initiatives, however, still leave us with the problem of how to ensure institutional safeguards to protect the independence and clout of such corporate ethical officers. How little ready business is for the GPD that Stone recommends may be judged by business's reaction to Purcell's milder proposal: "To be frank, top manage-

---

[13]For one account of such a suicide, see "Blowing the Whistle Begins a Nightmare for Lawyer Joe Rose," *Wall Street Journal* (November 9, 1977), p. 1. See also Avery Comaro, "When Conscience and Career Collide," *Money* (September 1976), 48–52.

[14]On this crucially important last point, see the suggestive article by Add. Langhold and Johs. Lunde, "Empirical Methods for Business Ethics," *Review of Social Economy* (October 1977), 130–42.

Christopher Stone's proposal is aimed at large corporations (assets or sales of $1 billion annually). Accountability problems are less acute for small corporations where feedback from customers and shareholders can be more directly felt and where individual responsibility for decisions can be more directly assigned.

[15]Theodore Purcell, "Electing an 'Angel's Advocate' to the Board," *Management Review* (May 1976), 4–11.

ment executives have given me mostly negative feedback on the ethical advocacy idea," says Purcell.[16] But however reluctant the business community is to change from SR to SA, the pressures in that direction are gaining momentum. As of this writing, FTC chairman Michael Pertschuk has announced the formation of a social accountability task force to "study the inside, decision-making process" of the corporation—processes hitherto private and sacrosanct, as we have seen.[17] Senator Howard Metzenbaum, Chairman of the Subcommittee on Citizens' and Shareholders' Rights and Remedies, is exploring what should be done "to make corporations more accountable to their shareholders and to the public,"[18] and the SEC is engaged in similar investigations.

Social concern departments. A more modest step in the direction of SA would be the establishment within the corporation of departments explicitly charged to look out for the interests of business's various social constituencies. To be sure, a business's main concern is not social good works, but economic profitability. But note that, although management sits down to make economic policy, it cannot help but make social policy. Economic policy has human and social impact, and so the SA model calls for formal and institutional recognition of and accountability for such impact. There could be, for example, internal departments concerned with pollution, with safety, and with consumerism. In this way, responsibility could be pinpointed for the actual social impacts that a business's economic decisions have on a community. In the SR model, these human impacts are either ignored, or dealt with ex post facto, or left to chance.

Many companies are beginning to introduce departments of social concern, especially in the area of consumer affairs—and these are not always just "public-relations" ploys. For example, a Consumer and Community Affairs Department was established by Pennsylvania Power and Light Company, which plans to have every division meet regularly with consumer panels. In Cambridge, Ma., Polaroid Corporation staffs a 300-person Consumer Services Department responsible for such things as monitoring and rewriting ads, lest they be misleading, and personally running quality-control checks on Polaroid camera repair centers.[19] Such institutionalized SA can be far more sensitive to social concerns than can the courts. Such departments can monitor the whole interface of business with

[16]*Ibid.*, p. 10.
[17]"New Fire in the Drive to Reform Corporation Law," *Business Week* (November 21, 1977), 98.
[18]*Ibid.* Ralph Nader's well-argued book in favor of federal chartering of corporations details concrete procedures for assuring such accountability. See Nader *et al.*, *Taming the Giant Corporation* (New York: W. W. Norton and Co., 1976).
[19]"Corporate Clout for Consumers," *Business Week* (September 12, 1977), 144.

society, whereas the courts hear but a small fraction of society's concerns. What these departments learn can be included as input into the business decision-making process itself to forestall social problems, whereas the courts must operate after the damage is done. In this direction of self-assumed accountability lies business's greatest hope of avoiding further external regulation of the kind that might eventuate, for example, from the much-feared proposal for a federal agency for consumer protection advocacy.

Officer Accountability. Ralph Nader suggests a more radical avenue for pinpointing responsibility. He would forbid management to sit on the board of directors, and he would assign to each director a specific area of social responsibility. One, for example, would be accountable for the company's environmental impact, another for employee welfare and safety, and another for consumer interests.

Former SEC chairman William Carey would leave the present structure unchanged, but would give shareholders the right to sue irresponsible officers. Again, this is an effort to pinpoint responsibility, but it suffers from the problems of the SR model in that it leaves the decision-making process itself untouched; it seeks to remedy problems, rather than forestall them.

Christopher Stone suggests that procedures be developed for disbarring offending officers from executive practice analogously to disciplinary procedures in the legal and medical professions. Clearly, before this becomes feasible, ethical norms and the assignment of responsibility for their observance would have to be spelled out much more objectively and clearly than they are today. Swedish economists Add. Langholm and Johs. Lunde[20] have proposed that we cannot talk seriously about business ethics until empirical methods are brought to bear both in the determination of norms and in their implementation. For example, consumers' expectations regarding a business can be objectively determined by compiling and analyzing all the complaints that consumers bring against a business. The nature of the complaints gives a fair picture of the standards that a particular business is expected to uphold. Conversely, an examination of the ways the complaints are handled can give an objective picture of the standards that a business actually does uphold for itself. From such studies, precise behavioral norms could be established. Such objectively determined norms would then be explicitly included in the objectives of a business project. The decision-making would consciously advert to the ethical constraints under which a project must operate. These would be just as real and objective as the economic restraints and the space-and-time con-

[20]Langholm, *op. cit.*

straints, and like these latter, subject to continuing criticism and reevaluation. Similar procedures could be applied to the ethical dimensions of business's interface with its other constituencies. An objective approach like this to business ethics would make more feasible an objective accountability on the part of business officers.

Social audit. A step toward SA that is feasible and, indeed, sometimes practiced right now, is the social audit. "Knowledge is power": this is the premise that puts teeth into the social audit. I'm careful about that part of my behavior that's going to make the headlines. The mere publication of information is itself an act of accountability. Stone suggests that corporations be mandated to publish in their annual reports not only a financial audit, but also a social audit. What, for example, are a company's assets and liabilities regarding worker safety? What are the employee injury statistics this year compared to last? What are the prospects for the future? Similar reports could be made on minority hiring, on product tests, on lobbying, and on pollution disposal. Such knowledge is not innocent; it is not value-free knowledge. For example, that a certain machine regularly injures its operators poses a moral challenge to do something about that knowledge. The publication itself of such data will force the company to give an account of its response or of its failure to respond to such data.

Indeed, much recent legislation has taken the truth-releasing path of the enforcement of accountability. We have seen, for example, the Truth in Lending Act, the Truth in Packaging and Labeling Acts, increased corporate disclosure requirements by the FTC and SEC, "sunshine laws," and the like. As of this writing, OSHA is studying the advisability of disclosure rules, such as requiring companies to report their accident rates in their annual reports. OSHA is also concerned with building up health and safety data banks to serve as information resources for ensuring proper working conditions.

The prospect of all this fresh air has not been welcomed with wild enthusiasm on all sides. Legitimate issues of confidentiality can be raised. Consider, for example, OSHA's laudable aim of limiting workplace exposure to carcinogens. To achieve this goal, the National Institute for Occupational Safety and Health wants undisputed access to all data that could show a cause-effect relationship between illness and working conditions. This entails the gathering and use of employee medical records for epidemiological studies. Issues of consent, of confidentiality, and of possible abuse come immediately to mind.[21]

The mid-70's has witnessed a dampening of initial enthusiasm for social accounting. The National Association of Accountants recently sur-

[21]See "Health Records Face a Privacy Challenge," *Business Week* (October 31, 1977), 38.

veyed 800 major corporations, only to find that there has been little effective implementation of the social audit. Accountants are not unconcerned with social responsibility. Indeed, the report states:

> (T)here is little doubt but that the pressures for increased levels of corporate social responsibility have led to the strengthening of the public affairs function and thus have created a more active force within organizations for social responsibility and social accountability.[22]

A genuine interest exists in translating SR into SA. But effective methods for doing this have proved elusive. One comptroller describes social accounting as "shovelling smoke." Perhaps accountants are not the best qualified to perform a social audit.

12. EVALUATION OF THE SA MODEL

Proponents of SR raise one major objection to the SA model that underlies all the others. The SA model is faulted for its reliance on governmental intervention into business's internal affairs, viz., into the internal structure of the corporation's decision-making procedures. And such intervention is especially intolerable because, in the SR view, government is even less accountable than is business. Lee Loevinger argues,[23] for example, that government is the real monopoly to be feared. There are no business monopolies except those established by the government. The fact that business critics must rely on the concept of "shared monopolies" or oligopolies attests to the fact that true business monopolies do not exist. But, the argument continues, governmental monopoly most certainly does exist, which is why it is dangerous to locate business decision-making power in government bureaucracies. True, some few top governmental officials are elected by the people, and are in this sense accountable. But the government's effective operations are carried on by regulatory agencies. These agencies, and the bureaucrats that staff them, are accountable, perhaps, in the sense that they need annual appropriations from Congress. But these bureaucrats have far more job security than do their career-manager

---

[22]"Social Accounting: A Puff of Smoke?", *Management Review* (November 1977), 4. Disclosure as a path to accountability is already being implemented and is in process of being extended. The SEC is drafting rules to require the disclosure of the composition, functions and compensation of committees of the boards of directors, as well as of the relationships between directors and management. The U.N. Commission on Transnational Corporations is recommending disclosure by multinationals of employment and production data, transfer pricing policies, significant new products and processes, new capital-investment programs, the cost and effect of announced mergers, and environmental-impact information.

[23]Loevinger, *op. cit.*

counterparts in business. These latter, when inefficient and ineffective, simply won't last in the job: that's accountability. But government bureaucrats, who control the flow of information, and who effectively shape policy and enforce it, retain their positions administration after administration: that's not accountability. The SA model wants the likes of these to be the ultimate moral monitors of business decisions. Their jobs are safe. There are no consumers or stockholders to monitor them, nor voters either. Misguided business decisions can hurt an industry. But misguided governmental decisions can hurt the whole society.

While SR rejects such governmental initiatives, it also rejects unbridled freedom for the business enterprise. In other words, SR does not embrace anarchical opinions like that expressed during an October 1977 conference at Menlo Park on "The Legitimacy of the Corporation":

> A private corporation should have the legal right to build an atomic bomb and drop it wherever it pleases, subject only to having to pay any damages it causes.[24]

The young philosopher who delivered himself on this sentiment is completely out of tune with business's present stance toward reforms in the area of corporate autonomy and governance. The Business Roundtable, for example, although it does reject the idea that such reforms should take place under government auspices, is increasingly responsive to pressures on business to legitimate its activities. Business is being called upon to show precisely why its traditional autonomy is beneficial to society, and precisely how abuses of this autonomy can be adequately controlled from within the business community without legal prodding from outside.

Which direction do you personally think an institutionalized business ethics should take—that of SR or of SA? SR assumes that business can clean its own house and introduce effective self-regulatory procedures on its own initiative. The Report of the 54th American Assembly exemplifies a concrete proposal for self-regulation through SR.[25] Some of the accountability structures there proposed resemble those suggested by Christopher Stone above—but the initiative for and the implementation of these is to

[24]*Business Week* (November 21, 1977), 100.

[25]Represented at the Assembly were viewpoints from commerce, finance and industry, labor, foundations, higher education, communications, all branches of government and law, the military, and civic organizations. The Social Responsibility recommendations covered every phase of corporate life including all of business's constituencies, the board, the audit process, communications, management, and the public sector. The general thrust of the report was that business must undertake immediate and comprehensive self-regulation, or government will rightly intervene. The background papers are published in William Dill (ed.), *Running the American Corporation* (Englewood Cliffs, N.J.: Prentice-Hall, Inc., 1978).

come from business, not from government. The SR and SA models both oppose business anarchy and unregulated free enterprise. Both models see the need for self-regulation and accountability on the part of business. The question is whether or not effective accountability can realistically be expected from initiatives by the private sector, or whether the path to it lies in the direction of government intervention and, perhaps, federal chartering of corporations. Is the corporate *persona* as it legally exists today with the rights and immunities described above a likely subject for self-reform and self-imposed accountability? This is the main decision you have to make as you evaluate for yourself the relative merits of SR, as opposed to SA, in business ethics at the institutional level. As you come to your decision, note the need for safeguards against zealotry and tyranny at the hands of nonaccountable government bureaucrats. But keep in mind that, the whole thrust of SA is toward assisting business to be *self*-policing, thereby diminishing the need for external regulation. And when *everyone* has to be accountable, self-policing becomes easier for all: virtue is rewarded instead of being penalized. As it is now, SR is left to the "conscience" of the individual corporation, and the exercise of SR can involve competitive disadvantage vis-à-vis the less conscientious corporations. SA does not suffer from this difficulty.

DISCUSSION QUESTIONS

1. Consider this statement by Milton Friedman: "Have you ever heard anyone suggest that the "Mom and Pop" corner grocery store should sell food below cost to help the poor people who shop there? Well, that would obviously be absurd! Any corner grocery that operated that way would be out of business very soon. The same is true on a large scale. The large enterprise can have money to exercise social responsibility only if it has a monopoly position: if it is able to hire employees at lower wages than they are worth: if it is able to sell products at a higher price than can otherwise be charged."[26]

a. Which SR model is assumed by Friedman? Is it SR understood as "good works" over and above the essential day-to-day business decisions? Or is it SR involved in the basic economic decisions a business makes in order to survive and grow? What kinds of activity would manifest SR in Friedman's sense of the term?

b. In *your* view, is a "Mom and Pop" store confronted with the di-

[26]Milton Friedman as quoted by Paul Haas, "Social Responsibility, an Indicator of Market Power," *Review of Social Economy* (October 1977), 189; reprinted from *Business and Society Review* (Spring 1967), Copyright 1967, Warren Gorham and Lamont, Inc., 210 South St., Boston, Ma., all rights reserved.

lemma of either bankruptcy *with* SR or survival *without* SR? If your answer differs from Friedman's, account for the difference.

c. Does your answer to the previous question also hold for large corporations? Explain.

d. What concerns of the SA model of business's responsibility are omitted from Friedman's apparent understanding of SR?

2. Increasingly since 1974, Nestlé has been the target of mounting criticism for sales policies it is pursuing vis-à-vis the Third World. Other companies could just as well have been singled out, but Nestlé has become the symbolic focus of this protest. Nestlé produced infant formula and, quite understandably, wanted to market it as widely as possible. The product is a good one, and there is no overt deception in the advertising campaign. With the birth rate declining in the West, Nestlé looked elsewhere to expand the market for its baby formula. It is the Third World these days that is producing babies. So Nestlé targeted this market with a super hard-sell campaign for the formula. Radio jingles and billboards touted the advantages of infant formula over mother's milk. Doctors and hospitals received films, booklets and free samples. Clinics were set up where women in white taught Third-World mothers the superiority of formula over breast-feeding. The campaign has had its effect. There has been a sharp fall-off in breast-feeding in countries where this campaign has been in force. Formula sales have climbed.

This economic success, however, has come at a human price. A 1976 UN Seminar on The New International Economic Order extensively explored the infant-formula issue. The conclusion was that in the name of profit, a good product can become a harmful one. The human problems revolve around sanitation and cost. Clearly, sterile water is essential to the use of infant formula, as are sterile bottles and nipples. The targeted women had no comprehension of such procedures nor the wherewithal to carry them out. Result: bacterial infection, diarrhea, dehydration, and death for the infants. The second problem is cost. The UN Protein Advisory Group estimated that it would take one-third to two-thirds of a family's income (depending on the country) to feed a six-month-old baby on the formula. So the mothers, not surprisingly, took to diluting the formula to stretch a four-day supply anywhere up to five weeks. Result: malnutrition and consequent brain damage for the infants, and higher death rates for babies on the formula, compared to those who were breast-fed.

a. If a company sells a good product complete with directions for its proper use, why should it be held responsible if consumers misuse it? Can the SR model be expected to forestall the kinds of human harm that seem to have occurred in the Nestlé case?

b. Along with economic impact studies, should a company make a human and social impact study of a product before marketing it? Privately, according to Nader, executives at Nestlé are realizing that the aforementioned misuses are foreseeable and serious. Is there any ethical duty to act on such a recognition of probable harm?

   c. Concerning products that are not only unnecessary but also likely to do harm, is it reasonable to expect companies not to market them if they can do so legally? This question could apply not merely to Nestlé and the Third-World poor, but also to the domestic liquor, tobacco, and handgun industries. Can you suggest modes of accountability that could forestall these kinds of social harm flowing from decisions that are economically sound?

SUGGESTED READINGS

1. *Readings on SR*
Davis, Keith. "The Case For and Against Business Assumption of Social Responsibility," *Academy of Management Journal*, June 1973, 312–22.
Dill, William R. (ed.). *Running the American Corporation*. Englewood Cliffs, N.J.: Prentice-Hall, Inc., 1978.
Friedman, Milton. "The Social Responsibility of Business Is to Increase Profits," *New York Times Sunday Magazine*, September 13, 1970, p. 146.
Hay, Robert and Ed Gray. "Social Responsibilities of Business Managers," *Academy of Management Journal*, March 1974, 135–43.
Loevinger, Lee. "Social Responsibility in a Democratic Society," *Vital Speeches of the Day*, April 15, 1973.
Taylor, John F. A. "Is the Corporation Beyond the Law?" *Harvard Business Review*, March-April, 1965.
Wilbur, Dr. James B. (ed.). *Human Values and Economic Activity*. Geneseo, N.Y: State University College at Geneseo, 1978.

2. *Readings on SA*
Langhold, Odd. and Johs. Lunde. "Empirical Methods for Business Ethics," *Review of Social Economy*, October 1977, 130–42.
Nader, Ralph, Mark Green and Joel Seligman. *Taming the Giant Corporation*. New York: W. W. Norton Co., Inc., 1976.
Purcell, Theodore. "Electing an 'Angel's Advocate' to the Board," *Management Review*, May 1976, 4–11.
Stone, Christopher. *Where the Law Ends: The Social Control of Corporate Behavior*. New York: Harper and Row, 1975.
Winter, Ralph K. *Government and the Corporation*, Washington, D.C., American Enterprise Institute for Public Policy Studies, 1978.

CHAPTER 8

THE PRAGMATIC vs. THE EXPEDIENT

If you follow the pragmatic method, you cannot look on any (purely verbal solution) as closing your quest. You must bring out of each word its practical cash value.

William James[1]

The life which men, women, and children actually lead, the opportunities open to them, the values they are capable of enjoying, their education, their share of all the things of art and science, are mainly determined by economic conditions. Hence we can hardly expect a moral system which ignores economic conditions to be other than remote and empty. . . . To many persons, the idea that the ends professed by morals are impotent save as they are connected with the working machinery of economic life seems like deflowering the purity of moral values and obligations.

This distinction between higher and lower types of value is itself something to be looked into. Why should there be a sharp distinction made between some goods as physical and material and others as ideal and "spiritual"?

John Dewey[2]

[1]William James, *Pragmatism and Four Essays from the Meaning of Truth* (New York: New American Library, 1974), p. 46; reprinted by permission of the David McKay Co., Inc.

[2]John Dewey, *The Quest for Certainty* (New York: G. P. Putnam's Sons, 1929), pp. 282, 283, 269–70.

OBJECTIVES FOR CHAPTER **8**:

1. To see how values translate into action;
2. To understand the premises of pragmatic philosophy:
   (a) the role of intelligence;
   (b) pragmatism's rejection of mere expedience;
   (c) pragmatism's radical sociality;
3. To understand the ethics that follows from these premises, and how to apply the five-step pragmatic method for making ethically responsible decisions;
4. To evaluate critically for oneself the main objections leveled against pragmatism as a business philosophy.

1. VALUES-CLARIFICATION EXERCISE AND THE "ACTION-TEST" OF VALUES

Business ethics remains nothing but empty moralizing unless it leads to an action payoff. So say the pragmatic philosophers to whom we now turn. William James, a founder of the movement, goes so far as to insist that you must bring out the "practical cash value" of what you say about ethics (or about anything else, for that matter). Self-deception about values is a common human failing that the pragmatists want to avoid.

The most frequent delusion is to claim devotion to values that one doesn't really cherish at all. Take, for example, an NBA owner who professes great dedication to and sense of responsibility for the city that his basketball team represents. What will you think of his values if at year's end he suddenly whisks his franchise off to another state without consulting the city fathers or anyone else? He might have felt himself to be a devoted community leader. He may even have come to believe his own propaganda. But his actions proved otherwise. Saying so doesn't make it so.

It is the "action test" that will tear aside the veil of self-deception about values. When I am tempted either to disclaim values that are really present, or to claim values that are really absent, the proof of the pudding will be my actions. To better understand how values translate into actions, take a moment now to do the following values test. Consider each item in the list. Is it a value to you? Write your answers in the appropriate columns as illustrated in the first example.

Psychologist Louis Raths has shown how action is the great revealer of where one's values really lie. If you want to know the Ten Commandments of a businessman's morality or of a business's corporate ethics, look

Item	Is it a value to you?	How you act on it.	How you could act on it.
(1) Higher income.	Yes	I opened a term-deposit saving account.	Could make cost/benefit analysis of owning a second car.
(2) More leisure time.			
(3) Better health & physical condition.			
(4) More effective relationships with employees &/or co-workers.			
(5) More satisfying job.			
(6) Cut down smoking/drinking.			
(7) Lower food costs.			
(8) More assistance from spouse re career advancement.			
(9) Lower car-insurance costs.			
(10) Less interference from family in my work & leisure.			
(11) Life in a pollution-free environment.			
(12) Vacation in (you name the place).			
(13) _____ (Name a value important to your business or to business in general)			
(14) _____ "			
(15) _____ "			

at the policies that are actually practiced. It is not the framed list of moral maxims hanging on your office wall, but your actions that reveal what brand of business ethics you follow.

So however much a person claims that there's no room for morality in the business world, his actions speak even louder of the morality and philosophy of life that actually guide him. One may or may not be proud of this morality, but it is there. And on the other hand, if the morality one claims to have is less a matter of practice than of public relations, then his actions will reveal this too, and give the lie to high-sounding press releases.

We tend to think of morality in terms of ideals existing somewhere in a moral heaven. Louis Raths, using John Dewey's pragmatism, brings the world of values down to earth. Values are observable and testable. In valuing something, three very concrete kinds of behavior are involved, viz., prizing, choosing freely, and acting. First, quite obviously, a value is something I prize and cherish, and am willing to talk about publicly. Consider the head of an advertising agency who once asked his vice-presidents to describe the aim of the company. The vice-presidents' answer to him was never in doubt—to produce the best ads in the business. "Wrong!" said the agency head; "the number one aim is to make money. Aim number two to make more money. Likewise aim number three." That man knew what he cherished and was willing to say so out loud.

But saying so isn't enough. A value is something I choose freely and with awareness of the consequences of my choice. A genuine value is the result of a free and rational decision. If a papermill introduces pollution controls only under the gun of a court order threatening to close it down, one rightly doubts such a company's genuine devotion to a clean environment. It would not act when it had the opportunity for free decision. Often, even the opportunity for free action is lacking. Ralph Nader and his Corporate Accountability Research Group (CARG), for example, would establish among other things an " employees' bill of rights." Companies would be prohibited from firing employees who disclose facts concerning corporate law-breaking to appropriate government agencies. Honest disclosure can't be a genuine value unless there is a climate of freedom in which disclosure can operate.

The third and final step in the valuing process is to translate these choices into a consistent pattern of action. This is the crucial acid test of value. It is conventional wisdom that American consumers value satisfactory goods and services. But do they? A consumer group, Call for Action, Inc., in a 34-city survey discovered that American consumers find something wrong with 28 percent of the goods and services they buy, but that they complain to the seller in only a third of the cases. Until the demand for consumer satisfaction gets translated into consistent action, it does not qualify as a genuine value.

In this section we have made two points. No business or business person is completely disinterested, "objective," and value-free. You may never give moral values a second thought, but the fact remains that a value system underlies your beliefs and actions. The task is to clarify what this value system is. The second point we made is simply this: Action is the acid test of value. Your free, rational decisions that translate into a working business policy give an accurate picture of where your values really lie.

Let's look now at the philosophy that underpins this action approach to values.

2. DIRECTION IN ETHICS WITHOUT DOGMATISM OR DRIFT

This value test assumed that values do exist and that values are revealed in action. So you should be suspicious about claiming to *value* what you don't take *action* on. Pragmatism is the name of this philosophy born in America that makes action the test of moral value. Action can point a moral direction in a climate where traditional guidelines have broken down.

We have been reviewing alternative philosophies that are used to anchor ethical values in corporate conduct. Business doesn't create moral values, but rather uses the values given by other value-shaping institutions. The Women's Movement, for example, highlights the value of equal opportunity for women; business lives with this. Civil-rights leaders, eventually backed up by the courts, have crystallized racial equality as a value; business is coming to accept it. Religion in the past more than now made a value of the "work ethic"; business adopted this to its own ends. The values of business mirror the values of the wider society. When the value-shaping institutions of the wider society falter, then the values of business lose anchor and are set adrift. Family, religion and education had been such value-shaping institutions, but have badly faltered in filling that role. Perhaps this trend is beginning to reverse itself, but American values do not find the strong anchor they once did in these institutions. Mainstream religions have become less dogmatic and even unsure about ethical values. The family has ceded moral education to the schools—schools that often boast of being value-neutral, and which on principle eschew the religious dimension of human life. So while often business people facilely appeal to family, religion and education for value-direction, these institutions have not been as responsive as their press would have them be. Whence a sense of drift in business ethics.

The drift is there, but the human need morally to justify behavior lives on. In this book so far, business behavior has been justified by appeals to human nature. These various philosophies of life—some might call them ideologies about human nature—each carry very specific consequences for business ethics. Spencerian dogmas about automatic progress and laissez-faire legislate a business climate in which it is believed that self-aggrandizement will inevitably work for the physical and moral improvement of society: what *is* and what *ought* to be are identical. Machiavellian ideology, on the other hand, saw the world of *what is* as the enemy of what *ought to be*. So Machiavellian human nature dictates that expedience must be the rule in business ethics. Ayn Rand, like Spencer, looks in objective reality for a guide to ethical behavior. Progress, however, is not inevitable. The business person becomes ethical only when he/she learns to follow unsentimentally the objective laws of reality. These three business philosophies have one thing in common, viz., a confidence that human nature and objective reality can supply a norm for business ethics.

Hobbes and Hume, however, were not so sanguine about the orderliness of objective reality and the lawfulness of human nature. They saw business ethics as involving subjectively constructed meanings rather than objectively imposed order. For Hobbes, as we've seen, the state of nature is a state of moral anarchy in which business and commerce would be impossible. It is only man-made laws, enforced by the state's supreme authority, that impose order upon this natural chaos. Hume also considered ethics to be subjective—rooted in the common feelings of mankind, especially in sympathy and fellow feeling, as expressed by society's conventions. The Jeffersonian tradition in America, sharing Hume's optimistic reading of human nature, would have confidence in the social responsibility model of business decision-making: people are to be trusted more than government. For John Adams, on the other hand, as for Hobbes, every man is presumed to be a scoundrel: so trust government more than people. The social-accountability model is congenial to this pessimistic reading of human nature.

Finally, the movement from conventional ethics and legalistic ethics to pragmatism is a movement from heteronomy to autonomy. The former two philosophies are other-centered. They look to the group, i.e., to society's conventions or to society's laws, for moral guidance. Pragmatism, on the other hand, places ethical responsibility squarely on the shoulders of business and the business person. The business philosophies to be considered in the final part of this book are prescriptions for autonomy in morals. This is not a return, however, to the egoism of social Darwinism and objectivism. Rather, it is an autonomy that is respectful of others, but without the moral conformism to others that characterized conventional morality and legalism.

Pragmatism as a business philosophy is neither completely subjective in ethics nor completely objective. It espouses neither optimism nor pessimism in its view of humankind. Pragmatism is ideally suited to mediate between dualisms such as these. It offers a method for arriving at responsible business decisions without the dogmatisms of some of the aforementioned business philosophies but also without relapsing into aimless moral drift. As such, it is a philosophy peculiarly suited to the American spirit, and especially to the temper of the American business person.

3. NOT NATURAL SELECTION BUT INTELLIGENT SELECTION

Pragmatic business people do not see themselves as slaves to iron laws of evolution. There is no inevitable force called natural selection ruthlessly weeding out the unfit and rewarding the fit. The economic environment of business does not stand as some fixed norm challenging them to meet its measure or go under. No. For the pragmatist nature is not in charge of man, but rather man is in control of nature. Problem-solving, not laissez-faire, is the pragmatist's basic stance toward business. Action is the watchword of pragmatism. You are what you do. The mind is what the mind does. And what the mind does is to solve problems. As problems arise in the business world, the human animal is blessed with intelligence, a tool or instrument for solving these problems. The pragmatist, like the social Darwinist, adopts an evolutionary stance toward the world. But for the pragmatist, the business person and not impersonal evolution is in the driver's seat. And intelligence is what puts him/her there. Intelligent problem-solving, then, is going to be the key to business ethics and the basis of a norm for discerning ethical from unethical behavior.

No Spencerian determinism here. Freedom is the rule. Human beings direct the course of evolution. This is a prescription for neither blind optimism nor despairing pessimism. Business can better the quality of human life or worsen it. "Better" is the key word. Pragmatic philosopher John Dewey calls this view of evolution meliorism, literally "better-ism." This down-to-earth, problem-solving approach to business ethics is situational and rational.

First, it is a situation ethics. No business person has to be told that the world doesn't stand still. Change is the norm. So an unchanging set of ethical prescriptions is not much help to the decision-maker who must operate in a context of change, process, and evolution. An inflexible ethics won't work in a fluid world. Situations are unique, and the decision-maker needs to respect this uniqueness. He rightly shies away from heavy-handedly imposing unbending ethical rules upon situations that change from day to day and from place to place. There is a standard of right and wrong, to be sure. But the pragmatist says that this standard must be able to cope with uniqueness and change.

Intelligence is such a standard. So we call this ethics rational. The intelligent decision is the morally good decision in a pragmatic ethics. The blind or irrational decision, the narrowly expedient decision—these are what the pragmatist calls moral evil. So you don't have to do dumb things in the name of morality. The case is quite the opposite. Intelligent problem-solving is the mark of virtue. Ethical values are not something up in the sky for our contemplation. No. They are woven into the concrete, tough, ever-changing situations in which business decisions take place.

So nothing is sacred in the sense that there is no moral value that we dare not submit to the scrutiny of human intelligence. John Dewey spent his life urging that we bring intelligence to bear on our moral and social problems the same way that we have so successfully applied it in the physical, technological world. He sought to heal the rift between the world of ethical ideals on the one hand and the world of scientific fact on the other. We tend to look on morality as somehow pregiven and settled, whereas the world in which science operates is unsettled and changing. We tend therefore to see ethics as a matter of heart and science as a matter of mind. Virtue, we think, means devotion to permanent ideals, while science grapples with the world of change. Not so, says Dewey. Ethics and economics operate in the same world. Both challenge mind more than heart. Both concern truth more than feelings.

4. THE MARRIAGE OF "IS" AND "OUGHT"

By placing intelligence at the heart of ethics, pragmatism heals the Machiavellian rift between what *is* and what *ought* to be. Moral decisions no less than economic ones are played out in the world of fact and action. Recall Machiavelli's claim that morality is confined to private life, while expedience must be the rule in public life, in the business world. Moral idealism is supposedly at odds with business realism. The pragmatist vigorously denies this Machiavellian claim. To be ethical is not to be unrealistic. Ethics is for public and private life alike. The method of intelligence demands realism in business decisions. The method of intelligence shuns the path of easy expedience. And the most intelligent business decision is by that very fact the most ethical business decision. "Is" and "ought" go hand in hand. There is probably no greater misunderstanding of this business philosophy than to confuse the pragmatic with the expedient. Wherefore, we have entitled this chapter "The Pragmatic versus the Expedient."

Narrow expedience looks to the short run; it has a tunnel-vision of business decisions. In other words, it puts blinders on the mind's eye. It blocks out inconvenient evidence, thereby failing to take the whole picture into account. This is irrational and therefore immoral, in the pragmatic view. True pragmatism's approach to philosophy and to ethics is holistic.

Businesses and business people alike exist in interlocking context of systems. An intelligent decision, then, must be responsive to the whole context within which a business decision takes place. In this holistic view, it makes no sense to oppose private morality and public expedience, as the Machiavellian would do. A businessman who is also a family man exists in both contexts. His identity comes from both; so his ethics must be responsive to both. To reserve ethics for the family and expedience for business ignores the fact that it is the same person who moves in both worlds. To deny either world in the name of expedience is to deny part of himself. This would be irrational, unpragmatic and, therefore, immoral.

5. BEYOND EGOISM AND ALTRUISM: THE SOCIAL SELF

Equally balanced and contextual is the pragmatic way of viewing the human person or "self." Ayn Rand puts the cart before the horse when she focuses on the individual business person operating in lonely autonomous isolation. A purely private ethics is as chimerical as a purely private existence. Human morality is something shared, something that is first and foremost held in common. Pragmatism's understanding of human evolution is profoundly social. It is wrong to conceive of society as made up of self-sufficient atomic individuals. Rather, it is because individuals, as humans, are born of society that they are enabled, as integral parts of society, to advance its evolution. The evolution of human selves is first and foremost social.

Pragmatist George Herbert Mead has done most to articulate the essentially social nature of human selves. Consider Mead's account of how an organism becomes a "self." Note the implied evolutionary approach. I am not born as a ready-made self. I must become a self. I must become the other in order to be myself. The individual is not the self. The self is the social process constituted by the interacting individuals. And it is their ability each to take the role of the other that enables them to play this social-selving game.

Childhood play and childhood games are ways in which children practice at becoming selves. First, at the stage of play, the child takes on different roles in turn. A boy pretends to be a policeman, Daddy, garbageman, Indian, bionic man. Thus, he exercises that unique human ability of getting in the shoes of the other, an ability so necessary to the socialization process by which he acquires a self. Secondly, at the stage of game, the process becomes more sophisticated. Consider a softball game. Charlie Brown standing all alone on the pitcher's mound in the pouring rain cannot be said to have a pitching self. Only through interacting with batter, catcher, infielders, outfielders, umpires, crowd and coaches does a pitching self come into existence. Only by taking the role of and responding to the expectations of my fellow players do I acquire a pitching self-identity. Soft-balling is a social-selving process in which by taking the role of their fellow players each acquires the social-selving identity of the soft-balling social act, the softball game. To play any position successfully, I must be able to take the role of all the other players simultaneously and to respond to their varying expectations. A first baseman, when the ball is bunted, anticipates that the pitcher will cover first, the catcher will back him up, the batter will run, the umpire will hover over the bag, and so makes the fielding and throwing response to these expectations accordingly. Note that unlike the stage of play, the softball player is not taking the role of others singly and in turn, but has somehow gotten into the varying roles of fellow players simultaneously. The first baseman is interacting now not with one other, but with what Mead calls a generalized other, and is thus enabled to respond to their complex expectations, thereby acquiring a rather sophisticated first-baseman self. The players together constitute the soft-balling selving process. No individual player alone has a softball self. Each participant in the game has a differing perspective on the same social act. The ability of each to take the role of the generalized other enables them to play and thereby acquire a soft-balling social self-identity.

The childhood game is a paradigm of the social acts that go on in society at large. It illustrates how I am constituted a social self, by taking part in my family game, in nation games, language games, job games, marriage games, church games, and more to our point, business games. The game metaphor is not meant to imply that these social processes are trivial. After all, it is through such social acts that I become the person that I am. There is nothing trivial about acquiring a self-identity. The game metaphor is simply intended to stress the social, processive, behavioristic, and structured character of the business process and of the way that ethics functions in that process.

Now let's look more carefully at this social self process that characterizes the business world. The business game can be viewed from two distinct but complementary points of view. First, there are the objective given rules of the game. This is the given predictable structure of the business process. Then there is the subjective side of the game, viz., the players' responses to these rules, responses which are unpredictable, creative, novel. Consider each in turn.

The objective side is what society expects of business. The roles and the rules are there. Defined responsibilities, hierarchies of authority, standard operating procedures, quotas to be met—all of these give an internal structure and form to the business process. Agencies, regulations, laws, private and public pressure groups add their own configurations to this structure. If this were the whole story, then Hume would be right. "Accepted practice" would be the moral guide. Business ethics would be no more than a matter of following the mores and conventions of business's various constituencies. But conventional morality is incomplete. It ignores the subjective side of the business game—the players.

In spite of all these objective constraints on individual business people, you still are never quite sure how the game is going to turn out. Ayn Rand's view of the autonomous individual opting for rational self-interest in splendid isolation fails to do justice to the very real outside constraints on business decisions. She does, however, understand that individuals need not surrender their autonomy to society. The business process, for the pragmatist, involves the interplay of subjective freedom in a context of objective constraint. Players in the business game can and do make an impact in the various creative and novel ways that each responds to the rules. Neither egoism nor altruism does justice to the business process or to business ethics. The pragmatic social self is an interplay of both, of subjective and objective, of individuals and institutions.

6. BEYOND ABSOLUTISM AND RELATIVISM: THE SCIENTIFIC MODEL FOR ETHICAL DECISIONS

It's time now to get down to specifics. We come to the very heart of pragmatism as a business philosophy, to wit, the *method* it proposes for making ethically sound decisions. It's all very well to advocate a balanced interplay between individuals and institutions. And few would quarrel with the proposal that moral ideals should be closely wedded to realistic practical action. But how? Pragmatism tells how: it offers a method of ethical decision-making based on the scientific model.

This is a radical departure from our traditional approach to moral values. We spoke above about the dogmatism on the one hand, and the sense of drift on the other, that pervades our current thinking about ethics and morality. The old morality looks to tradition and authority for its values. The so-called "new morality," having lost faith in traditional authorities, seeks to ground morality in the sincere feelings of individuals. Old and new share one thing in common: they are both mindless. Blind reliance on authority—moral absolutism—and blind reliance on feeling—moral relativism—are both alike blind. A main preoccupation of John Dewey's whole life was to bring the mind to bear on social and moral problems. The pragmatist sees the moral life not as surrender of will to authority, not as an expression of loving feelings, but as an exercise of intelligence: whence, the method.

So we'll not talk about *what's* good—moral rules. Rather our concern is with *how* to be good—moral method. Science, says the pragmatist, has given us the most powerful method for ascertaining truth that humankind has ever devised. We haven't begun to realize its full potential. This method has landed men on the moon, has generated technological marvels in communications, transportation, medicine and weaponry. But we haven't begun to bring this method to bear upon the determination of moral truth. The scientific model of thinking can illuminate and enrich our moral lives as it has done our physical lives. Of course, we don't live our moral lives under laboratory conditions. So the method will have to undergo some adaptations when applied to business ethics. But the overall pattern is similar whether we are talking about inquiry into physical truth or inquiry into moral and ethical truth. Ethics, like science, is basically a matter of problem-solving. And problem-solving involves five steps.

Step one: a felt perplexity. Doubtless, most of us get through the business day without the need to ponder ethical dilemmas or to make any decision that explicitly involves moral conscience. Our lives are routinized and our morality is built into our characteristic attitudes and patterns of decision. In other words, we have developed a character that spontaneously sustains our moral lives. Occasions for coming to grips with a moral decision may be few and far between. The pragmatist has no wish to disturb you in this happy state of "unproblematic experience," as Dewey calls it. He is prepared to deal with genuine problems, not artificially induced ones. So if in your daily work routines nothing bothers or challenges your conscience, just be glad and go about your business.

Alas, for most of us, this happy state of tranquil evolution is not destined to continue undisturbed for long. We stumble onto problems, yes even ethical problems. An alarm goes off inside of us, "something's wrong here." A shock, a disturbance breaks the happy course of our evolving lives. This, then, is the first step in making a moral decision. A "felt perplexity" triggers immediate awareness of a problem. We are pulled up short. The person who was cruising along so smoothly in the driver's seat of my conscience grinds to a halt. What am I going to do? What *should* I do? What is the ethically correct course of action in this situation?

Note that we are not dealing with abstract ethical principles. Moral decision-making takes place in the heart of concrete lived experience. Ethical dilemmas present themselves in specific situations and are to be dealt with concretely and situationally. It's not a matter of determining what's right in general, but rather of deciding the right thing to do here and now. Awareness of a concrete problem triggers inquiry into a concrete solution.

Suppose, for example, that sales manager Jones is troubled about Pete who used to be a star member of the sales force. Recently Jones notes a fall-off in Pete's performance. At first Jones ignores it. The problem may be temporary. Perhaps it will take care of itself. But the situation continues to deteriorate. Jones becomes increasingly uneasy. He begins to suspect that Pete has a serious problem with drink. Finally he can ignore it no longer. The job's just not getting done in Pete's sales territory. Things have come to a head. Something's got to be done about it. This kind of felt perplexity is the first step of a moral decision. Pete's performance, which has been an unproblematic part of Jones' work world, has become a problematic situation. This particular phase of the business process has ground to a halt. Jones has to get things moving again. He is like a laboratory scientist intrigued by observation of unexpected phenomena. "Hey, what's going on here?" the scientist asks, as he launches into the application of the scientific method. Similarly, Jones is perplexed. And if he is a pragmatist, his way of resolving the problem will be modelled on the tried-and-true scientific method. This brings us to the next step.

Step two: defining the data of the problem. The world changes. Situations are unique. Seldom is one problem exactly like another. It is unlikely that the solutions of yesterday's moral dilemmas will work today, because it is unlikely that yesterday's moral dilemmas resemble today's in every respect. So it is incumbent upon the decision-maker that he/she define the data of the problem at hand so as to appreciate it in all its uniqueness. No responsible laboratory scientist leaves out inconvenient data. To deliberately distort, ignore, or falsify the data would be a fundamental breach of scientific integrity. Fidelity to the method is the moral demand that his work makes on the scientist. Reason places a similar moral demand on the business person. His place of work may be anything but an antiseptic laboratory. But failure to make his work decisions with fidelity to the data would be a breach of moral integrity no less than a like failure would be on the part of the scientist. You see what this means. A good managerial decision is not *opposed* to a good moral decision. Rather, the two go hand in hand. Morality is not something awkwardly tacked onto managerial decisions. A management decision made with full fidelity to the scientific model is by that fact also a decision made with moral integrity.

Back to Jones's problem with Pete. Like the scientist, Jones must define all the data of the problem. Underline *all*. A moral perplexity is due to a *conflict* of interests. Spell out the conflicting data of the problem:

　　1. Pete has proven potential for excellent performance and Jones would hate to lose him.

2. His drinking problem is blocking that potential.
3. The consequent dip in sales is hurting the company and must be remedied.

It would be bad management and bad morals to pretend that any one of these factors did not exist. Inconvenient facts don't disappear of their own accord. A complete and accurate diagnosis of the problem sets the stage for an adequate solution. A scientist who fiddles with the data to make it come out right is drummed out of the community of scholars. Such wishful thinking is morally offensive in the business world as well.

Step three: entertaining hypotheses that take all of the data into account. The scientific, rational, and therefore ethically correct hypothesis will take all of the data into account. A hypothesis that ignores any of the data is irrational, and therefore irresponsible and unethical in this pragmatic way of looking at things. In the case of Jones and Pete, the company's sales process has broken down. Jones needs a hypothesis or plan of action that will reconstruct the situation, reconcile the conflict, so that the company can once again begin to move and evolve in an unproblematic way. Here are some possible plans of action that attempt to deal with the whole problem:

(a) Confront Pete with his recent performance record and drinking problem. Threaten to fire him if he doesn't stop drinking. Suggest Alcoholics Anonymous. Set a realistic sales quota you expect him to meet. Express confidence in him due to his past good track record.

(b) Confront Pete with his recent performance record and drinking problem. Grant him a three-month furlough with half pay to straighten himself out. At the end of this period the decision will be made to reinstate or terminate him. Tell him how you'd hate to lose him because he can be a good performer. Assign temporaries to cover Pete's sales territory.

(c) Call Pete in, and express your concern about his sales. Negotiate with him a mutually acceptable quota, and have him present a definite plan and schedule for achieving it. Tell him that you don't believe in interfering with employees' personal habits, but that you expect him to take care that they don't interfere with performance.

There are many other possible solutions, of course, and the more you can think of the better. Each of these three hypotheses tries to do justice to all the data. Each faces the necessity for improving sales. Each tries to salvage Pete's proven potential. And none ignores the drinking problem. "Solutions" that fail to take all of the data into account are irresponsible. Indeed, they are not really solutions at all. Here are some examples of incomplete and therefore irresponsible hypotheses:

(d) Fire Pete on the spot, and hire a replacement (ignores Pete's proven potential).

(e) Call Pete in, urge him to improve and set a quota for him to meet (ignores the drinking problem).

(f) Get Pete into the company's alcoholic rehabilitation program so that when he is recovered he'll perform at his former high level (ignores the company's immediate problem with sales).

Such incomplete hypotheses just don't work. That is their pragmatic sin. No workable solution can ignore part of the problem. This is the lesson that the scientific model of thinking brings to our moral lives.

Step four: consider the consequences of acting on each hypothesis. If you get the feeling that all this is obvious and that this is the natural way that any sensible person would tackle any problem, you are absolutely right. When faced with a problem, the most sensible thing to do is to take a good hard look at just what the problem is, think up solutions, decide which one will work best, try it, and see what happens. The scientific method is simply a formalizing of this natural experimental thought process. What is not obvious is that this experimental method should be applied to morality. The normal temptation, when faced with a moral dilemma, is to fall back on ethical maxims or traditional principles like, "drinking is evil," or "I should be kind to my employees," or "the lazy worker has no place around here." Such preconceived moral ideas take no account of the unique problem at hand. They are prejudices rather than experiments. Step four of the experimental method is to decide which hypothesis, which of the possible solutions, to employ. And in making this decision, not moral prejudices, but experimental consequences are to be the guide. The facile application of moral maxims may be expedient, but it is not pragmatic.

So take each of the hypotheses in turn and imagine what the consequences are likely to be if it is put into effect. For example, if Jones confronts Pete (see hypothesis (a) above), what is likely to happen? If Jones furloughs Pete (hypothesis (b)), would this resolve the conflict? Or maybe hypothesis (c) is the plan of action that has the best chance of working. So Jones compares the solutions one with another, asking himself where each is likely to lead. A moral decision is an experiment. Jones wants a plan that will pass the experimental test.

Step five: the test of action. The culmination of the process, of course, is to take what seems to be the best plan and act on it. Jones has thought his way through to a responsible decision. Now, acting on it will tell the tale. Suppose it doesn't work? Like the scientist's experiment, the test of action will soon reveal the weaknesses of any hypotheses. The pragmatic method is no more infallible than human intelligence itself. But the point is that this method is self-corrective. The test of action will show Jones how he has to modify his hypothesis, change his decision in order to make it work. If, instead of using this method of scientific intelligence he makes a decision on the basis of irrational feeling or of blind adherence to authority and tradition, such a decision is much less likely to work, much less likely to be suited to the particular problematic moral situation in which he finds himself. And what's worse, feelings, tradition, and authority give me no method of correcting unsuitable moral decisions. He's stuck with them. Decisions arrived at pragmatically are self-corrective; irrational decisions are not.

This is a situation ethics, but that does not mean that anything goes. Pragmatism does justice to both the subjective and objective sides of morality. On the subjective side, it realizes that the situation and circumstances of every business decision are unique. No universally binding objective code can be laid down for all. Business evolves, and business ethics must evolve with it. But there is also an objective side. The conflicting demands that are the stuff of ethical dilemmas in business are all too real. Intelligence is the tool for resolving these demands. Intelligent evolution is the meaning of human, and therefore the meaning of morality. Science has shown the way to using this tool effectively. Ethical dilemmas no less than economic dilemmas will yield to the experimental method, if only we are bold enough to use it.

7. CRITICAL EVALUATION

Recall the criterion by which we judge philosophical adequacy and ethical truth, viz., how comprehensively and consistently does the philosophy in question reflect and describe the realities of what it means to be a human being in society? How complete and accurate a picture does the philosophy paint? Does it leave out any aspect of human nature, or blur it over?

Time now to ask how true this pragmatic picture of human evolution is. How adequately is pragmatism able to handle ethical dilemmas faced in the business world? How do you evaluate for yourself the pluses and minuses of this business philosophy? We'll consider in turn criticisms that have been leveled against four of pragmatism's major themes: 1. against meliorism, that progress is an illusion; 2. against the stress of action, that there's no place for moral ideals; 3. against the rationality, that there's no recognition of the role of feeling and irrationality in morals; 4. against the fallibilism, that there's insufficient probing into true human needs and goals.

After restating in turn each of these four themes, a question (*Q*) or objection is presented to highlight a difficulty that could be raised against the theme in question. Then an answer (*A*) from the point of view of pragmatism is briefly stated. The intent is to help the reader weight the pros and cons of pragmatism so as to evaluate critically its adequacy as a business ethics. The intent is not either to endorse or reject it.

1. *Against Meliorism, that progress is an illusion.* Meliorism is the pragmatic faith that the secret of social and moral progress lies in the application of scientific intelligence. Herbert Spencer taught that because of natural selection, progress is automatic. He was wrong, says the pragmatist. The course of human evolution is determined not by the blind workings of nature, but by the free choices of human beings. Irrational choices will put us on a downhill course. Choices made methodically through the scientific model bring moral and social progress.

Q: Both Spencer and Dewey are wrong. Progress is an illusion. The price of scientific progress has been human suffering. Human beings have paid the cost of business's scientifically calculated decisions. The result is a society organized around the needs of technology rather than around the needs of human beings. Every scientific advance brings with it a retreat in the quality of life. The dark side of progress is unemployment, carcinogens, and a devastated natural environment.[3]

A: Such problems result not from too much science but from too little. Science has been used as a means of achieving various human ends. But science has not been applied to determining what those ends should be. The pragmatist urges precisely that the method be extended from the technological sphere to the moral sphere as well, *viz.*, to questions affecting the quality of human life. Consider, for example, the question, How do I produce a cola whose taste people prefer? That's a technological question and science is used as a means for answering it. Does cola fill a genuine human need? Should its production be allowed at all? This is a moral question. We don't apply our intelligence to questions like this one. Science is used as a means for reaching blindly accepted and often irrational goals. Dare we use it to examine these goals themselves?

2. *Against the stress on action: that there's no place for moral ideals.* Pragmatism brings morality down to earth into the heart of daily action. Dewey puts the matter well:

> To many persons, the idea that the ends professed by morals are impotent save as they are connected with the working machinery of economic

---

[3]These problems have a complexity that eludes easy rhetoric. At heart, they are the consequences of philosophical decisions about human life and values, as subsequent chapters will indicate.

life seems like deflowering the purity of moral values and obligations.

This distinction between higher and lower types of value is itself something to be looked into. Why should there be a sharp distinction made between some goods as physical and material and others as ideal and "spiritual"?[4]

Moral ideals are empty unless we devise ways of translating them into action. This translation requires the truly ethical person to immerse himself in the "dirty" world of the economic and political realities that condition every effective decision. "Every able-bodied man and woman should have the opportunity to earn a living": this is a nice moral ideal. But the ideal remains impotent until the practical question is asked of how to bring this about in a given place and time.

Q: Let's grant the important stress on action. Still, ideals too have an essential role to play, and pragmatism seems to neglect this. "Zero unemployment," "adequate health care for all," "the complete elimination of carcinogens from the environment," are at this present time very "impractical." Practically speaking we can entertain only more modest hypotheses concerned with reducing unemployment, improving some aspect of the health-care delivery system, or controlling one or other carcinogen. But it isn't enough to rest with the immediately practical. We need "impossible" ideals to shoot for. A completely functional and situational ethics like pragmatism tells us what we *are* (we are what we do), but it doesn't point the way to what we might *become.* Don't "impractical" ideals have the very practical role of giving direction and inspiration to our moral lives?

A: The pragmatist has no quarrel with ideals, as long as they play a practical role in keeping alive for us those values that we cannot put into practice. But he balks when ideals divert us from the practical problem-solving that is necessary for effective moral decisions. An industry can issue statements of ideal concern for employing blacks and women. But what is it *doing* to put this ideal into practice? The *ideal* value is empty and impotent until it is reduced to a *functional* value, i.e., to action. Suppose this is impossible. Suppose, for example, that a dental school would like to recruit blacks for its faculty. But there simply does not exist a pool of black dentists to draw on. In a case like this, it is vitally important to keep alive this presently impractical ideal. When functional action is impossible, says Dewey, we have recourse to ritual action. The dental school, for example, might sponsor an annual "Black Achievement" dinner in honor of outstanding black students in the area. Or it might establish a scholarship for minorities. Or it could institute in ghetto schools a series of talks on the

[4]Dewey, *op.cit.*, pp. 283, 269–70.

dental profession. These ritual gestures don't add any black dentists to the faculty, but they do serve to keep alive the ideal until such day as it can be rendered functional. In conclusion, then pragmatism stesses practical action—functional values. When this is impossible, it recurs to ritual action by which ideal values are kept alive. It insists that moral ideals that have no relation to action—either functional or ritual—are empty and impotent.

3. *Against the rationality—that there is no recognition of the role of feeling and irrationality in morals.* Pragmatic ethics is more a matter of mind than of heart. A loving concern for others is all well and good. But one must love *wisely*, which is where the method of intelligent problem-solving comes in. Ethical feelings may be well meant, but they may also be very wrong. With pragmatism, when you're wrong you know it and can correct it: this accounts for the pragmatic stress on rationality.

Q: Doesn't the pragmatist neglect the darker side of human nature? The business process is as much an interplay of irrational passions as it is of calculating reason. The desires of consumers, the demands of unions, the pressures of politicians, the greed of competitors—this is human nature in the raw forming the irrational climate in which business decisions are made. Pragmatism's stress on intelligence would be fine if human beings were basically rational. But they're not. Doesn't this unfortunate fact undermine the basic premise of pragmatic ethics?

A: This is a powerful objection. John Dewey professed an almost religious faith in what human intelligence could accomplish. Against this stands the long human history of blind passions and irrational emotions, above all when moral values are at stake. Dewey was aware of this history. His answer was education. People had to be trained to apply the experimental method to all problems, including their social and moral problems. Can human beings be educated to deal with ethical decisions in a rational way? You decide.

The pragmatist might also respond that there is no alternative better than the application of human intelligence. Surrender to irrational methods is no solution.

Finally, granting an irrational component in human decision-making, can we not deal with it in a rational way? Our hypotheses can factor in this irrational component. Suppose, for example, I am faced with the decision of firing an incompetent employee, who happens also to be a close friend. My irrational feelings are getting in the way of my making a sound business decision. So my hypothesis or plan of action should explicitly take these feelings into account. I will try to devise a plan that is sound from the standpoint of business, and at the same time does not violate my feelings of friendship.

4. *Against the fallibilism and piece-meal problem-solving—that there's no overall probing into genuine human needs and goals.* This objection takes an opposite tack from the previous one. It argues that pragmatism is not rational enough. We'll deal with it not here but in the next chapter, wherein are outlined some current criticisms of pragmatism and of the free-enterprise system.

CASE FOR DISCUSSION

International Management Consultant John Humble has pointed out[5] the increasing complexity of the environment in which business must operate. There is, first, a crisis of identity over the role business is asked to play as social agent for ecology, minority hiring, and enforcer of human rights overseas. There is the crisis of authority in which governmental agencies, consumer groups, labor unions, and environmental coalitions are infringing upon and eroding management's traditional decision-making prerogatives. And there is a crisis of integrity in the general skepticism about business's response to these competing interests. These interests are the spokes of the wheel with management at the hub keeping them in balance and thereby keeping the business wheel on course in the direction of its goal—the creation of economic wealth through profits.

Pragmatism claims to provide a rational ethical method for balancing out conflicts with a view to successful, practical and effective business decision-making; such decision-making is by definition also morally good. Keep clearly in mind the five-step method described in this chapter as a blueprint for responsible intelligent action. Show how you would use it to resolve the following value conflict.

We'll start out simply. You are the district manager in a large West Coast city responsible for 12 franchises of a national fast-food chain. The chain's policy is to hire part-time teenage workers who can legally be paid less than the minimum wage to carry out the routine operations of the franchise. The AFL-CIO Culinary Workers Union opposes this policy and has led the battle to oppose further franchise openings in the district. They are joined by the restaurateurs who must pay union scale, and fear further loss of business to the chains. You as district manager are aware that your competitors—other fast-food chains—also use part-time nonunion labor. You also point out that you employ 50 to 100 persons per store—more than any union restaurant does—and that these people would otherwise be

---

[5]John Humble, "A Practical Approach to Social Responsibility," *Management Review* (May, 1978), 18–22.

unemployed. Other franchises in your chain have been troubled by picketing, confrontations, and unionizing efforts by the Culinary Workers.

(a) National headquarters has given you authority to decide employee policy in this district, and the matter is in your hands. How would you apply the five-step method to arrive at a rational and responsible decision? Be careful to define the problem so that it takes *all* data into account. Be careful that your hypotheses under consideration not ignore any of the conflicting interests and values.

(b) You as district manager learn that your individual franchise managers have been forcing their teen-age employees to undergo lie-detector tests. Those who refuse are subject to dismissal. The PSE (Psychological Stress Evaluation) instrument or "lie-detector" being used is the type that measures subtle changes in the human voice, microtremors that increase when the subject is under stress and a subaudible 8 to 14 cycle tone that disappears under stress. Manufacturers of these PSE units claim that they are foolproof; they eliminate the need for interpretation of results that the ordinary polygraph requires. You are not so sure. You have read evidence that the PSE units cannot distinguish between stress caused by lies, or by ambivalence, or by misunderstanding. You also learned, however, that national headquarters does not disapprove of these tests. The main purpose of the tests is to ferret out employees who have union sympathies, and to keep abreast of unionizing activities. The PSE units are being used as a major weapon for maintaining the open shop.

How does this information modify your view of employee policy? Again using the pragmatic method, restate the problem. Show how you would proceed step by step to arrive at a responsible, intelligent decision. Be careful to define the problem so that it takes all the data (including this new information) into account. Likewise, be careful that your alternative hypotheses under consideration do not ignore any of the conflicting interests or values.

(c) A new headache has come to you, the district manager. A professor of nutrition at Harvard University's School of Public Health gained nation wide publicity by attacking the nutritional value of the typical menu served by your food chain. The menu was accused of being low in vitamins B and C, but very high in saturated fats. In a word, it's the kind of diet that increases cholesterol and leads to heart disease. You know that this indictment is true. You are personally very concerned with good nutrition, and you are very aware yourself of its importance for children who are the main targets of your company's syndicated advertising. You have little or no control over the national advertising campaign, and certainly have no say about changing the company's typical menu. You do, however, control a relatively generous budget to use for local advertising. The nutritional problem has always nagged at you in the background, and now the national publicity has brought the issue to a head as far as your own feelings are concerned. This conflict strikes at the heart of your commitment to and satisfaction in your work, and you feel you can ignore it no longer.

How would you apply the five-step pragmatic method to come to some rational and responsible resolution of this conflict? Be careful to define the problem so that it takes all the data into account—your personal concerns, your company's policies, and the nutritional facts. Be careful that your alternative hypotheses under consideration do not ignore any of the conflicting interests and values. Recall from the chapter above the role of *ideal* values, and how they can be kept alive even though they cannot at the time be translated into functional values.

SUGGESTED READINGS

Dewey, John. *The Quest for Certainty.* New York: G. P. Putnam's Sons, 1929.

Dewey, John and James H. Tufts. *Ethics,* rev. ed. New York: Henry Holt and Co., 1932.

Dooley, Patrick K. *Pragmatic Humanism: The Philosophy of William James.* Totowa, N.J.: Littlefield, Adams & Co., 1975.

Eames, S. Morris. *Pragmatic Naturalism: An Introduction.* Carbondale, Ill.: Southern Illinois University Press, 1977.

Gouinlock, James. *The Moral Writings of John Dewey: A Selection.* New York: Hafner Press, 1976.

Humble, John. "A Practical Approach to Social Responsibility," *Management Review* (May 1978), 18–22.

James, William. *Pragmatism* and *The Meaning of Truth.* Cambridge, Ma.: Harvard University Press, 1978.

Miller, David L. *George Herbert Mead: Self, Language and the World.* Austin: University of Texas Press, 1973.

Novak, George. *Pragmatism versus Marxism: An Appraisal of John Dewey's Philosophy.* New York: Pathfinder Press, Inc., 1975.

CHAPTER 9

MARXISM: THAT WHICH IS CANNOT BE TRUE

Thus economic freedom would mean freedom *from* the economy—from being controlled by economic forces and relationships; freedom from the daily struggle for existence, from earning a living. Political freedom would mean liberation of individuals *from* politics over which they have no effective control. Similarly, intellectual freedom would mean the restoration of individual thought now absorbed by mass communication and indoctrination, abolition of "public opinion" and its makers.

Herbert Marcuse[1]

On a view of man as a creature of limited cognitive capacity to organize his society and solve his social problems, the substitution of problem-solving interactions for impossible analytical tasks helps explain both the rise of the governmental interactive processes called democracy . . . and the multifaceted profusion of interactions called market system. A sufficient faith in science and reason makes both unnecessary. Lacking that faith many people will think both are indispensable.

Charles E. Lindblom[2]

OBJECTIVES FOR CHAPTER 9:

1. To understand why, according to the Marxist critique, the capitalist business system remains blind to its own antihuman defects and, specifi-

---

[1]Herbert Marcuse, *One-Dimensional Man* (Boston: Beacon Press, 1964), p. 4.
[2]Charles E. Lindblom, *Politics and Markets: The World's Political-Economic Systems* (© by Basic Books, Inc., Publishers, New York, 1977), p. 255.

cally, how operational thinking eliminates moral idealism and stifles genuine criticism;

2. To be able to outline the classical Marxist world-view, to wit,

   (a) the materialist theory of reality;
   (b) the dialectical logic;
   (c) the economic class struggle;
   (d) the economic determinants of philosophy and religion;

3. To contrast two views of human reason—Marxist rationalism and pragmatic fallibilism—and to draw the consequences of each for either a planned economy or a market economy;

4. To understand the objections and answers to Marxist criticism of operational thinking.

Introduction. Pragmatism provided a prescription for the ethical autonomy of business within the framework of capitalism. As autonomous, this ethics need not conform blindly to conventional and legalistic norms, but can evaluate these latter by the method of intelligence based on the scientific model, as we have seen. But pragmatism, according to the Marxist critique, remains infected with an unconscious moral conformism in its complacent adherence to the market system.

Ethics, as discussed so far, has left unexamined the overall character of the business system within which business philosophies operate. We have assumed that the market system as it now exists is a fundamentally sound, if not flawless, way of organizing society. Business ethics inquires into morally and socially responsible action within that system. Business interactions, when carried on ethically and responsibly, will result in an economic climate that is at once human and humane, we have supposed. Time now to consider the chorus of criticisms leveled both against industrialism and the market system itself. To these critics, the fundamental moral question is the antihuman character of the business process as it is now carried on. It is not so much a question of playing the business game fairly and responsibly, but of whether the game should be played at all under its present rules. We look at some of the hitherto unexamined assumptions of the system and at some of the alternative ways of distributing goods and services that have been proposed in the name of a better quality of life and of a more just society.[3]

---

[3]See, for example, Marcuse and Lindblom, *op. cit.* The next chapter will review assumptions shared by socialism and capitalism alike as criticized in the works of Ivan Illich, E. F. Schumacher, and Tibor Scitovsky. The Epilogue of this book will outline the current state of the question on justice and economic distribution in the debate between deontologists Rawls and Nozik against each other and against utilitarians like Smart and Hare in the tradition of Mill.

VALUES-CLARIFICATION

A major issue in the ongoing debate that reaches to the very roots of a business philosophy revolves around the issue of liberty in the economic sphere—the issue of a controlled economy vs. a free economy. On what do you pin your hopes—on the wisdom of planning or on the wisdom of pricing? We examine in this chapter the philosophy of a planned economy as the best cure for the exploitation of human beings. The following exercise introduces the discussion by asking you to highlight for yourself the factual issues upon which the debate often turns.

Suppose you have been commissioned by a middle-of-the-road political candidate to produce for him a series of spot TV ads. His opponent, who belongs to the Socialist party, is making surprising inroads with the following arguments which score the built-in injustices of the American economic system. If you were to devise an ad to counter each argument (a) what would you show in each case, and (b) what would the message be? Here are the arguments.

1. The many are being exploited for the benefit of the few. Three quarters of all private wealth in the U.S. is held by 18 percent of the families. The bottom quarter (over 50 million people) hold no assets at all. Four-fifths of the population (81 percent) own less than the top 5 percent. The top .008 percent own as much as the bottom half of the population and effectively control the corporations that dominate you.[4]

2. Work dissatisfaction abounds in capitalism. Unemployment is built into the system; dehumanized factory working conditions are the rule.

3. The rule of competition rather than of equality pits class against class, white against black, men against women, and rich against poor.

4. Base motivations grease the wheels of capitalism—pursuit of big bucks, looking out for number one, endless stimulation of false consumer needs, sexism, and scorn for the poor.

5. When humane planning is replaced by free enterprise, inhuman priorities take over. For example, more money is invested in cosmetics and pet food than in the necessities of life for the poor. Rock singers and professional athletes are rewarded far more than research scientists and teachers.

6. In capitalism, wealth, not merit, controls the political system. The presidency and the Congress belong to millionaires, lawyers, and businessmen, not to factory workers, or to farmers, or even to wealthy women. Lobbies with money are the lobbies with clout.

[4]See Dr. Lester C. Thurow, former member of the Council of Economic Advisors, in *Public Interest Newsletter* (December 1975).

7. Consider evils done in the name of profit: pollution increases (ecology is an unaffordable luxury in a competitive world); business seeks out the suburbs leaving urban decay behind; corruption and double-dealing become necessary evils in the climate of competition for profits.

If this list of injustices seems to you wrong-headed, exaggerated, and even false, this is not surprising, says the Marxist critic. You are trapped by your world-view. The very processes of technology and of thought that are meant to liberate you serve only to ensnare you. Let's see how this happens.

1. THE TRAP—OPERATIONALISM

One of the glories of the scientific method proclaimed by pragmatism is the open-mindedness fostered, and even required, by this approach to problems. Could it be that this openness is an illusion? Yes, say the critics of operational thinking.[5] Operational thinking locks us into our customary world-view and makes it impossible to be self-critical about our values. Briefly, operational thinking says this: "You are what you do." Things are defined by the way they operate. A "hammer" is whatever bangs nails into wood or pulls them loose. A "free election" is secretly voting for one of the candidates of the major political parties listed on the ballot. A "baby" is an eating, sleeping, screaming, excreting organism. In other words, if you want to know what something is, look at what it does.

So what's wrong with operational thinking? It does away with our ideals—that's what's wrong, says Marcuse. It locks us into the status quo. It blocks out alternatives. It reduces us. It says, you are *nothing but* what you do. When a mother looks at her baby, doesn't she see something more than "an eating, screaming, excreting organism"? Of course. She sees a possible doctor, lawyer, or president. Operational thinking blocks out the ideal person that the baby can become. When "free election" is defined as the process of voting for one of the major party candidates on the ballot, again we're locked into the status quo. We don't even consider alternative possibilities that could bring greater freedom than our present process of choosing from among nearly identical candidates. This same operational thinking blinds us when we define a "hammer" by the things that the ham-

[5]The following summary of Marcuse's critique first appeared in my book, *The Morals Game* (New York: The Paulist Press, 1974), pp. 41–45. For the best representation of Marxism that appropriates the capitalist picture as it exists today, see Ernest Mandel, *Marxist Economic Theory* (New York: Modern Reader Paperback edition, 1970), 2 Vols., and *Late Capitalism* (London: Verso Edition, 1978). I have chosen to work out of Marcuse who, together with Lindblon and Novak (see below), provides a particularly sharp foil to the pragmatic philosophy so characteristic of American business.

mer on your shelf can do. It keeps us from trying to create an "ideal" hammer, one, for example, that could drive in nails without banging or noise. Operational thinking makes moral pygmies of us. It keeps us so focused on what is, that we never raise our eyes to what ideally might be.

Operational thinking is enslaved thinking. This is no mere philosophical quibble over words. We have become literally slaves to the economic power structure, says Marcuse. But we don't realize it. We actually think that we are free. This type of thinking has pacified us, resigned us to our slavery. So each workday we obediently go through our paces as slaves in the "free-enterprise" system, cogs in the industrial machine. It never occurs to us that it is a strange kind of freedom that forces us to live, sleep, structure our hours and days, make purchases, and pay taxes all according to the demands of the economy. Our lives are not our own. And if we fail to meet these demands, the penalty is poverty, hunger, disease, and ostracism from the mainstream of social life. In our "free" society, a man without a job is less than a man and treated accordingly. It goes even further. Our "free" economy suspects a man without financial credit and a man who is not in debt. The hard-working, decent, safe, approved citizen is one who has bartered away his future until he is literally owned by his creditors. An industry will not hire the single man who has no strings attached in preference to the heavily mortgaged family man. The latter they can own. The tragedy is not so much that this is the case. The tragedy is that we accept it as inevitable.

Operational thinking makes this possible. What's good for the economy is good for the individual. We never dream of questioning this. We define our free economy by the way it actually operates. (You are what you do.) Then we set about getting human beings to do what is necessary to improve the economy. To this one end the whole system of laws, tax incentives, creditors, social pressures, job opportunities is brought to bear. These decide where the citizen will live, what he will eat, wear, and drive, and how much time he will spend with his family. The result is 100 million willing slaves of the economic power structure.

Does this sound excessive or even paranoid? If so, says Marcuse, you've been successfully pacified. You've been led to assume that what's good for the economy is good for you. The main decisions of your life revolve around the answer to this question: What do I have to do to earn a living, put food on the table and clothes on my children's backs? You've been so pacified into accepting things the way they are that you would never dream of asking the critical, the ideal question: What would I like to do with my life, and how would I like to spend all of my time? Unreal, you say? Yes. According to operational thinking it is unreal. This kind of thinking uncritically accepts the status quo, rules out alternatives, and eliminates ideals. Why is it that we would never dream of asking that basic human question: What would I like to do with my life?—instead of the enslaving question: What does economic necessity dictate that I do with my life?

What has happened in America, says Marcuse, is that "technological rationality" has taken over our lives. In theory, technology is neutral. This is not so in America. Our whole society is organized around the rationale of technology. Technological rationality is what guides political decisions. In other words, political decisions are based on what will foster economic productivity. Alternative goals are not merely ruled out. They aren't even considered. "Technological rationality has become political rationality," is the way Marcuse puts it. What's more, individual citizens are induced to swallow this whole process as only reasonable. In other words, technological rationality in the end becomes individual rationality. The logic of production becomes the logic of human thinking in our society. Dollars-and-cents thinking takes first place. All other considerations are subordinate. Money outranks sex and health as our central concern. Confer with that barometer of American preoccupations—the index of articles printed in the *Reader's Digest*.

Mind you, it's our very logic that is now governed by technology. If you presume to follow other rules of thinking, you're illogical, you're crazy. Suppose, for example, you tried to start a political party devoted to lowering production and productivity or to stopping progress. Suppose you quit work, claiming that freedom does not consist of having money or happiness in an abundance of goods. You'd be considered a subversive, good-for-nothing dreamer. We cannot imagine economic freedom outside the wage-price spiral rat race, political freedom outside the established paths of American democracy, or intellectual freedom apart from the cacophonous din of the media and the "free" press. Technological rationality has become the only rationality. Bluntly, man exists for the machine, not the machine for man.

If you don't believe that you are dominated by technological rationality, consider what a truly human freedom would look like. Here it is. Does it sound "crazy"? Consider a world in which you are free from the economy, free from the necessity of making a living. It would be a world not of idleness but of activity. However, it would be activity performed in freedom and leisure, more play than work. No more daily struggle for existence. Such would be economic freedom.

Political freedom would be freedom from the politics and politicians that control me instead of my controlling them. It would be a world in which politicians followed Aristotle's dictum: "Friends and truth are dear, but piety requires us to honor truth above our friends." No more voting

booths offering indistinguishable candidates vying for the chance to dominate and gouge you.

Finally, consider a world of intellectual freedom in which individual
thought would be liberated. No longer manipulated by indoctrination,
mass communication, and public opinion, the individual would be restored
and his unique creativity honored.

"A world in which I need not work for a living, in which I control my
government, and in which I think my own creative thoughts. It's unreal,"
you say; "it's utopian." How sad that a world in which I am not chained to
an economic machine, or victimized by a tyrannical politics, or controlled
by the mass media seems so unreal. What could be more natural than to
imagine that a man during his short space on earth could exercise his powers with dignity, master of his own fate and his own thoughts? The problem is not that this ideal is utopian. The problem rather bears witness to
the power of those forces that separate us from our freedom to be who we
really are.

Granted, Marcuse's diagnosis of capitalistic unfreedom goes against
the grain of established American thinking. Economic slavery? We have
the best standard of living in the world, don't we? Political tyranny?
Where else are elections more free? Controlled thinking? Our freedom of
speech is notorious around the world to the point of scandal. True, responds Marcuse. We can raise the standard—of *administered* living. We
live well, provided that we remain cogs in the technological machine, serving rather than served by the laws of productivity. We are well-fed slaves,
perferring this security to freedom because we see no other way to becoming well fed and also free. We don't even dream of an alternative. We are
likewise inextricably caught in the web of established politics and established thinking, never dreaming that there might be a way out. The political trap and the free-speech trap are closely connected. In both areas we
practice a tolerance that isn't tolerance at all, but oppression. By giving every political viewpoint, every voice and every opinion a hearing, we emas-
culate them, good and bad alike, and cause them to be not worth hearing.

A glance at your corner drugstore's paperback bookrack illustrates
Marcuse's point. The pornographer shares space with Plato, as does the
racist with the humanitarian. Bright packaging, not nutrition, sells cereal
at the supermarket. So it is with our highly touted "marketplace of ideas."
Every discussion panel has its token radical, every school committee its token student, every governing board its token black or female. Thus the opposition is institutionalized and thereby welcomed into the establishment.
The man of experience and the silly exhibitionist, the truth-teller and the
liar receive an equally respectful hearing. Thus, truth and criticism are
trivialized and incorporated into the established order of things. All voices

become merely different accents in our cultural milieu. Truly radical criticism is impossible. It used to be possible for a few people to live outside the established order of things and thereby challenge it; the adulteress, the rebel poet, the great criminal and the revolutionary did not walk the normal path. However, today we have not the adulteress but the neurotic housewife, not the rebel poet but the hippie, not the great criminal outcast but the gangster, not the revolutionary but the protester. The opposition has been enlisted to affirm rather than negate the established order.

In summary, it is Marcuse's claim that technological rationality has put us in a moral prison. Our politics and our very thinking are subject to its laws. Our so-called intellectual, economic and political freedoms are conditioned by this slavery. Opposition and freedom alike are part of life within the prison. It is impossible to assault the prison walls from the outside.

2. THE CAUSE—FALLIBILISM

Such sweeping Marxist indictments will strike the practical business person as all too easy and all too remote from the complex world where hard decisions are made. The business world has little place for utopias. And conversely, critics of the "antihuman" character of the free-enterprise system have little patience with appeals to the impracticability of their revolutionary solutions. In today's world, the planned society and the market system, though they are moving gingerly toward each other, are conceptually at loggerheads. At heart, the issue is epistemological, as Charles Lindblom has pointed out:

> On a view of man as a creature of limited cognitive capacity to organize his society and solve his social problems, the substitution of problem-solving interactions for impossible analytical tasks helps to explain both the rise of the governmental interactive processes called democracy . . . and the multifaceted profusion of interactions called market system. A sufficient faith in science and reason makes both unnecessary. Lacking that faith many people will think both are indispensable.[6]

The philosophical division here is so profound that it is almost impossible for either party to hear what the other is saying.

Not all criticisms of Western capitalism, however, come from the revolutionary camp. But all such criticisms, be they revolutionary, liberationist, or existentialist, share one thing in common. In one way or another,

---

[6]Lindblom, *op. cit.*

they are reactions to the economic doctrines of Karl Marx. His teaching forms the fundamental paradigm that consciously or unconsciously underlies most contemporary socio-economic criticism. The Marxist myth inspires action or reaction; it is virtually impossible to prescind from it. Let's look at the broad outlines of this picture that to a certain extent divides our economic policies and political parties, and which more fundamentally divides our globe.

Reality—dialectical materialism. For Marxism, as for the other business philosophies we have seen, it is the philosophy of life that underpins the ethical judgments of right and wrong. Marxist criticisms of the American economic system flow from a very specific philosophical picture of the world. We start with the nature of reality. First, reality is *materialistic*; secondly, this materialism is to be understood *dialectically.*

The *materialism* of Marx is not gross or reductionistic. It is very much kin to what Dewey called "naturalism." Along with Dewey, Marx rejects claims for reality and truth as coming from "supernatural" or "revealed" sources. Reality is confined to what emerges from observation, experiment and logical analysis. Also with Dewey, Marx has a faith in humankind and a faith in human reason. In fact, as we will note, his faith in human reason surpasses even Dewey's. But this faith is not supernatural and arbitrary. It is grounded in what reason has accomplished in the past and can be expected to accomplish in the future. Materialism does not degrade human nature, but rather keeps it focused on that material world of which it is a part, with all its qualities, powers, and potential for growth. Thus undistracted by false mysticism and supernaturalism, humans can rationally explore and develop the natural material world where true moral and social progress lies. Religion's stress on unreal "otherworldly" goals has often served to oppress and stifle social justice in this world. Marx's materialism closes off this escape route.

Material reality is also *dialectical.* Put simply, reality is in process of change at every level—physically, intellectually, economically, socially and aesthetically. And this change is not merely mechanical—more of the same. A thin person grows fat; one school district is divided into two; MacDonald's adds three fast-food franchises to a town. Such changes are mechanical, quantitative. *Dialectical* materialism stresses that matter is in process of *qualitative* change, viz., not merely change in degree, but also change in kind. Revolution, and not merely evolution, is the rule at every level. Qualitative leaps are not confined to physical and biological evolution. The Marxist is prepared for, and even expects, basic changes in social institutions, economic systems, laws, and power structures; more strongly, such revolutions are inevitable. It is at this point that Marxism and pragmatism part ways, as we will see.

Logic—"that which is cannot be true." The nature of thought is guided by the nature of objective reality. It takes a dialectical logic to understand a dialectical reality. Classical formal logic, as expounded by Aristotle, cannot deal adequately with change. Marcuse's statement, "that which is cannot be true," is an affront to the Aristotelian. Formal logic is based on three principles: the principle of identity (A is A); the principle of noncontradiction (A is not non-A); and the principle of excluded middle (A given X cannot be both A and non-A in the same respect at the same time). These formal principles seem self-evident: and they are—for *static* reality. But a reality that changes fundamentally and dialectically demands a logic which can grapple with this dialectic. The principle of identity (A is A), for example, must be complemented by the principle of unity of opposites (A is A and non-A). Ontologically this accounts for change. I am I (identity), to be sure. But since I'm changing, there is something in me that is not me, and hence is pulling me to change. I am at once myself and not myself (unity of opposites). So in a changing world, what a thing *is* cannot be the last word; as Marcuse says, "that which is cannot be true."

This dialectical character of reality and thought is disturbing, especially when we come to examine our most precious economic, moral, and social institutions. Dialectical logic is, quite literally, subversive. It faces up to the fact that our cherished institutions contain the seeds of their own destruction (A is A and also non-A). Pragmatic problem-solving, on the other hand, operates within an established unquestioned social framework with a view to the conservation of that framework. Marxist dialectic, however, questions the established framework with a view to its subversion. The first is guided by the formal logic of identity; the second by the dialectical logic of opposites in dynamic tension.

These conflicting logics (based on conflicting views of reality) will have profoundly conflicting consequences for business ethics and social justice, as we will see. By way of a quick small example, consider the plight of an executive faced with a minor rebellion by his secretarial staff. These employees, newly enlisted, say, in Boston's secretaries united group called Nine to Five, will no longer fetch coffee for the midmorning office break. The pragmatic problem-solving executive would seek a compromise plan of action that would enable established office procedures to go on as undisturbed as possible. The dialectical thinker, on the other hand, might radically question the established office structure itself that could give rise to such a problem in the first place. The pragmatist assumes that the office "society" is fundamentally just and that problems can be resolved while leaving the basic framework of that society undisturbed. The Marxist would see the problem as a symptom of "class struggle" pointing to a fundamentally unjust office structure that needs somehow to be overturned. For the pragmatist office life is what it is (A is A). The Marxist, in viewing office life dynamically, sees both what it is and what it is in process of becoming (A is A and also non-A).

Society—revolution toward utopia. To appreciate Marx's analysis of this class struggle, we need an exact definition of "class." Class is a function of production and of a person's relationship to the forces of production. So we now define (1) forces of production, (2) relations of production and (3) class. This will give us the economic structure or foundation of society. Finally, built on this economic structure is (4) the ideological superstructure that legitimates the economic foundation. Let's consider in turn each part of this Marxist anatomy of society.

(1) *The forces of production* include natural resources such as fossil fuels, minerals, wood, land, water, and the like. Included, too, are the tools, techniques, and skills for transforming these resources: machinery, computers, chemical processes, lasers, and lathes. Finally, there is the actual human labor that applies the tools and techniques to natural resources. Some level of productive labor is necessary for human survival and comfort. In this, every society is alike.

(2) *The relations of production,* on the other hand, can differ from society to society. We are talking now about property relations in this production process. People stand in different relationships to the forces of production, and hence in different relationships to each other. Some are owners; others are workers. Some work on what they themselves own; some work on what is owned by others. Some workers, i.e., slaves, legally are owned by others. Some are bound by legal contract to work for wages on what they do not own. Class struggle is the result of the conflicts of interest inherent in these property relations.

(3) A *class,* then, refers to any group that shares the same relationship to the forces of production. The *proletarian class,* for example, is comprised of industrial wage-earners who own neither the forces of production nor the product of their labor. The *capitalist class* is the group that owns the forces of production, without necessarily working on them.

We will not review here Marx's account of how the changing forces of production and consequent changing economic relationships led to the emergence of capitalism from feudal society. Suffice it to say that Marx saw this emergence as a truly progressive step. Land and natural resources under capitalism were no longer immobilized as hereditary fiefdoms, but became commodities on the open market. Monopoly-type barriers on trade were dropped, and proletarian workers became mobile and not land-bound as were the serfs. And from this economic structure, i.e., from this particu-

lar relationship of the capitalist and proletarian classes to the forces of production, emerged the political, moral, and religious belief systems that
served to support and legitimate this structure.

(4) *The ideological superstructures* are shaped and determined by the
economic structure of society, says Marx. Belief systems do not determine
the physical arrangements under which people live. Rather, it is the other
way around. He who controls the forces of production that people need to
survive also controls the supporting ideological superstructures. This
Marxist premise underpins Marcuse's critique outlined at the beginning of
this chapter. You would no more expect the dominant class to morally
condemn the private ownership of capital than you would expect the owners in a slave state to outlaw slavery. The moral belief flows from the economic status quo and is designed to reinforce that status quo. In this way
the ongoing established economic arrangements are made to appear as
"common sense," at the best and only way of doing things. It becomes virtually impossible to ask a truly subversive question. Belief systems pacify
the mind: they make us contented slaves.

Much modern sociology of knowledge assumes the Marxist premise
about the primacy of economic structure over philosophical belief. By way
of illustrating this model, consider the following imaginary scenario that
takes place on a desert island on the north shore of which a young American named Joe lands after a shipwreck. Suppose, coincidentally, that a Mi-
cronesian woman, Oaga, is cast upon the south shore a few days later. Unaware of each other's presence, each goes his and her own way. Oaga
doesn't go hungry. She knows how to fish and eats her fish raw. Joe, meanwhile, forages for nuts and berries. At mealtimes when Oaga squats on the
beach to eat her fish, she thinks to herself, "Here I go again." And Joe,
too, a former boy scout, as he builds his fire to roast the nuts and berries,
mutters to himself, "Here I go again." This is *habitualization*, the first step
by which we structure our actions and lives.

Oaga sees the smoke. She realizes that she's not alone. She approaches
Joe warily from a distance. For a couple of days they cautiously observe
each other. "There she goes again," says Joe, as Oaga eats her fish. "There
he goes again," thinks she, as Joe builds his mealtime fire. They cast each
other into roles. One is the fisheater, the other the firebuilder. *Typification*
is the second mechanism at work in the formation of society. What for
each at first was a casual search for food, has now become a personal habit
and a public role.

Joe would love the taste of some fish, but not raw. So one day after
her catch, Joe beckons Oaga over to the fire. He broils the fish. They sit
and eat. How good it tastes! Thenceforth at mealtime, she brings the fish;
he builds the fire and cooks. And as they sit down together they think,

"Here we go again." Their respective roles of fishcatcher and firebuilder have melded into a single mealtime institution—thus *institutionalization*, the third mechanism that makes society work.

One thing leads to another, and in due course little Joey is born. When Joey looks around, he doesn't see a once-deserted island. This is the world that is, the only world he's ever known. He sees bushes, beaches, rocks and trees; and he also sees that women catch fish and men build fires. That's simply the way things are done. What Joe and Oaga do at mealtime is for Joey an objective fact of life just as real as the bushes, rocks, and trees. This is the social mechanism of *objectification* whereby institutions harden into objective social facts. An economic social structure is taking shape. The fish, the firewood, and the skills that apply these to human survival: these are the forces of production. And just as real are the relations of production that build up around these, such as, for example, a matriarchal society in which Oaga and the women who come after her are the owners of the food, the wood and the fireplace, with Joe, Joey and their male successors as servants of the female owner class. Such are the fundamental mechanisms that shape the social structure. It is not philosophical, moral, and religious beliefs that bring this structure about, but the material forces of production and the objective relations of production. It is the structure that gives rise to the beliefs which in turn serve to legitimate it.

Men build fires and serve women; women catch fish, own the land, and command the men. Joey sees this and really can't imagine how things could be otherwise. But to make sure that he and his descendents don't get any subversive ideas, societies erect philosophies, theologies, and moralities that justify the reigning economic structure. This is the process called *legitimation*, which explains why women *must* catch fish and be superior to men, and why men *must* build fires and obey women. There might, for example, develop a theology in which the first woman was sprung from the sea goddess, and the first man from the fire god of the mountain. Woman's nature built in the image of the primeval seagoddess is meant to catch fish, whereas man's nature and role is modeled on the father fire god of the mountain. But the sea is superior to the mountain because the mountain arose from the sea, and the waters of the sea can quench the mountain's fires. So women, born of the sea, are naturally superior to men, born of the mountain. In such fashion the economic structure is legitimated. Not only do people know their place, but they feel they *must keep* their place. The established order comes to be seen as logically correct, morally right, and even divinely ordained.

Pragmatism, in Marxist eyes, serves as a legitimation of the capitalist way. Marxism's main quarrel with it is that pragmatism makes it seem that the political, economic, and philosophical arrangements of capitalism

form the most intelligent and moral human social structure. Thus pragmatism keeps us from analyzing the hidden class struggle and the suppressed
human needs that characterize capitalism, and from realizing the potential
for subverting this system in favor of a truly human and just society.[7] True,
there is a kind of political freedom, a kind of intellectual freedom, and a
kind of economic freedom in a capitalist society. And pragmatic logic legitimates these kinds of freedom. But because pragmatic logic is not dialectical, it does not realize the revolutionary possibilities of even higher levels
of freedom pointed to by Marcuse, as we saw above:

> Thus economic freedom would mean freedom *from* the economy—
> from being controlled by economic forces and relationships; freedom
> from the daily struggle for existence, from earning a living. Political
> freedom would mean liberation of individuals *from* politics over which
> they have no effective control. Similarly, intellectual freedom would
> mean the restoration of individual thought now absorbed by mass com-
> munication and indoctrination, abolition of "public opinion" and its
> makers.[8]

What we have are two opposing visions of human society and its possibilities. Following Lindblom,[9] we'll call the Marxist vision Model 1, and contrast it with the pragmatic vision, Model 2. We'll outline the Marxist critique of Model 2's version of political, intellectual, and economic freedom.

The Marxist critique. Both models favor democracy and political freedom. In Model 2, freedom lies in the political *process*, in the *method* of arriving at political decisions. One thinks of the multiparty system, of free
speech and civil liberties, of one man one vote and organized political opposition, of congressional balloting and the representation of special interests. Model 1 looks to content rather than method, to social needs and
goals themselves rather than the process by which these needs and goals

---

[7]See, for example, George Novak's *Pragmatism versus Marxism: An Appraisal of John
Dewey's Philosophy* (New York: Pathfinder Press, Inc.), 1975, especially Chapter 15, "The
Metaphysics of the Bourgeois."

Some recent Marxist economists have been critical of Marxism's own current dogmatism. While Marx's critique of capitalism may have been appropriate to the nineteenth century, capitalism today presents a different picture. Thus Barry Hindress, Paul Hirst, Arthur
Hussain, and Anthony Cutler in *Marx's Capital and Capitalism Today* (Boston: Routledge
and Kegan Paul, Ltd., 1977–78), 2 Vols., point to the distortions of capitalism that arise due
to overstressing the forces of industrial production in the traditional Marxist critique. The
Marxist vision has tended to ignore the expanding role of the service sector of the economy,
the impact of governments' regulations on companies, and the large place that money, credit
and financial institutions have in the economy. We have, however, outlined in the text classical Marxism, since it is the prevailing orthodoxy.

[8]Marcus, *op. cit.*
[9]Lindblom, *op. cit.*, Chapter 19.

are determined. From this perspective, two serious and related flaws show up in Model 2. American democracy conceives itself in terms that are too narrowly political, and hence is blinded to the economic determinants of that political process. Model 1 is able to diagnose these flaws because Model 1 is confident of the power of reason to analyze society in terms of genuine human needs. To clarify this distinction, consider how each model would approach the question of television programming. Model 1, for example, would urge and enforce the kind of programming that serves genuine progress and social justice. Model 2 would not presume to take such a substantive approach to television programming. Model 2's recommendations look not to content but to process: let the viewers decide content by turning off their sets or switching channels. If they let their children watch ads for sugar-coated cereals, so be it; if they boycott such sponsored programming, so be it. Model 2 does not directly attack the substantive question of whether children should be exposed to such ads. It does not question whether the encouragement of such products serves the genuine interests of children. Decisions about needs and goals result not from reasoned conclusions but from majority preferences.

Ostensibly, a philosophy of free speech and freedom of choice is operative here. But recall Marx. The philosophy is a superstructure, a mechanism of legitimation. The underlying economic structure is primary. The economic structure dictates the philosophy, not the other way around. So it would be hypocritical to proclaim a concern for the health and welfare of young TV viewers without establishing an economic structure that will assure this health and welfare. If it is socially desirable to keep children from eating too much sugar, the solution lies in the economy, i.e., in planning the production and distribution of sugar products. The solution does not lie in a philosophy of free choice that merely legitimates a market system of using sugar as bait for maintaining sales and profits.

Model 1 envisions a socially just society. This involves more than Model 2's narrowly political conception of democracy: one man, one vote, and then you're on your own. The goal is democracy and equality at every institutional level, and above all at the economic level. It will be a society without classes. When those who work the means of production also own the means of production, the division between exploiter and exploited will be overcome. Then equality of opportunity will be an effective reality, and not the empty shibboleth it is destined to remain in Model 2. The so-called "civil liberties" of Model 2 come at the price of wage-slavery of the majority to the privileged minority. In a class-divided society, there is no genuine economic freedom and security. Workers are hostages to capitalist owners. A business, for example, can devastate a town by a decision to move out, and there's nothing anyone can do about it. The fear of unemployment is the price of freedom to compete for jobs. Capitalism is the story of massive inequality and insecurity of the proletariat.

For Model 1, then, civil liberties take second place to social justice. It views the "freedoms" of Model 2 as highly qualified and often illusory freedoms. The censorship of ideas is covert but real. Advertisers are not about to sponsor programs designed to expose and destroy the power of those advertisers. The winners of free elections are beholden to those who bankroll their campaigns. Model 1 can do without such "liberties" in the name of advancing a genuinely just and egalitarian society. It is customary to suspend civil liberties in time of war. And the class struggle for a socially just society has the urgency of a war. Every state uses physical coercion. To this extent, every state can be called a dictatorship. Socialism at least has the merit of being a dictatorship of the proletariat. Its coercion is not exercised on behalf of the monied class. And the state, with its coercion, is destined to disappear when the battle is won against this determined minority class.

Not only does Model 1 have a battle plan, but it sees the victory as assured. Model 2, lacking a predetermined plan for matching production to consumer needs, will be plagued with gluts on the market, layoffs, depressed buying power, and all the psychological, physical, and moral misery that unemployment entails. The prevailing technological rationality in Model 2 is a blueprint for human misery. As E. F. Schumacher has pointed out,[10] the ideal toward which capitalism tends would be maximum production with minimum or zero employees. Technological progress signals layoffs. Better machines mean fewer employees, pared salary costs, higher profits. Technological progress serves the few, not the many. Model 1, on the other hand, puts human beings first. Technology serves the proletarian majority, not the other way around. Technological progress, therefore, will not signal layoffs but fewer working hours for all, because the workers own the machines. They are working for themselves. They are not working to fatten the profits of a capitalist class. So technological progress will benefit all, not just a few. Since production is planned and industries are not in competition, there is no motivation to get one up on competitors by grinding down the workers. The worker receives full value for what he

[10]E. F. Schumacher, *Small Is Beautiful: Economics As If People Mattered* (New York: Harper and Row, 1973), P. 51.
Schumacher joins with Marx in condemning an economic system that subordinates human needs and fulfillment to the impersonal dynamics of capitalistically organized technological production. Schumacher, however, sharply diverges from Marx's reductionism whereby all the higher expressions of human life—religion, philosophy, and art—are said to be mere disguises designed to foster the underlying class struggle: more on this in the next chapter.

contributes. He is not burdened with earning profits for those who do not work.

Rationalism versus fallibilism. The last chapter presented pragmatism as a business philosophy based on reason operating by the scientific method. But pragmatism's faith in reason is puny compared to the rational vision of society proposed by Model 1, as Lindblom has shown.[11] Marx, as we have just seen, was confident that there is a correct way of organizing society economically, and an incorrect way. And the intellectual elite can tell the difference. A true ideology, then, can be formulated to express what the genuine physical, psychological and social needs of human beings are. And having discovered what human nature is, political leaders rightly organize and direct society according to this true picture. In the tradition of Plato's *Republic*, Model 1 postulates a fundamental harmony and complementarity in the needs and goals of human beings in society. Those who by their deviation disrupt this correct social organization are wrong, and the silencing of such people is perfectly justifiable.

Model 2 has no such all-embracing confidence in the ability of human reason to diagnose the human condition and prescribe for it. We are fallible creatures. The world is far too complex to yield up a masterplan that our puny minds could comprehend. As we saw in our consideration of pragmatism as a business philosophy, problem-solving proceeds on a piecemeal basis. Within the overall business process, particular breakdowns occur. To these areas of conflict, methodical experimental inquiry is directed. But the assumptions of the overall process itself remain intact. The only overall vision in Model 2 is that there *is* no overall vision. Competition in the free-enterprise system will yield the best economic arrangement our fallible minds can hope for. And competition in the marketplace of ideas is the best test of truth. Such is Model 2's underlying epistemology:

> But when men have realized that time has upset many fighting faiths, they may come to believe ... that the ultimate good desired is better reached by free trade in ideas—that the best test of truth is the power of the thought to get itself accepted in the competition of the marketplace.[12]

This statement by Justice Oliver Wendell Holmes, Jr. is a classic expression of the partnership between free-enterprise economics and free-enterprise philosophy. It might also serve as a striking example of how a philo-

---

[11]Lindblom, *op. cit.*, Chapter 19.
[12]From: Dissenting opinion of Justice Holmes in *Abrams v. United States*, 250 U.S. 616 (1919).

sophical superstructure grows out of and legitimates the underlying economic structure, as Marx's analysis would contend.

If truth emerges from the marketplace of ideas, then "market surveys" become critically important in both the economic and political arenas. So free elections are essential to Model 2 as also in an unimpeded marketplace. Not merely freedom, but *truth* is at issue. The correct political policy will emerge from the ballot box in Model 2. It cannot be discovered ahead of time as in Model 1. Similarly, the correct economic distribution of goods will emerge as people vote with their dollars what to buy and what not to buy. Reason is not able to determine the correct economic structure ahead of time in Model 2. Free elections and free enterprise have a truth-producing function here that is lacking in Model 1. So it is not surprising that Model 1 can afford to be casual about such freedoms, and even view them as impediments to genuine human fulfillment.

This climate of freedom and competition allows for conflict. In the tradition of Hobbes, conflict and not harmony is the norm in human social affairs. Deviation is expected, not punished. There is no predetermined norm of truth by which the deviant can be judged wrong. In fact, it is from the clash of deviant views that the truth emerges in the view of Model 2. Therefore, fallibilistic pragmatism is skeptical about the utopias so confidently proclaimed by Model 1 with its confidence in reason and harmony.

Model 1 assumes that there is a correct answer to social problems and sets about to discover it by analysis. Model 2 shows no such confidence that there is a correct answer to be found. Wherefore policy-making proceeds not by analysis but by due process. Consider, for example, the question of whether to build nuclear power reactors in a given state. Model 1 will analyze the costs, benefits, and dangers with a view to arriving at a correct answer that will be authoritatively imposed. Whereas Model 2 is likely to submit the matter to referendum and vote. Obviously, analysis is not entirely lacking in Model 2. The ideal remains of an *informed* electorate. But the analysis occurs in a limited context of immediate problem-solving rather than in a context of a masterplan for society as a whole.

3. THE RESULTS—AN EVALUATION

We have been recounting some criticisms leveled at the free-enterprise business system as such. The flaws in the business system can be traced to a double philosophical blindness. Failures in the economy reflect failures in epistemology, i.e., in theory of knowledge and in methods of thinking. We have discussed these philosophical flaws under the headings of "operationalism" and of "fallibilism," each of which limits our ability to understand and alleviate our enslaved conditions, according to these critics. They blind us to alternatives.

Marcuse criticized the politics and economics of the business system for its flat "one-dimensional" way of looking at human society, which results from operational thinking. This is the negative side of the coin. On the positive side, we outlined Marx's diagnosis of what's wrong with the capitalist system, together with his implied program for a more humane society. Going beyond the tentative fallibilism of pragmatic decision-making, Marx confidently advances a revolutionary masterplan.

Comes time now for an evaluation of these critics of the business system. We suggest two defenses that can be marshaled against Marcuse's critique. Consider these for yourself. How valid is their critique of the business system as we know it? Is a truly just and humane society possible short of a complete revolution in the economic system as it exists today in the capitalist world?

Two defenses of operational thinking. Recall that Marcus criticized operational thinking because (1) it does away with ideals, and (2) it effectively suppresses genuine criticism. We'll restate in turn each argument by Marcuse. Then we will raise a question (*Q*) or objection that a pragmatist could make against this argument. After that, we'll give the Socialist answer (*A*) to this question or objection. Our intention is not to prejudice the issue one way or the other, but to help the reader arrive at a self-evaluation of the debate.

(1) Operational thinking, says Marcuse, canonizes the status quo. You are what you do. There is *some* novelty, to be sure. When problems arise, new solutions are found. But the economic, intellectual and political framework within which problems arise itself remains unquestioned. The question of what the *ideal* framework would be never gets asked.

Q: One can admit that pragmatic philosophy is inherently conservative. The human animal is a reluctant revolutionary. Fundamental paradigm-shifts occur only as a last resort. We prefer to tinker with the established economic and social system to make it work rather than to overthrow it. It is not at all clear that the Socialist's paradigm is the path to utopian freedom. Is the tyranny of the proletariat and of their elitist party leaders all that superior to the so-called tyranny of the capitalist class?

Furthermore, operational thinking need not in principle exclude revolution. It is conceivable that the capitalist economic system could become so unworkable, so unbearable, and so intolerably unjust that the only operationally viable hypothesis would be an economic and political revolution. The capitalist system is a long way from this extremity. For all its problems, it shows a strength and stability unmatched by many Socialist regimes.

A: The Socialist can readily concede that the ideal society is far from concrete realization anywhere today. A dictatorship of the proletariat, however, would be a step in the right direction—right, because society would then be organized around the interests of the majority worker class rather than around the minority owner class.

Moreover, while operational thinking may not in principle exclude the possibility of revolution, still it is more unlikely to entertain such a hypothesis—which brings us to the next point.

(2) Operational thinking effectively suppresses genuine criticism. Paradoxically, says Marcuse, tolerance of critical ideas becomes an instrument for undercutting the effective critical power of those ideas. When every idea, however inane, silly, or false, has an equal right to a hearing in the "marketplace," then the critic of the established structure gets co-opted into that very structure. When the token black, the token woman, and the token revolutionary have had their say, then they can safely be ignored.[13]

Q: There is some truth to this objection. The one who succeeds in defining the terms of an argument has gone more than halfway toward winning the argument. This insight underlies the traditional maxim: "Possession is nine-tenths of the law." Operational thinking starts with the given actual ongoing economic, political, and intellectual system. Actual events and institutions define the situation within which criticism takes place. To complain about this is to complain that society does not easily tolerate discussion of its own overthrow and suppression. It prefers to accommodate and adjust to critics within the ongoing institution rather than to aid and abet critics in their goal of overthrowing established institutions. Is socialism any *more* willing to cooperate with those who would overthrow *it*? Is it not even less tolerant of those who would subvert the Socialist system?

A: Socialism does not favor an indiscriminate tolerance of human and antihuman ideals alike. The propagation of false ideas that would delay the coming of a genuinely humane society is intolerable. Error has no rights.

Summation: We reach the parting of the ways. Pragmatic business persons are not all that sure of their ability to tell who is right and who is wrong. Too many fighting faiths have been overturned by time, as Oliver Wendell Holmes, Jr. has pointed out. Truth yields itself up only to the

---

[13]See, for example, Herbert Marcuse in "Repressive Tolerance," in Robert Wolff *et al.*, *A Critique of Pure Tolerance* (Boston: Beacon Press, 1969).

painstaking, cautious, and experimental inquirer who refuses to exclude out of hand any hypothesis. Tolerance even of apparently wrong ideas is essential for discovering truth. Time and the test of action will prove them right or wrong. Such is the modesty of pragmatic fallibilism.

But perhaps socialism's masterplan for economic justice will have the last word in the verdict of history. Today, 53 nations controlling 42 percent of the world's population proclaim allegience to some type of socialism, though not always of the Marxist variety outlined above. The outcomes of our daily economic and political decisions are the arguments that will determine which business philosophy most truly does justice to human life and to the quality of that life.

We come now to an economic philosophy that cuts deeper still. It views the Socialist-capitalist debate as comparatively trivial. For these latter two philosophies both fail to diagnose the antihuman direction in which industrial civilization is taking us. I'm talking about what Schumacher has called "Buddhist Economics," or Ivan Illich, "The Age of the Disabling Professional," which is the subject of the next chapter.

DISCUSSION QUESTIONS

1. Operational thinking canonizes the status quo. We address ourselves to problems within the system, but it never occurs to us to question the system itself. Hence we are doomed never to escape from systemically induced injustice.

2. Operational thinking stifles genuine criticism. Even Alexander Solzhenitsyn, no friend of Marxism, has pointed out how the very freedom of the American media can be a force opposing freedom. Where every opinion is tolerated, the bite of real criticism is blunted; error mingles with truth, and all opinion tends to gravitate toward the center of established opinion. But error has no rights. True is true and false is false. Humane ideas have a right to be heard; destructive ideas enjoy no such right. The proper propagation of ideas is not a matter for the marketplace, but for the humane planners.

These are two Marxist criticisms of a philosophical epistemology that enables the business system to flourish in spite of all its attendant evils. Can you escape these traps of operational thinking? Is your attitude one of, "What's the use? We can tinker with the system, but we can't change it." Or, on the other hand, can you accept criticisms of the market system as it now operates and entertain genuine alternatives?

Try the following exercise. Return to the list of evils imputed to the capitalist system in the test at the beginning of this chapter. Evils exist and evils call for remedy. The planning vs. pricing approaches to the allocation of goods and services represents a genuine value-conflict. Consider in turn each of the indictments against capitalism:

(a) Does the alleged evil really exist? Does the American business system as it is now organized result in the injustice in question?

(b) If so, list all the arguments you can muster to show that the remedy lies in government intervention and planning.

(c) Then list all the arguments you can to show that a market-remedy is the best cure for the evil in question.

(d) What are the points of seemingly irreconcilable disagreement between the two plans?

(e) Which of the differences between the two economic philosophies are fuzzy and not so clearcut?

(f) Then, sort out the elements that both sides share in common.

(g) Repeat the process for each of the alleged evils of the American business system as viewed through Marxist eyes and listed at the beginning of this chapter.

SUGGESTED READINGS

Cutler, Anthony, Barry Hindress, Paul Hirst, and Athar Hussain. *Marx's Capital and Capitalism Today.* Boston: Routledge and Kegan Paul, Ltd., 1977–78, 2 Vols.

Duncan, Graeme. *Two Views of Social Conflict and Social Harmony: Marx and Mill.* Cambridge: Cambridge University Press, paperback edition, 1977.

Garaudy, Roger. *Karl Marx: The Evolution of His Thought.* New York: International Publishers, 1967.

Leonhard, Wolfgang. *Three Faces of Marxism: Political Concepts of Soviet Ideology, Maoism, and Humanist Marxism.* New York: Holt, Rinehart and Winston, 1974.

Lindblom, Charles E. *Politics and Markets: The World's Political-Economic Systems.* New York: Basic Books, Inc., Publishers, 1977.

Macintyre, Alasdair. *Herbert Marcuse: An Exposition and a Polemic.* New York: Viking Press, 1970.

Mandel, Ernest. *Late Capitalism.* London: Verso Edition, 1978.

———. *Marxist Economic Theory.* New York; Modern Reader Paperback edition, 1970, 2 Vols.

Marcuse, Herbert. *One-Dimensional Man: Studies in the Ideology of Advanced Industrial Society.* Boston: Beacon Press, 1964.

Marks, Robert W. *The Meaning of Marcuse.* New York: Ballantine Books, 1970.

McLellan, David. *Karl Marx.* New York: The Viking Press, 1975.

McMurty, John. *The Structure of Marx's World-View.* Princeton, N.J.: Princeton University Press, 1978.

Novak, George. *Pragmatism versus Marxism: An Appraisal of John Dewey's Philosophy.* New York: Pathfinder Press, Inc., 1975.

Tucker, Robert. *The Marxian Revolutionary Idea: Essays on Marxist Thought and Its Impact on Radical Movements.* New York: W. W. Norton and Co., Inc., 1969.

———. *Philosophy and Myth in Karl Marx.* Cambridge: Cambridge University Press, second edition, 1972.

Wolff, Robert Paul, Barrington Moore, Jr., and Herbert Marcuse. *A Critique of Pure Tolerance.* Boston: Beacon Press, 1969.

CHAPTER 10

TOWARD A HUMANE ECONOMY

For every activity there is a certain appropriate scale, and the more active and intimate the activity, the smaller the number of people that can take part, the greater is the number of such relationship arrangements that need to be established. . . .

While people with an easy-going kind of logic believe that fast transport and instantaneous communications open up a new dimension of freedom (which they do in some rather trivial respects), they overlook the fact that these achievements also tend to destroy freedom, by making everything extremely vulnerable and extremely insecure, unless conscious policies are developed and conscious action is taken, to mitigate the destructive effects of these technological developments.

E. F. Schumacher[1]

I use the term "radical monopoly to designate . . . the substitution of an industrial product or a professional service for a useful activity in which people engage or would like to engage. A radical monopoly paralyzes autonomous action in favor of professional deliveries . . . from the assumption that those activities which we designate by intransitive verbs can be indefinitely replaced by institutionally defined staples referred to as nouns: "education" substituted for "I learn," "health care" for "I heal," "transportation" for "I move," "television" for "I play."

Ivan Illich[2]

---

[1]E. F. Schumacher, *Small Is Beautiful: Economics As If People Mattered* (New York: Harper and Row, Colophon Books, 1973), pp. 62 and 65.

[2]Ivan Illich, *Toward A History of Needs* (New York: © Pantheon Books, a division of Random House, Inc. 1978), pp. 39 and 36.

OBJECTIVES FOR CHAPTER 10:

1. To understand the distinction between the primacy of the economic as a methodological assumption, and the primacy of the economic as a given human goal;

2. To examine the tendency to equate the human with the economic, specifically, in our pursuit of:

    (a) the consumerist ideal of "the good life" (see Scitovsky);

    (b) the professionalist ideal of the "well-managed life" (see Illich);

3. To understand the philosophical roots of this equation of human and economic, i.e., reductionism and relativism (see Schumacher);

4. To test for oneself the practicability of these criticisms in daily decisions about economic living.

Introduction. We have viewed business in this book as the process of distributing economic goods and services, especially as this occurs in the private sector. We have examined alternative philosophies that more or less consciously guide individual and corporate decision-makers through the moral dilemmas that economic realities impose. These philosophies from Machiavelli to Marx, for all their differences, share an assumption and starting point in common. They each tend to assume as a given the answer of Adam Smith to the meta-economical question of what economics itself is all about. They each assume that economics concerns the creation and distribution of wealth in the form of goods and services. It is the science of how to get more wealth out of existing resources. This economic process can be placed in the service of various moral and social goals. These goals, of course, represent value-decisions. But the economist precisely as economist, and the business person precisely as agent of economic science, abstract themselves from such teleological considerations. Rather they tend to view human nature through the rather narrowly focused eyeglasses of economics as defined above. And this is not surprising. Business's whole reason for existing is to optimize the wealth creation and distribution process, and an ever improved technology is the instrument for achieving this more and more efficiently.

We have seen how pragmatism provides a prescription for the ethical autonomy of business within the framework of free-market capitalism. As autonomous, pragmatism, using the model of scientific intelligence, is in a position to pass judgment on heteronomous conventional and legal norms rather than blindly conforming to them. Marxism, as we saw, challenges pragmatism's unconscious conformity to the market system; this challenge is made in the name of ethical idealism and of a more just society. The value critique in this present chapter cuts more deeply still. The debate on the merits of a free versus a planned economy is relatively trivial according to these critics. For both pragmatism and Marxism leave unexamined much more fundamental human issues than this one. Both share the goals of the economic game as played in the industrial world; they differ only as to the best means for achieving these goals. But the goals themselves need to be scrutinized. And that's what we proceed to do now.

VALUES-CLARIFICATION TEST

This final chapter invites you to examine the broad question of human happiness and its relationship to the economy. We will be looking at the things you can buy—consumer goods and services; we'll be looking, too, at what makes you happy—human pleasure and satisfaction. A healthy economy and happy human beings: to what extent do these go together? What would a truly humane economy look like?

The following test is to get you thinking about these questions, to clarify your own present feelings about consumer goods and human goods and the relation between the two. Consider one at a time the following dogmatic claims typically found in advertising copy. Together with one or more other persons, answer the following questions about each claim in turn:

(a) What consumer-need or human value does the claim intend to promote or urge?

(b) List some underlying facts and examples that could support the truth of the claim.

(c) List some underlying facts and examples which tend to show that the claim is fallacious or untrue.

1. "There is no time like the present to lose those ugly pounds."
2. "If you own a digital watch, you deserve the very best scotch."
3. "There's no substitute for activated GR-342. That's why there's no substitute for Smooth-Ease Talcum Powder."
4. "Natural bread is best."
5. "Break-resistant plates are the solution to this summer's casual living."
6. "People who like people drink cold beer."
7. "Your own views are enriched when you listen to our Famous Scientists' Taped Lectures."
8. "For cheap delicious protein, peanut butter has no rival."
9. "Every bride deserves a modern kitchen."

10. "Only at the Aquarium can you see how the other half lives."

11. "Watching home movies is a great way to spend a winter evening."

12. "Spring is a time for growing."

13. "The Surgeon General has determined that cigarette smoking is dangerous to your health."

14. "Less is More."

15. "Spend money to get money."

  (d) Now ask yourself, is the need or value that each claim proposes also a need or value to you?

  (e) Does the value in question have a dollar value on the market? If so, approximately how much?

  (f) Is the market price worth it to you?

Such advertising copy sells not only a product but also a way of life. It is precisely the way of life that we come to examine now. First of all we can have no quarrel with the primacy of the economic and the technological as a methodological assumption. Viewed in this manner, the assumption will yield hypothetical imperatives for action. *If* I want to manufacture goods as efficiently as possible, what techniques should I adopt? What uses of labor, capital, resources, and time will yield the best returns on investment compared with other uses? What techniques should be brought to bear, *if* I want to maximize the delivery of services? How can be arranged the universal availability for human consumption of the comforts that money can buy? So far so good. The problem comes when these goals lose their hypothetical character and come to be viewed as absolute ends; when, for example, the maximization of comfort and the optimizing of technological efficiency become unquestioned goods in themselves.

There is a tendency, not always explicit, to *reduce* human nature to this economic dimension. What starts as a methodological assumption becomes a dogmatic statement about human nature. The human person comes to be viewed as identical with the economic person, and this equation of the human with the economic and technological becomes normative in a moral sence. There is a tendency, in other words, to identify the technologically better with the socially better, a tendency to prefer the professionally licensed expert to the amateur, a tendency to equate human satisfaction with consumer satisfaction. Once a primacy has been granted to these goals of technological efficiency and consumerism, then whatever best works for these goals becomes good business and good management.

In the course of examining business philosophies throughout the book, we have indirectly raised questions about whether technological efficiency, professionalism, and consumerism do indeed exhaust the meaning of human. Economists and business people are beginning more and more to face these meta-economic value questions head on. We will now briefly review three recent critiques of the economic system as it exists in the industrial world, both East and West. The critics in question are re-introducing the value issue into economics. They show how the primacy of the economic, technological view has become more than a methodological assumption about human nature. They see it as a dogmatic metaphysical statement about the meaning of human that therefore legitimates the ethical judgments which would flow from such a meaning. They challenge this metaphysics and this ethics. They seek to drive a wedge between the meaning of human and the meaning of economic in the conventional sense. Economic philosophers like Tibor Scitovsky, Ivan Illich, and E. F. Schumacher urge a revolution in perspective that transcends the Marxist strictures against capitalism which we saw in the last chapter. These men challenge assumptions about technology and humanity shared alike by today's rival political and economic camps. Each in his own way attacks the equation of the human with the economically efficient and the technologically rational. They raise a meta-ethical challenge to the established ethics of the industrial world.

Consider these three related angles on the antihuman consequences of the economic game as played in this industrial world. Tibor Scitovsky probes the ideal of consumer comfort, Ivan Illich questions the reign of professionalism, and E. F. Schumacher examines the rule of efficiency and of value-free economics. Critiques such as these are perhaps of little help to the business person in his or her day-to-day decisions, which must be made within the established framework of the business game as it is actually played. Still, they can have a heuristic value. Alternatives to the institutionalized injustices of the given world are at least conceivable. It is possible for economics to be pressed into the service of other goals. These proposals point to directions for institutional change that would support the primacy of the human. Indeed, you will recognize that individual business people are already acting on such humane concerns. Can such concerns be institutionalized into the economic structure? Can we look forward to what E. F. Schumacher calls "economics as if people mattered"?

1. THE CONSUMERIST IDEAL: THE GOOD LIFE

The American ideal of "the good life" is the first symptom of our tendency to equate the human with the economic. Americans in their pursuit of consumer comfort tend to aid and abet the view of themselves as economic persons, and little more. Economist Tibor Scitovsky,[3] a relatively mild yet incisive critic of our economic attitudes, examines the paradoxes inherent in our view of ourselves as "consumers." We value ourselves and others in terms of consumption, in terms of the goods and services we can afford to buy. Business as an institution is perfectly equipped to respond to this consumerist ideal of the good life. And business and society mutually feed upon and reinforce the illusion that human happiness lies in the fulfillment of this ideal. It is just this equating of consumer satisfaction with human happiness that Tibor Scitovsky attacks. Of course, the distinction between human being and consumer is obvious on the face of it, but too easily forgotten. Scitovsky brings to bear on economics the resources of psychology to show how fatal for human happiness it is to forget this distinction. Schumacher and Illich, to be considered below, will drive an ever deeper wedge between the ideal consumer and the ideal human being.

Human satisfaction: comfort and pleasure. Business as well as consumers, the clientele of business, are primarily sellers and buyers of comfort, Scitovsky argues. The substance of human satisfaction is comfort in the form of market products and services. Comfort, however, does not exhaust the range of satisfactions sought by the human person. So a comfort-centered life can be, in human terms, a very unhappy life. In some ways the consumerist ideal is the enemy of human happiness. Such in a nutshell is the thrust of Scitovsky's argument. To the extent that business and consumers, sellers and buyers, are comfort-oriented, they could be construed as purveyors of unhappiness rather than of satisfaction. For, in psychological terms, human satisfaction involves not only comfort but pleasure too. Indeed, it is possible that pleasure is incompatible with comfort. In other words, it is possible that the consumerist ideal fails even in terms of hedonism.

How can this be? Let's contrast comfort and pleasure. Comfort is merely a negative good. First, comfort is what assuages my appetites. Food and clothing, tranquilizers and television sets, beer and golf carts, all serve human comfort in this sense. As food assuages hunger and tranquilizers calm the nerves, so golf carts pamper weary limbs. Such comforts are concerned with drive reduction. In this consists the negative good: aroused appetites like hunger, anxiety, and weariness are appeased. The drive is reduced, the pain of arousal goes away, whence we are rendered "comfortable." The unending parade of media ads for goods, services, and conveniences keeps alive the ideal and desirability of comforts of this kind.

[3]Tibor Scitovsky, *The Joyless Economy: An Inquiry Into Human Satisfaction and Consumer Dissatisfaction* (New York: Oxford University Press, 1976).

These are the satisfactions that money can buy that businesses can best supply.

But note, too, that our arousal level can also be too low. Appetites not only need to be appeased, they also need to be stimulated. Such stimulants form a second type of comfort. We often, however, neglect the appetite-stimulating comforts to the detriment of human happiness. What was comfortable can become boring. This is the psychological version of the Law of Diminishing Marginal Utility. The more you have of a comfort the less you want of it. Consider, for example, routine sex with an accustomed partner, the "ice-cream diet" (no other foods allowed), or football bowl games on New Year's Day television. In each case, the appetite is not merely slaked, but sated; the result is not comfort but boredom. The appetite has sunk below the optimal arousal level. It requires not quelling, but stimulation. Comfort—the optimal arousal level—requires uppers as well as downers. So, what does an organism do when all its needs are satisfied? The answer "nothing" is wrong. Excessive tranquility can be as dissatisfying as excessive anxiety. Much of the defect in the consumerist ideal lies in its tendency to ignore drive-arousal comforts, chiefly found in the pursuit of novelty. So the single-minded quest to satisfy every aroused appetite will not lead to the good life, even as narrowly conceived by the consumerist ideal. This is the first fatal flaw.

The good life requires stimulants, mental and physical; the good life requires novelty. Physical stimulants, for example, include jogging, swimming, tennis, and other participatory sports, as well as the more rudimentary yawning, scratching, stretching, pacing. Mental stimulants would be activities like reading, entertainment, conversation, spectator sports, art, games, puzzles. More generally, the comforts that stimulate instead of satiate involve the pursuit of novelty in all forms. We stave off boredom by seeking out the new, the surprising, the unexpected. As psychologist Carl Rogers has pointed out,[4] Freud missed the mark completely in hypothesizing that "the nervous stystem is . . . an apparatus which would even, if this were feasible, maintain itself in an altogether unstimulated condition." Rather, the organism develops its potentials by seeking out ever more complex stimuli. The pursuit of stimulating comforts serves growth values as well as hedonistic values. Such is the usefulness of "useless" activities.

So it is no easy matter to lead a comfort-oriented life that is also humanly satisfying. An optimal arousal level requires of novelty-bringing comforts an intermediate newness. If they are too new (e.g., a severe electrical storm on an open golf course), they are stimulating to the point of

---

[4]Carl Rogers, *On Personal Power* (New York: Delacorte Press, 1977), p. 241.

anxiety, and the arousal level will be too high. If they are too redundant (e.g., a tennis game with a very inept and mismatched opponent), the result is boredom and the arousal level will be too low. Ideal are "safe dangers," novelties that can be coped with (e.g., a lightning storm viewed from indoors or a murder-mystery story—but not a real murder). Scitovsky's point is that business and consumer alike often neglect the stimulating side of comfort. The resultant focus on drive-reduction comforts leads to the paradox of boredom in the midst of plenty—consumer satisfaction that fails to yield human satisfaction. But the hedonistic case against the American version of the good life is sharper still, says Scitovsky.

Even supposing a nice balance of stimulants and relaxants, even granting the right mix of comforts that assures an optimal arousal level, there is still missing an essential ingredient of human happiness. And this missing ingredient points to the second fatal flaw in the consumerist ideal of the good life that views the person in purely economic terms. So far, we have been looking at comfort, a negative good involving the removal of excessive or defective stimulus/arousal. This negative good needs to be supplemented by a positive one, viz., the missing ingredient of *pleasure*. Human satisfaction, even in hedonistic terms, involves much more than the comforts that money can buy. A life of comfort is empty if not spiced by pleasure. And pleasure need not accompany comfort at all. Indeed the pursuit of comfort can be the enemy of pleasure. Let's see why.

Feelings of comfort or discomfort refer to the *level* of arousal, whereas feelings of pleasure are a function of *change* in the arousal level. It's like the difference between speed and acceleration. For example, "I'm hungry" = discomfort due to high arousal level; "I'm full" = comfort: appetite satisfied; while hungry, I might have said that my appetite was at a level of 30 mph, to use the speed metaphor; when sated, the appetite is gone: zero mph. Pleasure occurs in the *change* from hunger to satiation, i.e., in the eating process, in the *deceleration*, to continue the metaphor, from 30 mph to zero. When the eating is done, i.e., when the *change* in the arousal level ceases, so does the pleasure. This explains the fleeting nature of pleasure, the "let-down" when the experience is over and the goal is achieved. The achieving of comfort is the cessation of pleasure. A comfort-centered life can mean a pleasure-empty life.

So pleasure and pain are not opposite sides of the same coin. The absence of pain need not imply pleasure. And lots of pain is compatible with lots of pleasure. If anything, it is comfort and pleasure that are opposed to each other, not pain and pleasure! This paradox explains how the consumerist ideal can bring built-in disappointment in terms of human satisfaction. A high standard of living can translate into a high degree of boredom. Comfort gained is pleasure lost. And awareness of pleasure lost becomes regretful acquiescence in pleasure lost when comfort turns into addiction. The consumer in settling for comfort pays a human price, for the human craves pleasure as well as comfort. Scitovsky does not intend to attack either the business-marketers of comfort or the economic blueprints for their effective marketing. Any economist worth his salt is perfectly aware of the wide range of human satisfactions that need not and do not pass through the marketplace (sunbathing, chess-playing, girl-watching, for example). And any good business person will be responsive to "consumer" demands for stimulation and even for pleasure (indeed, the consumer is all too willing to take this route, Illich points out below). The fact remains that the American consumer economy is heavily oriented towards comforts that pacify, reassure and sedate the consumer. And since the acquisition of these is the prevailing definition of the good life, business and society conspire to organize the economy so as to bring this about. Scitovsky simply points out that money can't buy happiness, if human happiness is defined according to the consumerist ideal. And this is not bad news, but good, he concludes.

What is the good news that follows from this critique of the American way? Simply this. If money can't buy happiness, then perhaps happiness can be found in ways that are not directly related to disposable income. If a clear distinction is maintained between self as consumer and self as human, perhaps the human being can find nonmarket sources of satisfaction, especially in stimulations and pleasures that the market does not readily supply.

But the good news goes beyond the individual's pursuit of happiness. If the direction of human happiness does not lie in the ever more conspicuous consumption of exhaustible energy and resources, then a redefinition of the good life away from such extravagance holds out hope that human satisfaction and happiness is available for the teeming millions who can never expect to emulate the excesses of the consumerist ideal. Indeed it is doubtful whether even future American generations can afford to emulate this ideal. And this is not bad news once it is realized that the comforts sought by this ideal can crowd out the enjoyments of life instead of enhancing them. The challenge of society and of business's response to society is to reorganize the economy so that it recognizes the limits of growth and resources, and serves the cause of human happiness within those limits. This will involve a thorough revolution in values away from the extant consumerist ideal at home, an ideal looked up to as a leader of fashion and model life-style abroad. Can you think of examples of how this revolution is already underway? How would you redefine the ideal of human happiness? How would you make the business ethos responsive to this redefinition? Ivan Illich paints one picture of what such a revised economy might look like.

2. THE PROFESSIONALIST IDEAL: THE WELL-MANAGED LIFE

A consequence of the dedicated pursuit of comfort, as we have seen, is a kind of undefined dissatisfied malaise. For a cure of this malaise, it is tempting to look to the marketplace of stimulating pleasure-giving goods and to the marketplace of therapeutic potions, pills, and services. As we saw above, although consumers most zealously pursue pacifying comforts, the marketplace is equally ready to supply stimulating comforts and pleasure-giving novelties if the demand is there. And indeed novelty upon novelty crowds the marketplace—we call them fads—and they quickly wear out; the pleasure they give is short-lived. And the therapeutic market is booming both in pharmaceutical goods and in the health-care professionals who peddle the goods along with their services. Scitovsky diagnosed addiction to comfort-producing *goods* as a cause of human unhappiness. For Illich, the problem is the much more pervasive and entrenched dependence on *services* that deprives us of our identity as autonomously functioning human beings. Is this the direction of human happiness and salvation? Ivan Illich's answer is a resounding "No!" In the course of defending this answer, he gives a much more profound diagnosis than we have seen so far of the antihuman consequences of the economy as now dominated by the so-called "helping" professionals.

The price of progress, says Illich, has been loss of autonomy. As area after area of human life becomes professionalized, individuals lose the ability to take charge of their own lives. The focus of individual well-being has been transferred to forces that lie outside of the self. What masquerades as human progress has been a prescription for increasing human powerlessness. Scitovsky had preached liberation from debilitating affluence in the form of addicting comforts. Illich calls for liberation from disabling dependence on domineering professionals. This latter crisis cuts across all economic, political and cultural lines. The problem is as acute in Hungary as in Canada, in Andean villages as in American suburbs. From this perspective it is ironical to see the Third World, in the name of liberation, clamoring for the kinds of human enslavement in which the industrial world has enmeshed itself. The marketers of professional services have more insidiously and more completely enslaved the consumer than has any Madison Avenue huckster of comfort-addicting goods. If this seems to be hyperbole, consider now Illich's meaning for "professional," the domineering relationship that professionalism induces, and the professional myths standing in the way of restored human autonomy.

Development and progress have come to mean the substitution of industrial commodities (market exchange values) for autonomous activities (nonmarket use-values). What humans used to do for themselves autonomously and for free, they now must purchase in the market from professional "cartels." In Chile, for example, the commodity, infant formula, is replacing mother's milk, an autonomously produced use-value. In the mid-Pacific Caroline Islands, imported canned food, including canned fish, has replaced native fishing, an autonomous art now completely lost on those islands. In Mexican villages, bands of native music-makers have been replaced by loudspeakers attached to juke boxes; music now becomes a market commodity . Everywhere in the world, "education," a commodity on the market expressed by a noun, has replaced the autonomous activity expressed by the verb "I learn." The autonomous use-values such as "I move," "I walk," "I peddle," have become "transportation" or "mass transit," now an exchange-value: I pay to *be* moved. "Health care" is a commodity to be "delivered" at ever more exhorbitant cost, replacing autonomous responsibility like "I heal," "I take care of myself." Thus the measure of "progress" is the conversion of use-values into exchange-values.

Domains of autonomous and responsible human activity like self-learning, self-care, and self-movement have been surrendered to professionals and licensed experts who "know what is best" for me, and deliver to me their "expert" services at a price in the shape of commodities called education, health care and transportation. The scientist, the therapist, the executive, the professional, the licensed experts form a new "priesthood," says Illich. Such professionals as educators, physicians and social workers, under the guise of services delivered, in fact deprive their "clients" of the power and confidence to serve themselves. Their services are "disabling" rather than "enabling," whence Illich calls today "The Age of the Disabling Professional." The mark of the professional is not high income, arduous training or exalted social status. Rather the professional is characterized by the claim to special knowledge hidden from the amateur. The professionals deem that this knowledge confers on them the power to decide what others need, why they should need these things, and how their needs should and should not be administered. In other words, to them belongs the power to define who is a client or patient, to determine their need or disease, and to prescribe a solution or remedy. They have succeeded in co-opting the legal system to back up their authority, Illich goes on to say, and seduced their clientele to defer to this authority. To give a small but significant example, you address your physician as "Doctor," while the physician uses your first name in addressing you.

A slave is a person whom another legally deprives of the freedom to make certain voluntary decisions. The disabling professionals, says Illich, have achieved such a domineering, enslaving position over their "clients." Their monopoly over the power to diagnose gives them authority to create ever new constituencies of "clients" whose "needs" then must be prescribed for. The role of the physician in American society is the archetypal model of the "disabling professional." It used to be only on rare occasions that one would require the services of a physician. The role of "patient" used to be the exception; now it has become the norm. For example, pregnancy has come to be viewed as a disability bordering on disease. The best health-care professionals recommend frequent electronic monitoring of the fetus-become-patient even before it leaves the womb. It's all but impossible to arrange a birth without an attendant physician. Thenceforth each stage of human life and growth takes place under the supervision of the appropriate medical specialist. Natural functions become ailments. The pediatrician, the dentist, the gynecologist, and the orthodontist certify the stages and cycles of developing life; and at the annual checkup during the middle years the physician solemnly records the patient's slow demise: these lifelong patients are all terminal. The hypochondriac used to be the neurotic soul who haunted the doctor's office; now the deviant is considered to be the person who declares independence from doctors, who insists on birthing and dying at home, tends his own ordinary health needs, and takes primary responsibility for his own life and common human ills.

In the perspective of the medical model, consider the other disabling professionals. How free does the mortician, backed by legal sanction, leave you to arrange the funeral rites of your loved ones? What liberty do you have to educate your children outside of the legally mandated public and private system of tracked-in, lock-stepped certifications of conformity to professionally established norms? Of what weight on the open market is your personally acquired knowledge and experience—unless indeed it be certified and accepted by the educational professionals for "credit as life experience"? Reflect on how the police professionals decide which drug usage is permitted and which other usage defines you as a "client" of the legal system. Consider how judges determine which thefts by what socioeconomic classes render them "clients" for the prison system, and which not. Note, further, how hearsay evidence is banned from court proceedings unless it is hearsay rendered by the professional court psychiatrists certifying arcane and slippery issues of competence and incompetence, responsibility and nonresponsibility. How free do the traffic-planning professionals leave you to walk and bicycle where you will? How many legal roadblocks thrown up by the trade professionals will a person confront if he decides to build his own house, or put in her own electrical wiring? And more than this, when not legally coerced, we have even surrendered our food preparation to the professional purveyors of fast food and packagers of convenience.[5]

The antihuman consequences of this rampant professionalism infect every dimension of economic life and every political persuasion. It has come to be assumed that social progress consists in widening the access to such professionally offered commodities. If this be social and economic justice, it is doomed to remain an empty dream, above all for developing nations who aspire to live according to this model. What would be the economic cost, and more to the point the human cost, of world-wide cradle-to-grave care of every human being by an army of professional medical specialists, psychiatrists, lawyers, builders, social workers, city planners, educators, and the list goes on? Civil rights have come to be defined as equal access to these costly and disabling "services," at cost of surrendering the liberty to serve oneself. Welfare is seen to consist in the appropriation of these standardized packages, professionally prepared and forcibly substituted for all the things that people used to do for themselves. In this framework, there is little difference whether these commodities be distributed by the mechanism of the free-enterprise wisdom of pricing or by the socialistic wisdom of planning. The result in each case is equally disabling, equally enslaving. The enabling use of nonmarket, self-sufficient values is replaced by disabling market exchange-values.

In summation, says Illich, three illusions keep alive our willing slavery. As Scitovsky also pointed out, we tend to define ourselves primarily as "consumers." Our happiness and well-being as humans is measured by the means we have to purchase not only comforting goods but professionally packaged services. We value ourselves not chiefly by our autonomous ability to produce and to serve, but chiefly by our access to consumption and our claims on the services of others. This is the first illusion that keeps us fixed in the disabling pattern. It "paralyzes autonomous action in favor of

---

[5]For detailed discussion of the professionalization of our lives, see Ivan Illich's books: *Celebration of Awareness: A Call for Institutional Revolution* (New York: Doubleday, 1971); *Deschooling Society* (New York: Harper and Row, 1971); *Tools for Conviviality* (New York: Harper and Row, 1973); *Energy and Equity* (New York: Harper and Row, 1974); *Medical Nenesis* (New York: Random House, 1976); *Toward a History of Needs*, cited above.

As a counterpoint to this, consider the ongoing dynamic toward deprofessionalizing our lives brilliantly described by Scott Burns in *The Household Economy: Its Shape, Origins, and Future* (Boston: Beacon paperbound, 1977).

[6]Illich, *Toward a History of Needs*, p. 39.

professional deliverances."[6] A second illusion is our tendency to confound efficiency with bigness and complexity. Illich estimates, for example, that the average American spends 2,000 hours per year driving, parking and maintaining his car, and earning the money for its depreciation, maintenance, fuel and fluids, for insurance, and other legal and parking fees. This does not include time spent in traffic court, in jails, in hospitalization from auto accidents, or in earning money to pay fines. If he drives 10,000 miles per year, the net distance per hours invested is 5 mph received from his car—less than he'd get from a bicycle! We have willingly conspired with town planners and traffic managers to maintain ourselves in this irrational situation, but it can hardly be defended on grounds of efficiency!

Present educational, legal, and medical mega-structures are tools that only professionals can manage. Can we devise more efficient, less complex, smaller scaled tools that will restore to the autonomous individual, family and neighborhood control over health, over the power to learn, and over the means of maintaining peace and well-being in society? Most of us learn the difficult and dangerous art of driving a car from amateurs. Could the art of self-learning and self-care be part of our common wisdom too? Can we break through the illusion that bigness and complexity mean progress?

A third disabling illusion we noted above. It is the dream that by attaining civil rights to enjoy disabling professional services, we are thereby rendering ourselves autonomous. Could it be that such civil rights are the enemy of civil liberty? Which is more liberating: a "do it yourself" will-making kit, or access to professional will-making services? Which is more valuable in a Nigerian village: safe water, or access to a new hospital built for high-priced surgery?

Business thrives on feeding these illusions and on marketing the services demanded under their spell. Government remains the main enforcer. But at least the illusions point to a value crisis in society itself. Here business follows rather than leads society, and it understandably doesn't pretend to do otherwise. If society's values change, economic values and business's role in producing and distributing these would follow suit. Already there are movements in this direction and business is responding to these. Do-it-yourself, self-care, self-repairs, natural foods are symptoms of this move away from professionalism and toward autonomy. And in response, business is devising tools that enable individuals to reappropriate mastery over their own lives in every dimension. Critics like Scitovsky and Illich can help business people understand the value-framework that their activity serves and tends to preserve. It can help sensitize them to the antihuman enslaving consequences of such service, and to possibilities for revising economic priorities toward enchancing human autonomy and happiness.

3. THE RELATIVIST IDEAL OF THE MORALLY TOLERANT LIFE

We have reviewed Scitovsky's hypothesis concerning the negative results that the consumerist ideal of the good life can produce. Illich has pointed out the enslaving effect upon us of pursuing the professionalist ideal of the well-managed life. These ideals are revealed as psuedo-ideals. They are moral flaws in our economic system to the extent that they harm us as human beings. What makes us succomb to such illusory ideals? Scitovsky and Illich point out the symptoms and the disease. Now we review E. F. Schumacher who endeavors to discern the philosophical roots of our self-deception and consequent malaise.[7] As noted at the beginning of the chapter, the axioms of the prevailing economic system are not God-given and inevitable. They are to a great extent the result of human choices, choices flowing from philosophies of life not always conscious or articulated. Schumacher's effort is to reveal the philosophical assumptions that have led to our present predicament. These assumptions might seem like a litany of the business philosophies recounted in this book. It is not surprising, however, that the prevalent philosophies would lead to the prevailing economic structure. A review of Schumacher's criticisms can provide a counterpoint to our consideration of these philosophies and a different perspective from which to evaluate them.

Schumacher points out leading philosophical ideas—most of nineteenth-century origin—that have become so much a part of our everyday thinking that it would never dawn on us to question their truth and reality. These ideas, however, are not as empirical as they seem. Rather, Schumacher shows that they are the result of philosophical choices made long ago, and which have become part of the intellectual and therefore of the economic air that we breathe. Evolutionism, positivism, and pragmatism have caused these ideas to flourish. Their result is a leveling off of our perceptions. They yield for us a reduced world—one-dimensional world. We can with their help make quantitative judgments of "more" and "less." But we have become powerless to discern levels of reality, powerless to make *qualitative* judgments concerning "better" and "worse," especially in the realm of values. The result, says Schumacher, is a relativism in ethics

---

[7]E. F. Schumacher, *op. cit.* and *Guide for the Perplexed* (New York: Harper Colophon Books, 1978). Illich and Schumacher both prescribe a lowered scale of living as a remedy for our ills; one might be tempted to translate this in quantitative terms as a lowered *standard* of living, but the point argued in this chapter is that what is quantitatively lower can yield what is qualitatively higher. Leopold Kohr anticipated and diagnosed the problems inflicted on social, economic and political institutions by their sheer size in his book *The Breakdown of Nations*, published back in 1957, and republished in 1978 by Schocken Books as *The Overdeveloped Nations: The Diseconomies of Scale.*

that benignly tolerates any ethical view or value because it knows not how to discriminate good from evil in absolute terms. We are able to answer the question, "what's new?" It's on our lips constantly. But to queries about quality we have no answer: we don't even raise the quality question, "what's best?"

Our penchant for pinning all hope for human happiness on market comforts and services is rooted in a philosophical disease whose virulent strains emerged from reductionistic and evolutionistic nineteenth-century thinking. There may be few business people today who call themselves Social Darwinists, positivists, or Marxists, but the leading ideas of these philosophies have become part and parcel of our thinking apparatus, and they infect our views about human life and values and happiness. The characteristic common to such thinking (which we examined chiefly in Chapters 3, 4, 5, and 9) is its *reductionism*, viz., its effort to reduce the higher manifestations of human life to something lower. We think that the higher reaches of the human spirit consist in the unobservable realms of the aesthetic, the moral, and the religious. But we are wrong, say the reductionists. These so-called higher qualitative realms are really just subtle and disguised manifestations of much baser empirical, quantifiable realities. While differing on just what this base empirical reality is, they all agree that quality considerations are reducible to quantitative ones.

Marx, for example, as we saw in the last chapter, views what passes for life of the spirit (art, philosophy, religion) as *nothing but* a superstructure that disguises the basic structure and stuff of human life which is the economic realm and the class struggle to promote one's interests in this economic realm. The so-called higher superstructures do not represent genuinely superior realms of the spirit. Rather they are covert instruments for manipulating economic interests, these latter being where true reality lies. The positivistic approach to ethics of conventional morality (see Chapter 5) even more directly *reduces* ethical values to the level of observable phenomena. Accordingly, prevailing standards of business ethics are nothing but the common feelings of a given society regarding approved or disapproved behavior. Such feelings are observable and measurable, and are normative by the mere fact of their brute existence. Such is the nature of reductionistic thinking: what seems "more" is reduced to "less."

The attraction of reductionistic thinking is that it takes fuzzy metaphysical notions like "ethical good" and "moral evil" and renders them exact and measurable. This application of scientific techniques to the area of values claims to get rid of metaphysics. It substitutes the clear quantifiable methods of the exact sciences. What the reductionist has actually done, as Schumacher points out so well, is substitute bad metaphysics for good. The reductionistic faith is a decision, *indefensible on observable grounds*, about what will count as real. A Marxist type metaphysical decision that only the economic is real automatically makes it impossible to perceive other levels of reality. They don't exist because they cannot: the metaphysical decision has ruled them out of court beforehand.

It is not only Marxists who appeal to such a metaphysical rule. Such a rule is all the more powerful when unconsciously applied, and apply it we do in the business world, says Schumacher.

> Call a thing immoral or ugly, soul-destroying or a degradation of man, a peril to the peace of the world, or to the well-being of future generations; as long as you have not shown it to be "uneconomic," you have not questioned its right to exist, grow and prosper.[8]

Air pollution, plutonium-poisoned energy, or the employment of Mexican "wet-back" children all become "rational" once the metaphysical decision is made that the economic is the norm of what is real and good. Such spiritual disvalues as destroying the soul, endangering world peace, threatening future generations, or making unsafe automobiles do not weigh in the balance when compared to the metaphysical priority given to the economic. The most that an enlightened and liberal economic reductionist might do is to put a price on the priceless. An auto designer might measure the likelihood of accidents caused by a dubiously safe feature of a new model. Then he could estimate the cost to the company arising from damage suits which resultant injuries and deaths might give rise to (after all, no car can be 100 percent safe). These estimated damages could then be balanced off against the cost to the company of eliminating the safety hazard. On the basis of a cost-benefit analysis, a decision could be made. In other words, the economic reductionist can deal with human values like safety, peace and beauty once these have been reduced to the economic level. The positivistic act of faith, however, makes it impossible to deal with health, peace, and beauty on their own terms as goods in themselves, qualitatively superior to quantitatively measurable reality.

The biological evolutionary hypothesis of Darwin, as extended by Spencer to philosophy and morality (see Chapter 2), did much to make this reductionistic kind of thinking appear to us today as "only common sense." Evolutionism is the name that Schumacher gives to this philosophy that turns a limited biological hypothesis into a universal metaphysical law. What at first purported to describe biological change suddenly becomes elevated into a universal philosophical principle that *explains* the development of consciousness, self-awareness, social institutions, values,

---

[8]Schumacher, *Small Is Beautiful*, pp. 39–40.

and the origin of life itself. Natural selection, as we saw, is the law that allegedly explains development in every dimension of human and social life. Herein lies the evolutionist version of reductionism. Competition leading to natural selection resulting in survival of the fittest tells the whole story. There's nothing else to understand about the cause of the development of life, of mind, of society, or of ethics. The ethical values that survive through natural selection by that very brute fact become normative. Natural selection, for example, accounts for the genesis of laissez-faire ethics in Social Darwinism. Natural selection purportedly *explains* the evolution from laissez-faire to the egalitarian ethics prevalent today when merit takes second place to equality. The question of which value system is better cannot arise. Such is reductionism. Values consist in nothing but the actions that people and societies choose for survival in a competitive world.

Again, this reductionism rests on an act of faith. Evolutionism purporting to do away with metaphysics itself becomes a metaphysics, albeit a bad one, says Schumacher. A limited use of evolutionary hypothesis as one tool to explain observable phenomena is a perfectly sensible and legitimate scientific approach. But evolution becomes evolutionism when it makes the act of faith that there are no other levels of meaning beyond changes in observable phenomena, that nature including humankind with its ethics and moral aspirations is *nothing but* the product of chance (spontaneous variation) and necessity (natural selection). Meaning, purpose, quality are all ruled out of court ahead of time. It becomes impossible to judge on their own merits the qualitative value of moral ideals like laissez-faire ethics or egalitarianism. One can only ask: Have they successfully run the gauntlet of chance and natural selection? There is nothing more to say. The latest sexploitation film is a box-office success; the new play that sensitively and aesthetically explores a human religious theme fails. The man who lies on his résumé gets the job; the truthful applicant gets rejected. The deli owner who closes his shop at Friday sundown loses business; his customers trek to the deli across the street. In each case, one person decides on the basis of a quantitative economic norm, while the other decides on the basis of a qualitative aesthetic, moral, or religious norm. The evolutionist can measure the former, but the qualitative nonobservable levels of meaning escape him. The reductionist act of faith has ruled them out.

Such metaphysics is bad because it is incomplete. It reduces reality instead of comprehending it. But the uncomprehended dimensions do not disappear. They remain, albeit unacknowledged, to haunt us. This gives us some clue as to the metaphysical reason behind the criticisms that Scitovsky and Illich made of our economy. We recur to quantitative measures of happiness in the form of comforts purchased on the market and professional services rendered. Questions of quality and human purpose remain baffling and unasked. Can the purpose of human life be the measure of goods and services, rather than the other way around, asks Schumacher? Can we start with a metaphysical act of faith that allows for rather than disallowing quality judgments? Could we tolerate the possibility that such quality judgments about human life might overrule sound and measurably superior economic decisions to produce certain goods or offer certain services?

Questions like these assume that people and values are not properly reduced to mechanical units manipulated by laws of natural selection. The subtitle of Schumacher's most famous work is "Economics As If People Mattered." "People" represent a higher level of reality qualitatively superior to the rest of nature, in this view. People are more than the sum of those characteristics that can be observed and quantified. Schumacher calls by the name of "Buddhist Economics" that economic philosophy which puts people at the center of consideration. (Doubtless a case could be made for calling it Christian economics or biblical economics.) The metaphysics underlying such an economics must be open to quality, open to describing different levels of reality. Some levels are higher and superior, others lower and inferior. There is order in the world. An economics which is respectful of that order will not, for example, subordinate the needs and goals of people to the needs and goals of economic efficiency, if the former are seen to be qualitatively superior to the latter. It would be a violation of this order, for example, to automate at great profit the harvesting of bananas in Ecuador at the cost of reducing to penury the resultant large numbers of unemployed workers and their families. The reductionist might veto such a decision on the basis of a cost-benefit analysis of what would benefit his company economically in the long run. Schumacher does not mean this. He means rather that superior human dignity could justify the decision not to automate regardless of the economic costs. It is a distortion to reduce people to their quantifiable contribution to an economic enterprise. People are qualitatively superior to the enterprise and ethical decisions should reflect this.

There is no place here to defend a full-blown alternative to reductionism. Such an alternative would abjure the narrow act of faith of the reductionist. Opened in this way to the perception of the ascending levels of being, a person could discern, with the blinders off, new qualities and powers at each superior level. Armed with a firm grasp on order and hierarchy, a person is enabled to make quality judgments about what is better and what is worse, what superior and what inferior, which values take precedence over other values. As we move up the ladder of being from the inanimate world of minerals to the living world of spontaneous growth, and thence to the animal world of movement, sense and consciousness, on to the human world of self-awareness and autonomous freedom, a qualitative progression can be discerned. There is a movement from passivity (a rock just lies there) to activity (plants grow); from exteriority (a chemical reaction needs an external trigger) to interiority (of itself, a kitten yawns); from necessity (a puppy's development is relatively predictable) to freedom (a child's development much less so); from dispersion (the relative instability of an untended vegetable garden from year to year) to integration (the increasing cohesiveness of a human society); from a little or not experienced world (an earthworm's horizon is greater than a dandelion's) to the universe-as-world (the unlimited object of human aspirations). These are qualitatively distinct and describable levels of reality. Note that as we move up the scale, reality escapes the observability, exactness, quantifiability, and predictability which make the lower level of reductionism so attractive. What we lose in exactness, we gain in comprehensiveness and richness. But by abandoning the reductionist faith, one must also abandon the security and predictability that go with it. If the world is truly ordered and hierarchical, then reductionism that reduces everything to the same level is a false philosophy. And relativism in ethics that follows from Reductionism is a false ethics, says Schumacher.

Ethical relativism states that one morality is just as good as another. The double blow dealt by reductionism and relativism to genuine philosophy has brought us to our present predicament. One morality is as good as another because one reality is as good as another, the story goes. The reductionist view which puts all goals on the same level gives us no norm for judging any one superior or inferior to another. The result is that the norm of moral good, the goals of human happiness are dictated by the whims of fashion or of temperament. This one lives by the goddess of success; that one worships at the shrine of self-fulfillment. For a third person, money is the be-all and end-all. A fourth lives only for her family. The reductionist has no way of judging the worth of these goals when compared to one another. They're all on the same level. Marx would reduce them to manifestations of economic class struggle. Freud would reduce them to the acting out of repressed unfulfilled incest wishes. Spencer would see them as enacting the evolutionary struggle under the iron law of natural selection. Such is ethical pluralism in America. When quality judgments are suspended all philosophies are tolerated as equals.

A non-reductionist philosophy, however, can legitimately put people in first place because there is such a thing as first place, and second place and third place. All are not on the same level. The human potentials for freedom, integration, activity and knowledge—however inexact these may seem to the quantitative science—are qualities that demand respect. An economist who puts people first can derive qualitative norms to guide the production of goods, the use of resources, and the proferring of services. He can measure their qualitative impact on human potential. Again, this is not the place to expand on such norms in detail.

4. QUESTIONS FOR DISCUSSION AND EVALUATION

Consider, by way of example, the following questions: Can you bring qualitative value judgments to bear on their answers? Can you transcend a reductionistic economic calculus? Since we have not been dealing with a formally articulated philosophy, these discussion questions will substitute for the usual end-of-chapter evaluation.

(1) From a reductionistic and quantitative point of view, $50 worth of corn = $50 worth of coal = $50 worth of paper napkins = $50 worth of dental care. Can you see any qualitative differences among these four various types of goods? Aside from dollar value, should any ethical considerations go into decisions about the use and conservation of these types of goods?

(2) "More is better" is a quantitative principle. "Less is more" is a qualitative principle; it means that less quantity can mean more quality. Recall Illich on "the disabling professionals" and Scitovsky on the paradoxes of comfort. How might you apply the "less is more" principle to:

(a) transportation
(b) diet
(c) medical care
(d) industrial expansion
(e) labor unions
(f) clothing
(g) worker supervision
(h) bank account

(3) A quantitative norm cannot tell you what is too big and what is too small. For example, I can know quantitatively that one family has no children and another 15: this tells me nothing about which size is better. Reflecting upon the quality of human life I might conclude that the ideal family consists of two parents and three children: this would be a qualitative judgment. Schumacher expresses the principle of such a judgment this way: "for every activity, there is an appropriate scale." In line with this principle, how large would you say is:

(a) the ideal city
(b) the ideal family
(c) the ideal grocery store

(d) the ideal car
(e) the ideal house
(f) the ideal tennis racquet
(g) the ideal welfare check
How long would you say is:
(h) the ideal working day
(i) the ideal working week
(j) the ideal span of life
(k) the ideal vacation
(l) the ideal school day
(m) the ideal dinner time

(4) Schumacher offers another quality-principle to guide decisions about appropriate levels of consumption. Overconsumption can lead to human dissatisfaction as Scitovsky pointed out. Overindustrialization can lead to enslavement and loss of autonomy, as Illich pointed out. At the same time, misery characterizes those countries where consumer goods are lacking and underindustrialization leads to frustration. Schumacher offers another quality-principle to guide us between these extremes. This principle is just as inexact as the others. But exactness comes only at the cost of reductionism that Schumacher rejects for reasons we have seen. This nonreductionistic quality-pinciple is: "Seek maximum well-being with minimum consumption." (Do you agree with this principle?) An example of this principle's violation would be the purchase of a new wardrobe cut and styled in the latest fashion to be replaced every three months. On the other hand, an example of the principle properly applied would be the *sari* worn by Indian women, a continuous piece of cloth with minimum styling always in season, that can be draped gracefully on the body by the skillful wearer. How might this principle of "Maximum well-being with minimum consumption" be applied to:

(a) men's clothing
(b) TV viewing
(c) TV programming
(d) home heating
(e) home water usage
(f) breakfast cereal manufacturing
(g) commuting to and from work
(h) telephone use

5. CONCLUSION

This chapter has reviewed briefly some of the critical voices raised against our economy as now organized. These voices are heretical ones to those who put the well-being of the economy or the well-being of any given economic enterprise above the well-being of the affected human beings. Scitovsky, Illich and Schumacher are heretics, too, to those who view people reductionistically as pieces to be manipulated by empirical quantitative laws in the service of the economy. The consumerist, professionalist, and relativist ideals have failed. Scitovsky showed that maximum consumption of human comforts can cause human unhappiness. Scitovsky challenges you to imagine a business or a society that would actually call a halt to the production of these comforts in the name of human happiness. Illich showed that the burgeoning helping professionals are smothering human autonomy and growth. He challenges you to imagine a society of people who protest such help and demand to be left alone to help themselves in the name of human freedom. Schumacher wants to restore considerations of quality to center stage, so that once again we not merely ask the quantitative question, "what's new?" but make qualitative judgments concerning "what's best." It is true that for the most part business is the follower of society's values, but society's values are changing, as these critics point out. And it is at least partially within the power of business to encourage such changes toward a more humane economy.

CASES FOR DISCUSSION

1. This assignment asks you to make a quality judgment. You are to distinguish economic value from intrinsic value, as Schumacher urges, and to discern pleasure from comfort, as Scitovsky proposes. Each person should purchase and bring to the next class an item worth about $2, keeping in the range of $1.80–$2.20. Try to make a "good buy." The item should be tangible, with an assignable monetary value, and not embarrassing to show others. In the next class:

   (a) Each person, *show* the item and give the price; it should have a *quantitative* economic value comparable (within the $2 range) to the other people's purchases.
   (b) *Tell* the *qualitative* criteria that make it a "good buy" in your judgment.
   (c) Take a vote on who made the "best buy." Why?
   (d) What did you learn about your quality criteria when you compared them with the norms of quality used by others?
   (e) Would you classify your item as more "comfort-giving" or more "pleasure-giving" on Scitovsky's scale? Why?
   (f) Is your item a potential source of human satisfaction or dissatisfaction? Why? Of consumer satisfaction or dissatisfaction? Why?

2. The situation created by agribusiness today highlights the issue of the "disabling professionals" raised by Illich, and the issue of a people-centered economy proposed by Schumacher. Agribusiness is a term applied to the corporate takeover of the food industry including the manufacture and distribution of farm supplies, the farming process itself, and the packaging and distribution of farm commodities.[9] Agribusiness consists in the 200 major companies which in a major way are involved in producing over half the food eaten on the globe, according to the United Nations Center on Transnational Corporations. This represents the professionalization of agriculture with all the human costs attendant upon this process as in other areas of life like medicine, transportation and education.

The first effect of agribusiness's advent into an area is the appropriation to itself of land that belonged to individual farmers. Land that had been used by farmers for their families' subsistence is turned over to one-crop farming for export to the affluent markets of industrial nations. The corporations either buy up such land directly or enter into compacts with governments and large landholders who hold the land with the same ends in view. With their subsistence crops gone the small farmers, now turned laborers in the employ of corporations, don't make the money they need to purchase what they formerly grew for themselves. Rampant malnutrition is the result.

Nations once able to produce independently their own food needs became dependent on the agribusiness corporations due to policies governing the import and export of farm commodities. During the last century, India was a major exporter of grain. Caribbean countries, too, supplied their own food and more for export, and South Korea and Japan were self-sufficient in the production of rice. Corporations conspired with governments to swing the pendulum from independence toward dependence by less-developed countries on agribusiness's parent nations. This state of dependence was effected by loans to customer LDC's for internal security (= cost of controlling rebellious peasants whose grain markets were being ruined by imports), for developing "taste" for manufactured process foods (like cola, canned food, and infant formula), and for transfer of farm workers to the cities with the resultant slums and blight. Note the classic enslaving effect of professionalization: loss of liberty and of self-reliance, the substitution of experts for ordinary individuals, the complexification of products that thereby become more expensive and less available to the formerly independent growers.

---

[9] For a detailed discussion of and further references on corporate agriculture, see "An Agribusiness Manual," published by Corporate Information Center, Room 566, 475 Riverside Drive, New York, N.Y. 10027.

Agribusiness's professional solution to world hunger is the very sensible, on the face of it, injunction to increase agricultural productivity. The mobilization of forces for productivity resulted in what goes by the name of the Green Revolution. Labor-diminishing capital-intensive resources were amassed in the underdeveloped countries. High-powered farm machinery made it possible for one man to do the work of 10 plus a team of horses. Chemically derived fertilizers, oil-based pesticides, and electrically pumped irrigation systems are all petroleum dependent and derived, and so increasingly scarce and prohibitively expensive for the developing nations, and completely out of the question for the individual farmers. The goals of efficiency and technology replace the goals of the people whom the technology was brought in to serve. The "miracle seeds" which feed the Green Revolution are designed to thrive in this climate of artificial mechanized irrigation and chemical fertilizers. The more frequent plantings and the greater number of seeds per stalk encourage, and even demand, machine harvesting, large storage and shipping facilities, and large banks of capital and credit. The costs and scale of professional agriculture devastates the individual farming entrepreneur. The Green Revolution drew like a magnet corporations and capital from industrialized countries. And the corporations were not bound by the E.P.A. and other constraints imposed by the parent country. So not only were individual farmers devastated, but their natural environments too. The small farmers who survived on their farms could not compete with the miracle seeds. As land values climbed, they were bought out, sold out. The devastating human cost of this technologically successful revolution has spawned a counterrevolution. The U.S. Agency for International Development (A.I.D.) is now embarked upon a campaign to discover "appropriate technology" for developing nations, to restore to people control over the agricultural tools that have come to control them.

This thumbnail sketch of agribusiness is a bare, simplistic outline intended as a peg upon which to hang the philosophical issues raised in this chapter. Consider.

(a) Give examples of "appropriate technology" (to use A.I.D.'s term) or of "enabling tools" (to use Illich's phrase) that could move agriculture in the LDC's in the direction of autonomy and self-reliance.

(b) Professionalism thrives on myths of technological omnicompetence. Name three factors that tend to demythologize the legitimacy of agribusiness's domination of food production.

(c) Give five rules for farming "as if people mattered" in poorer countries.

(d) Think of examples from agriculture of the principle "For every activity there is an appropriate scale."

(e) Recall the two opposing principles: "Less is More," and "More is Better." Give a valid application of each principle to the food industry. Can these two principles be reconciled? How?

(f) Buddhist economics suggests the following principle to guide a humane economy: "Maximum well-being with minimum consumption." Name five ways in which agribusiness seems to violate this principle.

(g) What arguments might agribusiness use to respond to the criticisms implied in the answer to the previous question? Where do you stand on this issue?

SUGGESTED READINGS

Burns, Scott. *The Household Economy: Its Shape, Origins and Future.* Boston: Beacon paperbound, 1977.

Illich, Ivan. *Celebration of Awareness: A Call for Institutional Revolution.* New York: New York: Doubleday, 1971.

———. *Deschooling Society.* New York: Harper and Row, 1971.

———. *Energy and Equity.* New York: Harper and Row, 1974.

———. *Medical Nemesis.* Random House, 1976.

———. *Tools for Conviviality.* New York: Harper and Row, 1973.

———. *Toward a History of Needs.* New York: Pantheon Books, 1978.

Kohr, Leopold. *The Overdeveloped Nations: The Diseconomies of Scale.* New York: Schocken Books, 1978.

Scitovsky, Tibor. *The Joyless Economy: An Inquiry into Human Satisfaction and Consumer Dissatisfaction.* New York: Oxford University Press, 1976.

Schumacher, E. F. *Guide for the Perplexed.* New York: Harper Colophon Books, 1978.

———. *Small is Beautiful: Economics As If People Mattered.* New York: Harper and Row, Colophon Books, 1973.

APPENDIX

JUSTICE AND ECONOMIC DISTRIBUTION: THE RAWLS DEBATE

First Principal [of Justice]. Each person is to have an equal right to the most extensive total system of equal basic liberties compatible with a similar system of liberty for all.

Second Principle [of Justice]. Social and economic inequalities are to be arranged so that they are both: (a) to the greatest benefit of the least advantaged, consistent with the just savings principle, and (b) attached to offices and positions open to all under the conditions of fair equality of opportunity.

John Rawls[1]

From each as they choose, to each as they are chosen.

Robert Nozick[2]

The principle of utility or the *greatest happiness* or *greatest felicity* principle (is) that principle which states the greatest happiness of all those whose interest is in question, as being the right and proper, and only right and proper and universally desirable, end of human action.

Jeremy Bentham[3]

[1]John Rawls, *A Theory of Justice* (Cambridge, Ma.: The Belknap Press of Harvard University Press, 1971), p. 302.

[2]Robert Nozick, *Anarchy, State and Utopia* (New York: Basic Books, Inc., Publishers, 1974), p. 160.

[3]Jeremy Bentham, "An Introduction to the Principles of Morals and Legislation" (1879), in *The Works of Jeremy Bentham*, ed. by John Bowring. (New York: Russell and Russell, 1962), I: 1, footnote.

1. CONFLICTS OF JUSTICE: MERIT VS. EQUALITY

It's hard to know what to do with the lively debate triggered by the appearance of John Rawls's monumental work, *A Theory of Justice*.[4] Since the debate is ongoing and still very current, it does not lend itself to the clearcut dispassionate lining up of issues that a historical perspective could afford. And while the debate rages heatedly in academic circles, it has not in this form filtered down into the thinking of the nonprofessional philosopher in the way, let's say, that Social Darwinism has. Still, the issues—social justice and the distribution of wealth—are perennial ones, though here expressed in slightly new accents. And certainly fundamental to business ethics is the basic question raised by Rawls, viz., what should be the basis for distributing economic goods and services in a society? Such distribution is the defining characteristic of the business enterprise. So while the discussion is as yet being carried on mainly in academic circles, students of business ethics are properly interested in finding out what it's all about. This Appendix outlines in broad strokes the state of the question of the Rawls debate. The presentation is necessarily oversimplified. The literature is voluminous and growing daily. It can serve to introduce students to the more nuanced treatments in the readings suggested at the end of the chapter.

The business perspective on the Rawls debate would focus on economic justice: who should get what and why? In answer to this question, utilitarians appeal to the greatest happiness principle of producing the greatest good for the greatest number of people.[5] Libertarians, on the other hand, see the fairest and most just distribution of wealth as that which results from the uncoerced choices of free individuals: the best way to ensure a just state of affairs is to leave people alone. Rawls's theory challenges both of these views, as we will see. But first, let's define "justice" and the issues of justice with which these theories are grappling.

(a) *Justice as equal treatment.* Justice in its simplest terms means that *equals should be treated the same.* Women deserve the same pay as men when they do work that is equal to men's. People, since they are equal as human beings, deserve equal access to minimum human food, shelter, and medical care. Claims such as these are made in the name of justice—equal treatment for equals. But people are equal in different ways. Not all kinds of equality require equal treatment. No one would argue that all blue-eyed

---

[4]Some of the discussion of discrimination and reverse discrimination in this chapter first appeared in slightly different form in my book *The Morals Game*, Chapter 9.

[5]John Stuart Mill, "Bentham," in *Dissertations and Discussions* (London: John W. Parker and Son, 1859), Vol. I, Chapter 3, p. 17.

salespersons, even though they enjoy the same eye-color, deserve the same sales commission. The company's security guards and the company's president are equal as human beings. Does justice demand that they be treated in every respect the same? Surely not. So the principle of justice must be qualified as follows: "Equal treatment should be given to those who are equal *in relevant respects.*"

Next question: when is the equality among persons *relevant?* The answer to this question has taken two directions. In the first, *merit* is the relevant factor. You must *earn* your just deserts (e.g., "equal pay for equal work"). This is the view of *meritarian* justice. In the second, humanity— *equality as human* beings—is the relevant factor. Justice is not something you have to earn. You are entitled to justice simply by being born human (e.g., in justice a starving person has a right to food, even though unable to pay for it). This is the view of *humanitarian* justice. When equality as human conflicts with merit as earned, that's where problems arise. Discrimination or unequal treatment highlights this conflict.

(b) *Justice as "discrimination" or unequal treatment.* "Discrimination" has become a bad word.[6] It was not always thus. In fact, it is still a compliment to call someone a "discriminating" person. "Discriminating," according to the *American Heritage Dictionary,* means "perceptive," "able to draw fine distinctions." A discriminating connoisseur could distinguish good wine from bad. A discriminating football scout could distinguish promising young players from the run-of-the-mill variety. A discriminating editor can distinguish manuscripts that will sell from those that will flop. The word discriminating, then, is often used to mean the ability to distinguish good from bad. The discriminating man distinguishes in favor of one item and against another. So discrimination takes on the character of making a value judgment.

To discriminate in the area of sex seems to mean not merely to distinguish men from women, but to discriminate in favor of men as against women (or the other way around). In the matter of race, to distinguish black from white seems to mean not merely that black and white are different, but that black is superior to white (or the other way around). Discrimination, then, which originally meant a neutral recognition of differences, now comes to imply a negative value judgment, a discrimination *against.* Discrimination against poor wine is harmless enough. But when you are talking about human beings, isn't it unjust and immoral to discriminate against your fellow-man? The answer is no, at least not always. Let's see now how we can distinguish discrimination that is just and moral from that which is not.

[6] *Ibid.,* pp. 51–52.

Remember that discrimination can be a neutral word. In this sense, human society is unimaginable without it. Discrimination rests upon two incontrovertible facts: (1) all persons are not equal; (2) persons are different from one another. Discrimination is a recognition of these inequalities and differences so that one's conduct may be guided accordingly. This is the basis of *meritarian* justice, as we have seen.

On the other hand, it is true to say that "all persons are equal" and that "persons are not different—they share a common humanity." To discriminate among human beings as if some were superhuman, some human, and some subhuman is unintelligent, unrealistic and therefore immoral. Refusal to discriminate here is a recognition of the common humanity that one shares with others so that one's conduct may be guided accordingly. This is called *equalitarian justice*, as we have seen.

Failure to discriminate, then, where discrimination is due is injustice. To take an absurd example, you wouldn't hire a kleptomaniac as a store detective in preference to a retired police officer in good standing. Here, discrimination is clearly just. It recognizes merit and talent and rewards it accordingly. And conversely, discrimination can also be unjust. Take the not unknown case of a woman who is refused entrance to medical school in favor of a less-qualified male applicant. To discriminate thus on the basis of sex is to treat her as a second-class human. This is a violation of equalitarian justice.

Therefore, discrimination is sometimes just and sometimes unjust; it's not always easy to decide. For example:

(1) Poverty discriminates, placing the poor in a class apart; welfare regulations are an attempt to discriminate between the deserving and the undeserving poor; guaranteed annual income is a proposal that refuses to discriminate among the poor. Here, which is just and which unjust—discrimination or refusal to discriminate?

(2) College entrance exams are an attempt to discriminate between qualified and unqualified applicants: open college admissions is a policy that refuses to discriminate on the basis of merit or talent. Here, which is just and which is unjust—discrimination or refusal to discriminate?

(3) Work rules in a factory forbidding women to lift heavy weights discriminate protective working conditions for the "weaker sex"; a policy subjecting women to the same conditions as men is a refusal to discriminate on the basis of sex. Here, which is just and which is unjust—discrimination or refusal to discriminate?

Note, too, that even the nondiscrimination proposals just mentioned involve discriminations on other levels. Guaranteed annual income does discriminate between the rich and the poor. Open college admissions do discriminate between those who have high-school diplomas and those who don't. Equal working conditions for women do not extend to rest room facilities shared with males. How do I discern just discrimination from unjust? In these conflicts between equality and merit, between humanitarian justice and meritarian justice, what moral norm will provide a just and ethical basis for the distribution of economic goods and services? We will now state without detailed elaboration three alternative answers proposed by participants in the debate provoked by Rawls's *Theory of Justice*.

2. CONFLICTS OF JUSTICE RESOLVED: THREE ALTERNATIVES IN THE RAWLS DEBATE

"Who should get what and why?" is the question of distributive justice. "You should get what you earn" is the meritarian answer, and indeed *merit* is a plausible norm for the just distribution of economic goods and services. "Economic benefits should be equally distributed" is the humanitarian answer. And the fact of our common humanity does lend a plausibility to an equalitarian norm of distribution that inspires the communistic view of society so popular around the world. But serious misgivings result from the doctrinaire application of either merit or equality alone as the sole norm for resolving conflicts of justice. Both seem required. Wherefore, philosophers have sought a more general principle that transcends both merit and equality to serve as a guide for balancing the claims of each. We'll now briefly review three such general principles. Their respective merits are now hotly under debate:

(a) The Utilitarian Norm—The Greatest Happiness Principle;
(b) The Rawlsian Norm—The Social Contract Principle;
(c) The Libertarian Norm—The Historical Entitlement Principle.

(a) *The utilitarian norm—the greatest happiness principle.* For the utilitarian, the primary moral imperative is not that justice be done, but that the greatest happiness be produced for the greatest number of people in a society. The utilitarian, to be sure, cares about justice and the welfare of individuals, but the welfare of individuals is viewed as part of the general welfare. The maximization of the general welfare or happiness is the norm that the utilitarian uses to resolve problems of economic distribution like the following: Should peanut farmers be subsidized? Should corporate profits be taxed at 50 percent? Should the minimum wage be $4/hour? The utilitarian will weigh the *happiness-producing* quotient of these policies, and on this basis will decide the moral merits of each.

Jeremy Bentham (1748–1832), most influential of the British utilitarians, wanted to take ethics out of the realm of blind intuition and give it a solid intellectual foundation. Bentham's disciple, John Stuart Mill

(1806–1873), shared this aim. The principle of utility is grounded on the nature of human action. The utilitarians point out that we cannot help but seek pleasure and avoid pain in everything we do. The norm of moral good and evil, then, is what respects this character of human conduct. Since the goal of human life is to seek pleasure or happiness, then moral good consists in fostering this goal, i.e., in maximizing the sum of human pleasure or happiness. "The end of human action," says Mill, is "necessarily also the standard of morality."[7] And how does Mill prove that happiness is the end of human action?

> The only proof capable of being given that an object is visible, is that people actually see it. The only proof that sound is audible is that people hear it. . . . In like manner, I apprehend, the sole evidence it is possible to produce that anything is desirable, is that people do actually desire it.[8]

It is a direct appeal to experience. So the norm of moral good and evil lies in an action's tendency to promote or destroy happiness—the happiness of those affected by the act.[9]

Granting that it is possible to calculate the happiness-producing potential of actions (a possibility that many dispute), utilitarianism becomes an ethics of the bottom-line common good. Just as a business must sometimes sacrifice individual markets and products for the overall profit picture, so according to utilitarian reasoning individual welfare may be sacrificed in the name of maximizing the happiness of the greatest number.[10]

---

[7]Later utilitarians introduced important refinements that we won't go into here, such as the distinction between act-utilitarianism and rule-utilitarianism. Rule-utilitarianism looks to the happiness producing potential that as a rule flows from a certain kind of action in order to judge its morality. Murder taken as an isolated act, e.g., killing an evil person, might be adjudged morally good since it would increase the sum of human happiness. But as a rule, murder does not promote human happiness, and so it fails the rule-utilitarian's test of goodness. Act-utilitarians are much more situational. They tend to judge moral goodness by the happiness-consequences of the particular act in question. Mill tended toward rule-utilitarianism. Mill, too, refined Bentham's understanding of pleasure or happiness by introducing *qualitative* considerations into the hedonistic calculus. Thereby, a lesser amount of higher quality spiritual happiness could outweigh a larger amount of material happiness. Any complete treatment of utilitarianism would have to explore issues such as these.

[8]Of course, utilitarians try to defend against such objections that are continually lodged against this philosophy. See especially the books of R. M. Hare and J. J. C. Smart suggested for reading below, and judge for yourself whether they succeed.

[9]Rawls, *op. cit.,* pp. 25–26.

[10]As you recall, pragmatism like utilitarianism judges morality by *consequences.* It differs from utilitarianism in two important respects. First, pragmatism does not set up ahead of time any predetermined moral goal like that of maximizing the general happiness. Rather, pragmatism is concerned with *specific* moral ends that emerge from *particular* problem-solving situations. The ends of moral action are not pre-given but are open-ended. Secondly, while utilitarians stress the *subjective* ends of human happiness and satisfaction, pragmatism

The utilitarian wants to argue that what promotes general good or happiness will redound to the individual's happiness. The focus, however, remains on the general happiness, and individual happiness is derivitive from the general. As Rawls points out:

> The striking feature of the utilitarian view of justice is that it does not matter, except indirectly, how this sum of satisfaction is distributed among individuals.[11]

So the utilitarian requires only that the net amount of the general welfare be maximized, with no one individual's welfare counting as more or less than any other's. The utilitarian does not require that the individual's welfare be maximized. Justice is concerned that individuals receive their due; the general welfare comes second. Utility is concerned with the total amount of benefits in society; the individual comes second.

What we see here is the distinction between *consequentialism* in ethics, and *deontologism*. The Utilitarian is a consequentialist: he judges moral good and evil by the *consequences* of the act or rule. Actions are not good or bad *in themselves*, but are good or bad according to their consequences for the general welfare or happiness. For deontologists, on the other hand, morality is not chiefly a matter of consequences. Rather, certain actions and rules of action are good or bad *in themselves* of their very nature regardless of the consequences. For example, the deontologist would consider the killing of an innocent human being as wrong in and of itself, and not merely on utilitarian grounds. The Rawlsian and the libertarian positions, as we will see, are in the camp of the *deontologists*, as opposed to the *consequentialism* of the utilitarians.[12]

(b) *The Rawlsian norm—the "social contract" principle.* As a deontologist, Rawls rejects *aggregate utility* as an answer to the question, "Who should get what and why?" Justice of its very nature demands that we seek first and foremost that *individuals* get what is justly due to them. In the tradition of equalitarian or humanitarian justice, Rawls insists that inequalities in the distribution of economic goods and services must be justified. Equal distribution is the norm; inequalities represent deviations from the norm that need to be justified or corrected. Fundamental is Rawls's first or general principle of "greatest equal liberty," viz., that "all

---

focusses on *objective* human goods that are objectively testable on the scientific model. The rather vague general hedonistic calculus of the utilitarian gives way to the specific objective problem-solving method of the pragmatist.

[11]Rawls, *op. cit.*, pp. 62 and 83.

[12]See R. M. Hare, "Rawls's *Theory of Justice*," in *Reading Rawls* (New York: Basic Books, Inc., Publishers, 1974).

social values—liberty and opportunity, income and wealth, and the bases of self-respect—are to be distributed equally. . . ." This is qualified by the second or special principle by which inequalities are justified, viz., that "social and economic inequalities are to be arranged so that they are to the greatest benefit of the least advantaged": he calls this the "Difference Principle" which in turn is qualified by the need to consider "fair equality of opportunity."[13] In oversimplified terms, equal distribution is to be the norm unless unequal distribution would work to the benefit of all, especially of the worst off.

Why should we follow the Rawlsian norm? What sort of proof can be offered for it? Rawlsian principles should be followed because they are reasonable. How does one guarantee that the principles by which a society distributes goods and services are indeed reasonable principles? Rawls recurs to the "social contract" tradition (recall Hobbes, above) as an alternative to utility as a norm of social morality. The end of morality is not to ensure the greatest sum of happiness or the benefit of the greatest number of people. No. Morality is based on a social contract to ensure that benefits be fairly distributed to all members of society. The fairness of this social contract is to be guaranteed by the special conditions under which the contractors are hypothesized to draw up the terms of the contract. We are to imagine an original state of nature in which people come together to draw up the rules for society. The people in this state Rawls names the "people in the original position," irreverently dubbed "POPs" by Hare.[14] The POPs are assumed to operate under self-interest. But this self-interest does not go unchecked. Rawls stipulates that the POPs also operate under a veil of ignorance. They are not to know what their own individual characteristics or circumstances will be when they become "people in ordinary life" (called "POLs" by Hare) in society. So, as a POP, I don't know whether I'll be rich or poor, dumb or smart, male or female, black or white, nor do I know the values I'll want to pursue when I become a POL. Thus ignorant, it is to my self-interest, says Rawls, that I draw up principles that will assure my basic liberties and maximum benefit even though I should end up as the most disadvantaged of the POLs. Self-interest, operating under the veil of ignorance, forces the POPs to draw up a social contract that is universally beneficial to all, and is thus reasonable and fair. Equality, then, should be the norm. And if there is inequality, as there must be, it can be justified only if the inequality benefits all, especially the least advantaged. For example, privileged people, like educated surgeons and rich investors, could make the POL world a better place, even for the disadvantaged, than

[13]Nozick, *op. cit.,* p. 160.
[14]*Ibid*

that world would be if such inequalities of education and wealth did not exist. In such cases, inequalities of distribution could be justified even in the equalitarian world of Rawlsian justice. Under the Rawlsian rules of the game, it is only reasonable for POPs to recur to a maximum strategy. I'll best protect myself as a POL by stipulating a "best worst case" policy as a POP.

The overriding value for Rawls is respect for the individual humanity of every human being. Accordingly, equalitarian justice becomes the norm. In this, he parts ways with the utilitarian and libertarian justifications for inequalities in society. Is the unequal justification of wealth just and fair? Yes, says the meritarian, if the wealthy earned their wealth. No, says, Rawls. You can't ignore the poor and the worst off in society on grounds of the general welfare or even on grounds of merit. Justice is owed to every person: it need not be earned. Unequal wealth is justified only if those at the bottom of the heap will benefit more from the inequality than they would without it. In conclusion, consider how you would judge the justice of the free-enterprise system on each of these three norms—the utilitarian norm, the meritarian, and the Rawlsian.

(c) *The libertarian norm—the "historical entitlement" principle.* Like Rawls, Robert Nozick is a deontologist, i.e., he holds certain acts and rules to be morally valuable in themselves, and not just because of their consequences. Whereas Rawls put equality first, individual liberty is the central value for Nozick. In terms of the political spectrum, Robert Nozick has been Rawls's sharpest critic on the right. Individual liberty is his deontological absolute. The talents and efforts of people are not community resources, as Rawls claims, to be appropriated by all, especially by the most disadvantaged. Rather, the fruits of individual talent and effort should redound to the individual. The structure of society and of the distribution of benefits in society does not drop out of the blue according to some idealistic plan, as Rawls would have it. Social arrangements are encumbered by the realities of concrete history. A central respect for liberty and for historical concreteness leads Nozick to his Historical Entitlement Principle of Distributive Justice. In this he parts ways with both Rawls and the utilitarians. People are entitled to what they earn, he says. They should be rewarded at the price that their talents command, and not primarily on the good that they do for the community. A baseball pitcher can command a $5 million-dollar contract, while a nun devoted to ghetto health and education can barely acquire income to continue her work. So be it: coercion of others would be unjust as a means of helping her. Rawls, as a good equalitarian, assumes that what benefits the least advantaged will benefit all of society's members. But liberty, and not equal benefit, is the libertarian's central concern. And inequalities are justified quite simply: Free individuals enjoy the right to benefit from the free agreements they make about the use of their talents and efforts. Rawls relies upon his moral intuition about equality, and finds it confirmed when he applies it as a concrete norm of distribution. Nozick, on the other hand, relies upon an intuitive primacy for liberty that he finds confirmed when applied as a norm for the distribution of benefits in society.

So Nozick has recourse to the liberalism of John Locke and Adam Smith in his opposition to Rawls. The right not to be interfered with—negative rights—in the pursuit of one's freely chosen life-values is the primary bulwark of liberty. Only this absolute right to follow one's own path without interference respects the unique individual autonomy of human persons. This individual autonomy is the defining characteristic of what it means to be a human being. So, whereas with Rawls the central deontological value is human sociality, with Nozick it's human individuality. The distribution of benefits in society, then, should respect this individual autonomy. There is no predetermined pattern to which society should conform, as Rawls's principles would like to pretend in their concern for the least advantaged. Thus Nozick rejects what he calls "patterned theories" of economic justice. And there is no end-state condition toward which society should be aiming at—such as the greatest happiness of the greatest number as proposed by the utilitarians. Nozick rejects "patterned theories" and "end-state theories" in favor of what he calls the "Historical Entitlement" norm of the just distribution of benefits in society. Benefits should be distributed as we *choose* to distribute them. Distributions that are the results of past choices should be respected so long as such distributions did not violate the negative rights of others. Such historical choices entitle you to the benefits in question: such is the Historical Entitlement norm. It is not a question of *re-distribution* of wealth (or of other benefits) as Rawls and the utilitarians would have. What matters is the freely chosen distribution of benefits. I can and may *distribute* what I produce. *Redistribution* ignores the production factor—i.e., ignores where the benefits came from in the first place. They can't drop out of the sky.

Nozick, then, would not forbid "capitalist acts between consenting adults." The Historical Entitlement Principle he expresses as follows:

> From each according to what he chooses to do, to each according to what he makes for himself (perhaps with the contracted aid of others) and what others choose to do for him and choose to give him of what they've been given previously (under this maxim) and haven't yet expended or transferred.[15]

---

[15]See the work of J. J. C. Smart cited in the suggested reading for this Appendix. I except R. M. Hare who is suspicious of the validity of moral intuitions and founds his utilitarianism

Noting the defects of this statement as a slogan, Nozick restates it in simplified maxim form as:

From each as they choose, to each as they are chosen.

Individual freedom to be left alone—the primary libertarian value—demands that I be able to distribute my property as I see fit, so long as I do not encroach on the freedom of others to do the same. Rawls in stressing the equalitarian distribution of benefits ignores the *production* of benefits. And those who produce obtain entitlement to what they produce. And this entitlement is to be respected. Rawls is wrong, says Nozick, in viewing the free productive efforts of individuals as community property. The primary beneficiary of such efforts should be the person who exerts these efforts. The veil of ignorance under which Rawls's POPs must operate is biased in favor of a patterned or end-state view of society. But concretely, society does not operate under a veil of ignorance, and the principles of just distribution quite reasonably reflect free choices justly and historically made; the so-called objective justice stipulated by the Rawlsian POPs is biased by the subjective conditions that Rawls imposes upon their decisions.

Conclusion. Each of these norms flows from a moral intuition about what values should predominate in particular situations involving the distribution of benefits. And the primacy of each of these particularized values receives a generalized justification. It's a dialectic between the particular and the general. Particular applications interact with generalized justifications. The utilitarian intuition appeals to the inevitability of pleasure or happiness as the motive of human action and to the natural feelings of benevolence or of fellow-feeling that this state be maximized—so that maximum benefit becomes a universal principle. For Rawls, the equalitarian, the logic of the original position assures the universality of his two principles. Nozick's intuition of the primacy of unfettered freedom as the defining characteristic of the autonomous human being is the basis of the libertarian norm of distributive justice. In a sense, each of these founding intuitions is a philosophical option to be tested in particular cases and justified by general argument.

---

on the logic of moral language as prescriptive. In fact, he feels that his position is close to that of Rawls in that he, Hare, puts himself in the shoes of others in order to arrive at moral prescriptions, thereby universalizing, as do Rawls's POPs, the just principles of distribution.

3. REVERSE DISCRIMINATION: A CASE FOR DISCUSSION

Consider the following issues raised by "Compensatory Hiring" in business, pejoratively known as "reverse discrimination." How does "reverse discrimination" fare when tested by the utilitarian norm, the Rawlsian norm, and the libertarian norm: What is your evaluation of the issue and of these three positions?

On the basis of race alone, blacks have been discriminated *against* in the past in educational and job opportunities. This justifies today discrimination *in favor* of blacks on the basis of race, so the argument goes, to remedy past injustice. On the basis of sex alone, women have been *excluded* from certain careers in the past. This justifies today the *inclusion* of women in these careers on the basis of sex alone, even to the exclusion of equally or better qualified males. Unjust past discrimination is to be remedied by present-day reverse discrimination.

This may seem just to formerly victimized minorities. But it seems unjust to the newly discriminated against victims. Discrimination in favor of blacks, the objection goes, is clearly discrimination against whites. It is immoral racism in a new guise. Only the names of the victims have been changed. Discrimination in favor of females is clearly discrimination against males. Carried to a logical extreme, if women are to be equally represented on today's job market, this means either firing half the presently employed males, or else excluding a generation of male job applicants until the female quota is attained. Nothing so radical is seriously proposed. But the principle is clear. Discrimination in favor of females can be achieved only at the cost of male opportunities. It is sexism in a new guise. Only now the male replaces the female as victim. So on the face of it, reverse discrimination seems not to be justice but a mockery of justice.

Basically, reverse discrimination rankles the white and the male precisely because it does not recognize and reward their merit. It assumes that merit alone is not everything. But if equalitarianism is the most basic ideal of human society, a strict meritocracy would be inhuman and immoral. Let's look at the philosophy of man underlying these assumptions that claim to justify a policy of reverse discrimination.

Equalitarian philosophy clearly views all humans as belonging to one species. There is no subgroup, or class, or caste of humans that is inferior to or to be subordinated to another. Human dignity is something that every person already possesses. Respect for this dignity need not be earned or merited. It is morally demanded by the mere fact of one's membership in the human race. This philosophy rejects, for example, a sexual caste system in which the female is inferior to the male, and hence subordinate to him and owing him obedience, or weaker than he and demanding his often patronizing "protection." This philosophy rejects a racial caste system in which essentially inferior races are to be dominated by master races. A person might have to *qualify* to be an astronaut, a pro quarterback, or a public school teacher, but no one has to qualify to be a human being equal, as human, to any other human being. There is no specification sheet for membership in the human race besides being conceived and born. This all may seem obvious enough, but it has radical implications for the application of meritarian justice.

There are times, it is claimed, when *merit* is used to determine the qualifications for being treated as *human*. And the lack of certain merits equivalently relegates certain classes of people to a subhuman status in society. In other words, sometimes the rigid application of meritarian justice equivalently violates equilitarian justice. This is the key argument of the reverse discriminator. Treatment on the basis of merit alone sometimes means treatment of certain persons as less than human. In these cases, considerations of merit must give way to considerations of equality. This is what reverse discrimination sets out to do. It refuses to let considerations of merit alone disenfranchise certain classes of people from the human race.

It is precisely this disenfranchised status that has been laid upon women, blacks and other minorities. Or say, rather, that these groups had never been enfranchised to begin with. One remedy is "reverse discrimination." But this phrase has misleading connotations. It seems to imply that if the *original* discrimination was unjust, then it is legitimate to turn the tables on the original perpetrators and do an injustice to *them* via *reverse* discrimination! Reverse discrimination as understood by its advocates is not against anybody. Its whole focus is positive—to bring about a society that treats in a human way those groups that are now being treated as somehow subhuman. Phrases like compensatory discrimination and preferential hiring better express this positive goal. These policies are directed toward a society in which no one, whites and males included, will be used as the subhuman tool of an allegedly superior caste, and in which every person will have equal access to participation in the society in which he lives and enjoy the fruits of that participation.

This ideal state of affairs does not exist for women and blacks in America today. Law schools, for example, may not have intended in the past to keep blacks out of the legal profession. But the criteria for admission have just as effectively produced that very result. Less than 1 percent of American lawyers are black out of a black population of 12 percent. And what's the last time you saw a woman physician in the country where women outnumber men in the general population?

This is not simply a question of a numbers game. If that alone were the issue we'd be hearing a louder clamor than we do urging, for example, equal representation of women in the ranks of professional baseball. What's at issue are social needs as well as proportionate representation and individual justice. Without indicting all male psychiatrists and gynecologists, women have been complaining more and more about the patronizing and unsympathetic treatment accorded them by male physicians in these areas of particularly female sensitivity. There have indeed been increasing claims of out-and-out abuse.

Moving to the legal profession that is entrusted with the delicate task of mediating conflicting public interests in the American melting pot, let's hear from the American Bar Association's brief filed in the Marco de Funis case:

> Training lawyers for the work of accommodating and ordering conflicting interests of a pluralistic society requires a diverse and heterogeneous student body; a segregated law school will not afford an adequate education for a multi-racial practice.

I would conclude, then, that, as in the medical profession so, too, here in the legal, both concrete considerations of social need and abstract considerations of equalitarian justice urge a redress of current injustices by some policy of preferential treatment of minorities.

This idea of preferential treatment is not some wild recent invention by blacks or by women's liberation. The favored treatment accorded by schools to the children of generous alumni, or by politicians to generous corporations is not unheard of in American society. Such long-practiced exceptions to a rigid meritocracy have often operated against justice and the common good. The preferential policies that we have been discussing are based upon justice and the common good. They are unusual only in that they favor the oppressed minorities rather than the established holders of power. Accordingly, it is from this latter quarter that the shouts of anguish are the loudest.

Reverse discrimination, however, is no panacea. It's not without its problems: (1) How far should this principle be extended? (2) Will the results be truly effective? (3) Is it fair to the newly discriminated against victims?

To the first problem. Not *all* blacks, Puerto Ricans, and Chicanos (and certainly not all women) are "disadvantaged." Nor are all whites "advantaged"! And is reverse discrimination to be practiced in favor of other ethnic groups that are in some degree hindered by discrimination, i.e.,

Jews, Poles, Italians, Hungarians, Arabs? When merit gives way to quotas, an epidemic can be unleashed.

Second, maybe what minorities need most of all are not lawyers and doctors of their own kind, but lawyers and doctors who are optimally qualified. Of course, sex might enhance a woman doctor's effectiveness with women patients as also race might enhance a black judge's ability to make judicious decisions for the black community. There is no assurance, however, that minority professionals will hasten to serve their own "constituencies." And finally, we might note that a double standard of admission to professional schools can easily lead to a double standard of grading or evaluation and the consequent stigma that minority professionals are not as well qualified as their "majority" colleagues.

Third, as we have noted before, discrimination in favor of minorities almost always involves discrimination against "majorities"—against qualified white males to cite the case in point. The community is asking the white male to pay the price of its past inhumanity. Advocates of reverse discrimination should face this cost squarely. True, meritarian justice may not be the absolute norm for all human relationships. It may occasionally have to give way to equalitarian justice. But the fact remains that meritarian justice *is* justice. *Quid pro quo*, equal pay for equal services, equal reward for equal merit, equal opportunity for equal qualifications— these demands of justice do not disappear even in a society that is trying to compensate for past wrongs. As a matter of fact women, blacks, and other minorities are striving to bring about a climate in which precisely their own *merits* will be recognized and rewarded. To do away altogether with the principle of merit is to defeat the ultimate good at which reverse discrimination is aiming. The temporary and selective suspension of the merit system in the case of qualified white males remains an evil to be tolerated, not a good in itself. Though it is an evil, it may be in present-day America the lesser of two evils. The greater evil would be the continued relegating of minorities to a subhuman caste system.

How would the Rawlsian, how would the utilitarian, how would the libertarian confront the above conflicts arising out of a policy of reverse discrimination? On the one hand, a doctrinaire meritocracy would put some groups in a master race or master sex, dominating and using their "inferiors" to their own ends. No longer would there be one human race, all of whose members receive equal treatment as humans. A doctrinaire equalitarianism, on the other hand, ignores merit and talent and reduces all human beings to a least common denominator where uniqueness, freedom and talent count for next to nothing. In political terms, both laissez-faire capitalism ("merit is everything") and uncompromising communism ignore a dimension of human reality that is present and will not go away. Men are equal. But they are unique and different from each other too. Justice is the virtue that guides the relations of persons among themselves, and these two dimensions must be observed in any balanced philosophy of man.

DISCUSSION QUESTIONS

1. Consider the following description of the "American Way":

The basic problem of injustice in America is not racial or sexual or ethnical discrimination. The problem goes much deeper, and racial and sexual inequalities are simply conspicuous surface symptoms of it. American society, maybe more than most others, has an unequally skewed reward system that results in great disparities of wealth. This consequently divides Americans into the top group of superhumans who are most admired, the middle group of average humans, and the poor who hardly count as human at all. Money is the main determiner of which group you belong to and of how humanly or subhumanly you'll be treated. In India the *sanyassin* who wanders about half naked begging for his bread is an object of respect and admiration. But such a character wandering about on American streets would be charged with vagrancy and thrown into jail. Granting the religious and cultural problems with this little illustration, the point remains that in America money is the main source of the social esteem one receives as a human being and consequently of one's own self-esteem as a human being.

Next question: Who gets the money? In the capitalistic West, the answer to this question is that economic reward is a function of demand. Which humans are in greatest demand? Look at the salaries and benefits: professional athletes, top executives, doctors, talented singers, etc. In a word, the intelligent, the graceful, and the "beautiful" people are in demand. They are the ones who are rewarded. They count even as superhuman if they are supersuccesses. The ugly, the defective and the stupid are lucky to get enough to eat and stay out of the cold. That is to say, they are lucky to receive any minimum human treatment at all. You are human in America to the extent that you are productive and marketable. Membership in the human race indeed does have to be earned in America. This is the basic injustice that all the racial, sexual and ethnic quota systems don't touch at all. In this framework, minority quotas are simply a way for minorities to get their piece of the action in this unjust meritocratic system of determining who is human and who is not. This is understandable and even morally commendable, but it leaves untouched the problem of the lack of respect in America for the individual human being, however poor and talentless he may be.

It would take nothing less than a revolution, however, to break the automatic link in America between productivity, money and humanness. Our system of taxation, our salary structure, and most importantly, our materialistic goals would have to be profoundly altered. Reformed college-admissions policies and preferential hiring didn't touch the surface of *this* problem.

> How would Rawls and Nozick debate the justice or injustice of the "American way" as here described?

2. Note one very important difference between compensatory discrimination and "unjust" discrimination. When blacks and women are kept out of the American mainstream, it is a blow to their self-esteem. We inevitably regard ourselves as others regard us. We behave as we are expected to behave. And as long as women and blacks were expected to be and to act as inferior and as less than human, they tended to live out their lives in such an inferior role. The phenomenon of "the self-fulfilling prophecy" is a fact of human behavior. In this, more than in anything else, consists the viciousness of unjust discrimination. It makes persons relegate themselves to the realm of the subhuman. Compensatory discrimination has, for example, no such effect on whites or males. Those belong to the favored group. Their self-esteem is relatively secure. Though in a sense they are the new "victims" they are not victims in the sense that blacks and women were and often still are. Reverse discrimination does not touch on their humanity. The goal of reverse discrimination is not a system in which every subgroup will be proportionately represented in every area of human life. The goal is rather that every individual will have the opportunity to be viewed, and to view himself and herself, as the human equal of every other human.

> Would you accept on utilitarian grounds this argument in favor of compensatory discrimination?

SUGGESTED READINGS

Arthur, John and William H. Shaw. *Justice and Economic Distribution.* Englewood Cliffs, N.J.: Prentice-Hall, Inc. 1978.

Barry Brian. *The Liberal Theory of Justice: A Critical Examination of the*

Principal Doctrines in "A Theory of Justice" by John Rawls. Oxford: Clarendon Press, 1975 edition.

Bentham, Jeremy. "An Introduction to the Principles of Morals and Legislation," in *The Works of Jeremy Bentham*, Ed by John Bowring. New York: Russell and Russell, 1962, Vol. I.

Daniels, Norman (ed.). *Reading Rawls: Critical Theories of "A Theory of Justice."* New York: Basic Books, Inc. Publishers, 1974.

Mill, John Stuart. *Utilitarianism*, 12th ed. London: 1895.

Nozick, Robert. *Anarchy, State and Utopia*. New York: Basic Books, Inc., Publishers, 1974.

Rawls, John. *A Theory of Justice*. Cambridge, Ma.: The Belknap Press of Harvard University Press, 1971.

Smart, J. J. C. *An Outline of a System of Utilitarian Ethics*. Victoria, Australia: Melbourne University, 1961.

Wolff, Robert Paul. *Understanding Rawls, A Reconstruction and Critique of "A Theory of Justice."* Princeton, N.J.: Princeton University Press, 1977.